Mounted Police Life in Canada

A Record of Thirty-one Years' Service

BY

CAPTAIN R. BURTON DEANE

With a Map and Four Plates

PROSPERO

CANADIAN COLLECTION

TORONTO
2001

Mounted Police Life in Canada:
A Record of Thirty-one Years' Service

This edition first published by
Prospero Books in 2001
from the 1916 Cassell and Company edition

National Library of Canada Cataloguing in Publication Data

Deane, R. Burton, 1848-1930
Mounted police life in Canada:
a record of thirty-one years' service

(Prospero Canadian collection)
Facsim. reprint.
Originally published: London: Cassell, 1916.
ISBN 1-55267-181-X

1. Deane, R. Burton, 1848-1930.
2. Royal North West Mounted Police (Canada) - Biography.
3. North West Mounted Police (Canada) - Biography.
4. Frontier and pioneer life - Prairie Provinces.
I. Title. II. Series.
FC3216.3.D42A3 2001 363.2'092 C2001-930618-0
F1060.9.D29 2001

Prospero Books
90 Ronson Drive, Toronto, Ontario, Canada
M9W 1C1

Printed on acid free paper

Printed in Canada by Webcom Inc.

CONTENTS

CAPTAIN R. BURTON DEANE

LIST OF PLATES

MOUNTED POLICE LIFE IN CANADA

CHAPTER I

1883—84. REGINA

IT was a glorious morning, in the early part of July, 1883, when I left the Windsor Hotel in Regina, and started to walk the two and a half miles of rolling prairie that intervened between the hotel and the barracks of the North-West Mounted Police, some of the roofs of which were distinguishable in the distance.

Regina had been selected by Lieutenant-Governor Edgar Dewdney as the capital of the North-West Territories, and had been christened by H.R.H. the Princess Louise, whose husband, the Marquis of Lorne, was then Governor-General of Canada.

The Mounted Police had been ordered to make Regina their head-quarters, and the transfer from Port Walsh had not been quite completed at the time of which I write.

In order to facilitate the housing of the police in their new home, a number of so-called "portable" buildings had been shipped in from Eastern Canada. These had been made in sections, and were readily put together on the spot. Needless to say, they were cold habitations, and every room on the ground floor required to have a stove to itself.

Mounted Police Life in Canada

The prairie was carpeted with wild roses, and for a time I tried to avoid stepping on them, but they were so plentiful that the avoidance of them became irksome, and I hardened my heart and walked on.

I found the officer in command to be Superintendent William Herchmer, known all over Prince Rupert's Land as "Colonel Billy." Whence he derived his title of "Colonel" I do not know, but he assumed it and it stuck to him.

I sought him out and reported my arrival, and he took me round and introduced me to the other officers in the Post.

These were Dr. Jukes, the senior surgeon of the Force; Inspector P. R. Neale, the supply officer; and Inspectors A. R. Macdonell, Greisbach and A. B. Perry. The latter had served a short time in the Royal Engineers at Chatham, but the atmosphere of the School of Military Engineering seemed to have proved uncongenial, and he had returned to his native country to accept a commission in the North-West Mounted Police.

The Commissioner of the Force, Colonel A. G. Irvine, was not in Regina at the time of my arrival, and as he had more room in his quarters than he absolutely required for himself, I was installed therein for the time being. Having with me a folding bedstead which I had used in the Ashanti Campaign of 1873-4, and a light kit, I was easily housed until my quarters should be ready for occupation.

Inspector Neale was married and comfortably settled, and he and his wife were kind enough to ask me to take my meals with them, which I was very glad to do.

The empty shell of a house (a story and a half high) was placed at my disposal, and I was invited to partition it off to suit my convenience, which I did. Carpenters were at once set to work on it, and two rooms were added downstairs, which made it a sufficiently commodious and convenient habitation. Seeing that there was no rent to pay, and that the Government provided stoves, fuel and light, I considered myself supremely fortunate. After a few days the adjutant, Superintendent John Cottòn, arrived, and General Orders then announced the appointment, as Inspector, of R. B. Deane, Esq., although my credentials from Ottawa showed that I had been a captain in the Imperial Service.

The Mounted Police Force had been in existence for ten years and had not a standing order or regulation of any kind. I was expected to remedy this defect and, as I had been for five years adjutant of a division of Royal Marines, consisting of 3,500 non-commissioned officers and men, besides officers, and had served afloat and ashore for close on sixteen years, it was child's play to me to draft regulations for a little force of 500 men when once I had become acquainted with the conditions of life and service in the country.

Regulations were needed badly enough, but what was more urgently required than anything else was the driving power to compel the wheels of the machine to turn smoothly. I had been told in Ottawa that I should find the Mounted Police an "armed mob," and I certainly discovered them to be so.

I spent the best part of the months of July and August in Regina trying to teach the "hay-leg"-"straw-leg" business to some recruits, and when the Comptroller visited the Post towards the conclusion of that interval, he said that he noticed an improvement in the bearing of the men. At the beginning of September I went to Toronto to fetch my family, who were installed in a house there, and brought them all westward early in the next month—wife, five children, and a domestic servant whom we had found in Winnipeg. A telegram from T. C. Patteson to Mr. George Stephen, president of the Canadian Pacific (now Lord Mount Stephen), expedited the transmission of the car containing our household goods, and we soon settled down in our new home and awaited the advent of our first North-West winter.

The first line of study that it was incumbent upon me to take up was obviously that of the Criminal Law. I was familiar with Military Law, and it was fortunate that I was so, for there was no one in the country, either at the bar or on the bench, who knew anything about it, and it devolved upon me, a few years later, to teach the Supreme Court of the North-West Territories the true relations between itself and a court constituted by the Mounted Police Act. The particulars of this will be found under the chapter entitled "Mounted Police Law."

The study of the Criminal Law that we were to administer in the country was, at that time, a little complicated, for only certain statutes were in force in the North-West Territories; having ascertained from Colonel Richardson, the senior stipendiary magistrate, which those were, I set to work to epitomise them into the form of a manual which a constable could carry about with him, so as to inform himself as occasion might require.

Colonel Richardson was very kind, and devoted several hours to going over my work with me and to making corrections and suggestions.

I studied also all the police manuals which I could procure, the principal ones being those of the Royal Irish Constabulary and the Melbourne Force.

In this manner I spent the winter of 1883, in equipping myself for my future duties, and the time was well spent. So far as any idea of a "Constable's Manual" was concerned, the Police Department at Ottawa had no interest in, nor any sympathy with, any such project. My manuscript was promptly consigned to a pigeon-hole, where it remained until a sympathetic fire came along some years later and made an end of it and of other records in the departmental building at Ottawa.

I next turned my attention to the problem of "Standing Orders," which were very urgently needed, and with that object in view I studied all the literature that I could procure. I have already remarked that, however desirable regulations might be, it was equally desirable that there should be some driving power which would keep the machine moving, and an illustration of this may be offered. One of the officers stationed at head-quarters had been detailed for railway duty, and in pursuance thereof he used to travel on a pass, and to talk mysteriously about the people with whom he used to come in contact, and so on. After I got to know him better he told me that he did not know what his duties were, and that he had never received any orders on the subject. To my knowledge he never made a report, and his chief object in life seemed to be to buy scrip cheaply from the half-breeds. He had begun to acquire 1,000 acres of land in Manitoba, and thought of little else. I do not know what good the purchase did him, for when he died he did not leave a penny. Presumably he bought more land than he could pay taxes on, with the consequence that in time it was sold to cover the arrears.

This is an apt and true illustration of the go-as-you-please manner in which the Mounted Police Force ran itself in the year of Our Lord 1883.

In April, 1884, the Commissioner appointed a Board of Officers, of which I was one, to formulate a single rank drill for the Force and to draft Standing Orders. The drill was soon disposed of, and then glances of inquiry were cast at me. I asked if there were any means of ascertaining the contents of the Commissioner's office, as there was necessarily therein a certain amount of material which would have to be worked into Standing Orders, and this ought to be at our disposal. It seemed that there was no way by which we could obtain the required information, and I therefore said that I did not see how we could make any progress. The board died a natural death then and there.

The Commissioner, who had been to Ottawa during part of the session, returned on Good Friday and announced that I was to be promoted to superintendent and appointed adjutant from April 1. The appointment, however, did not actually reach Regina until May 14, and on that day I took charge of the Commissioner's office.

The staff consisted of Staff-Sergeant W. H. Irwin (now Clerk of the District Court at Lethbridge) and Sergeant (now Superintendent) Routledge.

The care and attention which my predecessor had not bestowed upon his office were evidenced by the fact that there was not even an index to the correspondence, and it was necessary for us to sort and examine the entire contents of the office and to make a correspondence register as we went along. This gave me the opportunity that I was looking for, of finding out what orders there were for incorporation in my new work, and, although the operation exhausted several weeks, the time was not ill-spent.

The lack of a correspondence register explained some funny little dockets, with which the table in the Commissioner's office was covered. These were all neatly folded up, with labels describing their contents, and an indiarubber band round each of them. When the office was properly fitted up I asked the Commissioner if he had any objection to my removing his treasures piecemeal and answering them. There was no very great difficulty in so doing, although I was a stranger to the country. One docket, I remember, related to a claim made by an old widow at Battleford, whose oat crop had been trampled by some police horses which had broken through her fence. I recommended payment of a hundred dollars to settle her claim.

Another prolific source of correspondence were the numerous claims made by men, when taking their discharge from the Force, for compensation on account of having received some injury while in pursuance of duty. One docket related to a claim for 5,000 dollars made by a non-commissioned officer, and it caused us a great deal of trouble to hunt up old ration returns and such-like documents to find out where he was on certain given dates. There was nothing on record to show that the so-called injury had ever been reported at the time, and this obviously called for a remedy in the future. In the Royal Navy I knew that when a man was injured on duty he was given what was known as a "hurt certificate," and I made a provision that, in cases where a man was injured in the Force a board of officers should be immediately convened to take the evidence of the persons cognisant of the facts, and to give an opinion in accordance with that evidence. That settled that question.

Another source of acrimonious correspondence was the question of discharge by purchase, which had never been either recognised or in contemplation, for the simple reason that it cost the country so much money to bring men into the West, that the least return the Government could expect was that the men should serve the term of five years for which they had engaged. However, so many men claimed that recruiting officers had led them to believe that they could "buy out" if they did not happen to be satisfied, that I introduced a system from my old corps, by which applicants for purchase had their names placed on a list, and were allowed to take their turn at the rate of three per month. Sir John Macdonald was pleased to approve of this suggestion, and it was adopted in the Mounted Police.

The principle involved was all right, but with the accession to power of the Borden Government in 1911 it laid itself open to abuse.

In the year 1912 no fewer than fifty men were allowed to purchase their discharge out of a force numbering only 654 men.

An amendment to the Mounted Police Act was made in the following year, increasing the pay of the various ranks and reducing the term of a constable's engagement from five to three years. In view of this reduction, I wrote to Mr. R. B. Bennett, M.P. for Calgary, advising that discharge by purchase should be abolished except in very special cases. He replied saying that he agreed with everything I had written, and would take the matter up with the Comptroller. The vigorous manner in which he did so may be gauged by the fact that in that year, 1913, out of a total number of 708 non-commissioned officers and constables no fewer than 71 had been permitted to purchase their discharge prior to November 1. Out of the aforesaid total number, 43 men deserted during the same time, and 49 were dismissed for bad conduct.

The figures are significant, as tending to show that, in spite of the shortened term of engagement and the increased pay, the Mounted Police was unable to obtain and retain desirable men. In my opinion a great mistake was made. The engagement should have remained at five years, and additional pay should have been given to bring the total wage up to the market level. As it has turned out, the Government took away with one hand what it gave with the other. That it increased the pay is true, but it took away from the issue of kit; and the price of some of the articles of clothing has been raised to a prejudicial extent.

Canadians as a whole are very proud of the world-wide reputation which the Force has made, but they may as well face the unquestionable fact that the Force is now on the down-grade and should be abolished before its reputation is quite gone. Five years were none too long a time to teach a constable the multifarious duties of a mounted policeman; but when, in addition to the reduced term of three years there is added the pestilential discharge by purchase whenever a man chooses to ask for it, it necessarily follows that the Force is able to render to the public nothing better than a very inferior kind of eye-service.

As an illustration of what I mean, a constable who had joined the Force on August 12, 1912, was in course of time transferred to my division, and was subsequently detailed for detachment duty at Bankhead, where there is an anthracite mine. He was by way of being a handy-man, and the manager offered him $2.90 per day to run an engine in the mine. He applied to purchase, was given instant permission to do so, and, on December 1, 1913, took his discharge upon payment of $61.50, that is $3 per month for the unexpired portion of his engagement.

Another constable was sent to replace him at Bankhead, and on February 5, 1914, he, too, applied for permission to purchase, which was instantly allowed by the Commissioner, and he took his discharge upon payment of $85.50. It seems that a surveyor had offered him $45 a month to join his survey party.

To an officer in charge of a police district such eccentricities as these are simply maddening and heart-breaking, and the public suffer as a result.

The worst case known to me happened in the early

part of 1914. There was a constable on detached duty at ——, but he was so utterly neglectful of his duties that I was in process of making arrangements to withdraw and replace him. To my intense astonishment I received a telegram from the Commissioner's office at Regina to give him his discharge by purchase. This order had, I subsequently learned, emanated from Ottawa, and, of course, governed both the Commissioner and myself; but any such proceeding cannot fail to be subversive of discipline, and is antagonistic to the best interests of the Force.

The people amongst whom I have lived and worked in the West for over thirty years will concede that I am as competent a judge of disciplinary administration as any person in Canada, and they will understand that I am telling them historical facts which they are likely to learn from no one but me, and which it is time they were told.

This constable was given his discharge, and his successor, quite a competent young man, had hardly been in his place for one calendar month when he, too, applied to purchase, and was allowed to do so.

From all the foregoing it will be seen that the Mounted Police Force has developed into a philanthropic organisation, whose objects are laudable enough, so far as providing young men with means of livelihood is concerned, but hardly so satisfactory to the lonely settler when "constabulary duty's to be done." Nor is it possible to regard the philanthropic provision of openings for young men as the purpose for which a police force exists.

To return, however, to the Commissioner's office in Regina, the muddle that most wanted straightening out was in connection with the medical staff.

Whether rightly or wrongly, the department at Ottawa had acquired the notion that the medical officers at the various Divisional Head-quarter Posts in different parts of the country were dispensing drugs, &c., supplied by the Government for the use of the non-commissioned officers and men, in their private practice.

Oddly enough, an officer could not get any medicine at the police surgery. In order to remedy this state of affairs, an oldish medical practitioner, at St. Catherine's, in Ontario, was persuaded by Sir John Macdonald to give up his practice there and bring his family to the North-West, in order to take up the appointment of senior surgeon. All sorts of promises had been held out to induce him to take this step, and the old man used to complain bitterly that faith had not been kept with him. However that may have been, and I have no personal knowledge of the matter, the appointment was not in any way acceptable to the various assistant surgeons, who seemed determined to do all they could to make Dr. Jukes's life a burden. Correspondence used to be carried on directly between the medical officers, and if the senior surgeon wanted any information or returns which were not quite palatable, the assistants frankly told him to go to the devil.

As soon as I felt myself securely seated in my chair I issued a General Order to the effect that in future direct correspondence between the senior and assistant surgeons was to cease and was to be carried on through the Commissioner's office and the Officers Commanding Divisions, each of whom would be held responsible that information required by the senior surgeon was promptly and accurately rendered, and that replies to correspondence were couched in proper terms.

As soon as the Order reached Ottawa the Comptroller at once wrote me a private note, saying, "General Order so-and-so settles the medical question," as, of course, it did in a very obvious and simple manner, and there was no more trouble.

Dr. Jukes became a great friend of mine, and was a very fine old gentleman, and also a very competent practitioner.

The Conservative party treated him abominably. When, in course of time, his memory failed and he became past work, they laid him on the shelf with a paltry superannuation of about twenty-five dollars per month. There was a clause in the Act whereby he could have been allowed to count ten more years than he had actually served, but therein lies the difference between the two political parties. The Liberals look after their friends, while the Conservatives do not.

Take my own case. When Sir John Macdonald's party met disaster at the polls in 1896, I was not mean enough to leave it at a time when it most needed loyalty and service, as so many of the old chieftain's appointees did, but remained in its ranks until the Liberals went out of power in September, 1911, over the reciprocity question. At that time both the Commissioner and the Assistant Commissioner were men who had been appointed by Sir John, but, after the fateful 1895 election they had turned their coats and had thus secured promotion over the heads of their seniors. In 1913 a new appointment was made, that of an Assistant Commissioner for the Province of Alberta, and as I was by eight years the senior superintendent of the Force I naturally expected to obtain the appointment. The whole Western country had the same expectation, but I reckoned without my host.

One of the superintendents had a brother in the Dominion Parliament, representing an Ontario constituency, and conceived the brilliant idea of obtaining promotion for himself over the heads of his seniors and betters. His amiable design in some way became known to another superintendent, senior to himself, and a scion of an old Quebec family. In self-protection, for

I do the man the justice to believe that he would never have done so otherwise, he set to work to pull political strings, with the result that he got the appointment. All such trickery as this is quite *comme il faut* in Canada. No one thinks any worse of a man for trying to supersede his superior, and it is this spirit which accounts for the numerous changes which have taken place in the past thirty years in the general officers sent to Canada from England to command the Militia. The two officers at the head of the Mounted Police of whom I have spoken are graduates of the Royal Military College at Kingston, Ontario; and Britishers do not sufficiently assimilate the principle that "Canada is for the Canadians," and, that when a Canadian wants a job no Englishman need apply. When General Colin McKenzie could not "get on" with the impossible Minister of Militia, whom most of his party take as a joke, nothing more needs to be said. Sir George French brought the Mounted Police into the West in 1873, and his treatment by the Canadian Government of the day is a matter of history. As a comment on the injustice with which he was treated by the Canadians, the Home Government gave him the Queensland Command.

CHAPTER II

1884. REGINA

The year of Our Lord 1884 was a very busy year for me. In addition to the work in the Commissioner's and Adjutant's offices, I had the work in the Post and its interior economy to look after, and the training of men and horses to supervise. My outside staff consisted of Sergt.-Major Robert Belcher (now Lieut.-Colonel Strathcona's Horse) and Staff-Sergeant Walter Simpson (ex-Staff-Sergeant Royal Artillery); and two old-fashioned soldiers such as these could be trusted to render good and loyal service without having to be watched. For the horses I employed Constable Montague Baker, who was probably the best rider in the Post, and for the clerical work of the division I had a smart young corporal named S. G. Mills, who subsequently obtained a commission, and after his retirement was visited by a terrible affliction—the loss of his sight. I am glad to know that, in spite of his trouble, he is to-day a happy and prosperous citizen of Hamilton, Ontario.

Montague Baker was a very useful man, and I finally appointed him to be sergeant-major of the newly-formed division "K," in the autumn of the rebellion year, when the strength of the Force had been increased to 1,000 men. I was sorry to learn the other day that he had recently "joined the majority."

In the summer of 1884 I made two notable engagements. Two men named Charles Ross and G. P. Arnold presented themselves, saying that they had crossed the line to homestead near Moose Jaw, but had come to the conclusion that farming conditions were hardly favourable, and that they proposed to join the Mounted Police. I sent them to Dr. Jukes for medical examination, and presently the old gentleman came across the square.

"Do you know that those men you sent to me for examination are very fine specimens of muscular manhood, but that they bear the scars of bullet wounds?"

"How do you account for them, Doctor?" I queried.

"Oh! well, they say that they have worked as scouts for the United States troops and have been wounded in 'scraps' with the Indians and so on."

"All right, Doctor," I replied, "if they have seen shots fired in anger they are the men for my money, and if you say they are sound I shall engage them and take chances on their respectability."

I had no occasion to regret doing so, and did not bother my head about their past history. They were dead shots; they could ride anything with hair on; they did not drink; and they were not afraid of work. What more did man want? Ross was, after a time, sent to Calgary and Arnold to Prince Albert, in the north. Arnold was killed at Duck Lake, at the outbreak skirmish of the rebellion. He received one bullet wound in the neck, but paid no attention to it, and continued to "peg away" at the enemy until he was shot through the lungs, and that was conclusive. He and Ross were great friends. The latter, early in the rebellion days in the north, whither he was sent, became known as "Charlie Ross, the famous scout," and stories were told of him during the fight at Cut Knife Creek how, whenever he had sent an Indian or half-breed to the happy hunting grounds, he would mutter to himself, "Another for Arnold." With a man who habitually shot wild rabbits with a bullet through the head, in order to avoid spoiling the meat, a poor Indian or "Breed" did not stand much chance so long as there was enough of his dusky carcass visible for Charlie Ross to draw a bead upon. In my company, he followed a horse's trail across the prairie for about fifteen miles at a gallop, and it was none too plain a trail either.

Another valuable recruit who offered himself for acceptance during the same year was T. J. Kempster, an upstanding specimen of a man who had served as a trooper in the 2nd Life Guards, and proved to be a very capable riding instructor. The wild eccentricities of the prairie-bred horse astonished him at the outset, but I induced him to undertake the training of them upon the principles of M. Baucher, of the French army. Montague Baker and he used to work together.

Baker, by the way, had a very narrow escape on one occasion. A broncho (i.e. an unbroken horse) from the wild and woolly West—a savage brute who was rather more intractable than his compeers—succeeded in planting a hind foot fairly and squarely in Baker's face, but under Dr. Jukes's care he recovered perfectly.

In the course of the same year, in company with the Lieutenant-Governor, I visited the famous Bell Farm at Indian Head, which consisted of I forget how many thousand acres. The climate and the country were not, at that time, conducive to any such experiment, and when the rebellion of 1885 broke out the management were only too glad to hire out their teams and men to the Militia Department for the transport of stores, etc., at the rate of ten dollars a day.

They had, I thought at the time, only one useful practice, which was a regulation requiring all their stables to be locked and the keys returned by nine o'clock every evening to the time-keeper of the establishment, who lived at the head-quarter farm. I thought that the principle was so good that I immediately adopted it. Our four stables stood east and west with doors at each end, the eastern end facing the barrack square. I secured the western end with Yale padlocks on the inside, and the eastern end with similar contrivances on the outside, and the stable picket had the keys strapped on to his belt.

On September 15, 1884, I received a telegram from Major Bell, that in the course of the previous night fifteen horses had been stolen from the Bell Farm and driven rapidly southwards towards the line. Sergeant Blight and a couple of men from Regina succeeded in recovering seven of the horses in Montana, and as the tracks of only nine animals could be found on the south side of the Missouri River it was conjectured that the others had been driven to exhaustion, and some of them possibly drowned in attempting to cross. I asked Major Bell afterwards how it was that the thieves managed to get the horses out of locked stables, and he replied, "Oh, we gave up that practice; it became too tiresome!"

I had an amusing experience with Bell in 1885, when Lord Lansdowne was touring the country in the autumn after the rebellion. The first stop he made in the North-West Territories was at Indian Head. There I had orders to meet him with an escort of a hundred men, all of whom we could not mount, and there was thus a most incongruous force of men riding in dead-axe (that is "heavy") wagons, and so on. Mr. Assistant Commissioner Crozier had recently come into Regina, and these were his ridiculous orders. However, on our arrival at Indian Head, Major Bell was promptly on deck, and said: "I have chosen a most delightful spot for you to pitch your camp. It is just in convenient view from my drawing-room windows, and I am sure His Excellency will be immensely pleased with the prospect."

"That may be so, Major Bell," I replied, "but I have hardly travelled over the fifty odd miles between this place and Regina to contribute to the aspect of your scenery. Canada holds me responsible for the safety of her Governor-General while he is in my charge, and I have already sent a non-commissioned officer ahead to select a ground for our camp in proximity to the railway station. That is where our camp will be pitched. I am sorry to upset any of your arrangements all the same."

We camped, therefore, just behind the station buildings. When the viceregal train came into the station (in the very early morning) a sentry was posted at each end of the Governor-General's car, and thinking that everything was seraphic I slept the sleep of the just.

His Excellency told me later in the day that he thought four sections (sixteen men) would be ample escort for him on the forthcoming forty-five mile ride next day. And so it was that we started out the next morning with a smart escort of sixteen men, under Sergeant Kempston, on route for Fort Qu'Appelle via Katepwa, where we had luncheon at Father Hugonnard's Indian School.

From there we went to Fort Qu'Appelle, where the Hudson's Bay Company had a store, etc., and there His Excellency had a pow-wow with the Indians of that neighbourhood, and made them the usual presents of food, tobacco, etc. Thence, at the suggestion of the Hudson's Bay factor, with whom Lord Melgund was driving ahead, we started by a roundabout road to Qu'Appelle station on the railway. We rode and rode and rode, and it looked suspiciously as if the factor had lost his bearings. So, after a time, His Excellency said to me, "Well, Captain Deane, I am in your hands. I think we had better head for our train."

I had taken care to provide a scout who knew every inch of that country, and he took us by a bee-line to where the viceregal train had pulled up westward from Indian Head. The Governor-General was due to address a small deputation on arrival, and he then asked me to dinner.

In the year 1884 an incident occurred which recalled to my mind an observation made to me by a very astute Indian named Osoup at Crooked Lakes earlier in the year. He intimated that the Indians fully recognised the power for evil that lay in their hands with regard to the railroad, and it is much to their credit that they have abstained from such mischief during all these past years. Probably if there was one individual who, more than any other, exercised an influence for good in this respect, it was the Reverend Father Lacombe, O.M.I., for he had great influence with Crowfoot, the honoured chief of the Blackfoot nation, and the Blackfeet made no trouble when the Canadian Pacific passed the northern edge of their reserve.

It was pathetic to hear the old man say in 1905, after the Province of Alberta had been formed out of the North-West Territories, amid great ceremonies at Edmonton, "They said everything nice about themselves, but never a word about the police or the priests." I replied, "Father, you have put the cart before the horse. Everyone who knows anything about it knows that the police would have been of little use without the help of the priesthood."

In the month of June it was reported that an iron rail had been found placed across the track at a point about seventy miles west of Regina, and a sergeant, an interpreter, and three mounted men were at once dispatched westward by rail, with orders to work back along both sides of the track. They returned next day, bringing with them three Indian prisoners, whom they had arrested on suspicion. As I was engaged in investigating the matter, it transpired that two of the Indians, who were Assiniboines, were brothers, and were able and willing to point out the real culprit. A passing freight train was detained, and men and horses, with one of the informers, were immediately dispatched westward again.

Two days later they returned, bringing in an Indian named Buffalo Calf; the brothers had seen him place the rail on the track, and he was subsequently convicted on their evidence and sent to the penitentiary for two years.

The year wore on with never an idle minute, until Christmas approached, and then it became my duty to write the Commissioner's annual report for presentation to Parliament. This entailed about a month's work, but the report was duly dispatched to Ottawa on Christmas Eve. The Montreal *Gazette* was good enough to say that it read like a romance.

CHAPTER III

REBELLION YEAR, 1885. REGINA.

On March 10, in response to a telegram from Ottawa, Colonel Irvine left Regina with four officers, eighty-six non-commissioned officers and men and sixty-six horses, en route to Prince Alberta, 291 miles distant. This journey was made in seven days, the average daily travel being forty-two miles, which, considering the short days and the severe weather, was pretty good travelling. His departure left the Head-quarter Post with myself and thirty-two non-commissioned officers and men, and no horses. Fortunately the Indian Department had a few ponies, which they were able to lend us, and with them we had to do the best we could.

At the end of March a cipher telegram from Ottawa announced that three hundred men in Chicago had bound themselves together, by oath, to invade Canada in the interests of the half-breeds, and that their objective point in the first instance would probably be Moose Jaw, forty miles westward of Regina.

Although I did not take this proposition very seriously, I could not, of course, neglect any reasonable precaution, and so opened negotiations with some Sioux Indians, who had been for some time camped in the neighbourhood of Moose Jaw, with a view to engaging them as scouts, but the negotiations fell through, chiefly owing to the difficulty in mounting them.

It happened that just about that time a man named

Louis Legarré, who lived at Wood Mountain, a settlement about 90 miles south-east of Regina, came into town to represent to the Lieutenant-Governor that a large number of half-breeds in his neighbourhood were in a starving condition, that they wished to remain where they were so as not to be implicated in any way with the rebellion, and that they would be glad of any employment which would keep the wolf from the door. Legarré undertook to see that the work was properly done, and to vouch for the good faith of the men for whose selection he would be held responsible, and, this arrangement having been sanctioned in Ottawa, forty scouts were engaged, and an officer was sent to Wood Mountain to supervise proceedings.

At this year's session of the Dominion Parliament the strength of the force was increased from 500 to 1,000 men, and in order to provide accommodation for them a number of large square tents, etc., were sent to us from Ottawa. These we pitched round the barrack square in the intervals between the portable houses.

On May 3 a telegram was handed to me: "One hundred and thirty recruits will reach you at midnight, and require supper." The men duly arrived.

It took us several days to get them all clothed and settled down, for our stock of clothing, etc., was entirely insufficient, and we ransacked all the shops in the town to buy the necessary underclothing, blankets, etc. Considering that there was not much money in circulation, this was a godsend to the local storekeepers. This consignment was the first of about 600 men who joined us in the course of the year. As soon as their training was completed, the men composing each squad were dispatched to one point or another in different parts of the country. Of the recruits I can only say that they were the finest and best behaved lot of men that I have ever been connected with. They gave no trouble, and settled down to learn their business with determination.

In consequence of a little incident that occurred when there were from 250 to 300 men under canvas, it occurred to me to have a heart-to-heart talk with them. I was impelled to this by various considerations, to explain the chief one of which I must hark back a little.

Colonel Irvine, soon after his arrival at Prince Albert on March 24, received from the Comptroller at Ottawa a telegram which read: "Major-General Commanding Militia proceeds forthwith to Red River. On his arrival, in military operations, take orders from him." Now, Colonel Irvine, having discussed the subject with the leading men of the neighbourhood, and being in possession of all the ascertainable facts, had come to the conclusion that it was his duty to place Prince Albert in as defensible a position as was possible in the circumstances and to protect the many women and children who gathered there. He accordingly refused to abandon his helpless charges and to move out into the field. The force at his command was not sufficient to admit of his doing both things.

General Middleton had enough men with him to eat the rebel half-breeds, moccasins and all, but seemed to have some ridiculous ideas about the risking of human life, and hesitated and demurred until Colonel Williams's regiment got tired of being made fools of and rushed the half-breed trenches, out of which the dusky occupants scrambled without any ceremony whatever, and were lost to sight.

It was this redoubtable outfit that General Middleton wanted Colonel Irvine's force to attack from the rear, without giving him any instructions to that effect and without making any plans to that end, and because Colonel Irvine did not do so, the gallant General permitted himself to say on one occasion, alluding to the

Mounted Police, "Where are these gophers? Why don't they come out of their holes?" That expression naturally ran round the country, and I made it the text of a sermon which I preached to my men, whom I formed up in three sides of a hollow square.

I began by telling them how very gratified I was at the manner in which they had got down to business, and hoped that they would continue in well-doing. I said in effect: "We are not playing at soldiers here; we have got the strictest and most tedious kind of duty to perform. We have upwards of fifty rebel prisoners to guard, and if any one of you men fail in his vigilance when on guard disaster may ensue. We have, as you know, nine sentries posted round the barracks at night, and the safety of all Government property depends upon the ceaseless attention of each of those nine men. Take the hay corral, for instance; what is there to prevent some evil-disposed person from crawling up to that haystack and setting it on fire? There is nothing to prevent it but the vigilance of the sentry. The stables are locked, it is true, but there are over a hundred horses picketed in the stableyard. What an easy matter it would be for two or three rebels to ride into those lines and stampede those horses while attention was being devoted to the burning haystack! Under cover of the double excitement it is conceivable that an attempt might be made to 'rush' the guard-room, but I want you all to understand that under no circumstances whatever are the guard to leave their prisoners. They have positive orders to that effect. Their rifles are loaded and they will not hesitate to use them. I tell you these things in order to impress upon each man of you the responsibility that rests upon you.

"The whole North-West knows, and you know, that the General Officer Commanding the Militia has so far forgotten himself as to apply the term 'gopher' to our comrades in the north. Are you content to remain under such a reproach? I tell you candidly that I am not, but I cannot remove it without your help. Will you help me to remove it? You are aware that Parliament has increased the strength of this Force from 500 to 1,000 men. That means that 500 additional men will be trained in these barracks this year, and you are part of that number. The addition of 500 men cannot fail to have an influence upon the Force as it existed a few weeks ago. Is that influence to be for good or for bad? Are we still to be called 'gophers' and to submit to the jeers of the criminal classes whom we are to control? or are we to earn the respect of all right-thinking men in this North-West world by proving ourselves to be the best disciplined and most efficient corps in Canada? It will be a proud day for me if ever that time should come, and I believe it will come. Will you think it over and make up your minds? Will you, in your barrack rooms, cultivate a little *esprit de corps?* Will you consider the responsibilities that lie ahead of you in policing these vast territories, and determine first to learn and then to do your duty with honour to yourselves and your corps and with benefit to the people amongst whom you may have to live and work? You can do it if each one of you will harden his heart and stiffen his back and say to himself 'I will.' But the issue rests with you and not with me. I can only hope for the best. Sergeant-Major, dismiss the parade."

As a matter of fact, the men were so keen that I do not believe a cat could have crept through the line of sentries unseen. They picked up one man who had the appearance of a tramp, but who had a pocketful of matches. He had, of course, a plausible tale to tell about having been trying to get employment from ranchers, etc., and, beyond locking him up for the night, there was no adequate reason for punishing him as a vagrant. He was thus sent away in the morning and advised not to stop in town. He went a few miles eastward, as far as a place called Balgonie, where there was a railway bridge, and to this he set fire. We soon gathered him into the fold again, and this time he went to the Manitoba Penitentiary for two years.

In the autumn of the year the town of Regina got up some athletic sports, and our men were invited to participate. One event was a tug-of-war, and for this there were three entries—namely, the town team, the Montreal Garrison Artillery, and ourselves. The artillery team were easily beaten by the town, who had a very good team, including a powerful, big man who stood about six feet six inches, and whose build and weight were in adequate proportion. Him they placed at the tail end of the rope as anchor, and they thought themselves unconquerable.

For my part, in my old corps I had seen a little of tug-of-war teams trained by expert gunnery instructors, and, when the police team was finally chosen and got down to work, my impression was that there was nothing in Western Canada to touch it. It turned out just as I expected. The police team never budged—they just held their opponents while they pulled themselves out, and then, very gradually but very surely, hauled them across the line.

As soon as the tug was over I turned aside to talk to the Lieutenant-Governor and Mrs. Dewdney, who were close by in their carriage, and had hardly had time to say a few words before a woman clutched my arm and said, "Stop them!" I looked to where she pointed, and saw that a merry free fight had begun between the men and the riff-raff of the townspeople. I ran into the fray, and the first man I came across was a hot-headed Irish corporal who held a townsman by the throat and was choking the life out of him. I ordered him to let the man go, but he affected not to hear me, or not to recognise my voice, so I took hold of his face with both hands, and, turning it so that he could not help seeing who I was, said, "If you don't drop that man this instant I'll give you six months to-morrow morning." He let go of the man, fell back and saluted, and I said, "Fall the men in over there," indicating a spot by a wave of my arm, "and tell them off into sections." I went to the judges' stand, told them I was very sorry that any unpleasantness should have arisen over a simple tug-of-war, in which the police were unquestionably the winners in a fair and square pull, that the police would not touch the prize which they had legitimately won, and that, as the Mounted Police were maintained in the Territories to keep the peace and not break it, it was my intention to take them all home immediately to their barracks.

By the time these remarks were concluded my men were fallen in and told off, and away they went. They sang themselves home over two and a half miles of prairie between the town and the barracks, and the town was left. The Lieutenant-Governor and some of the prominent residents left the ground in disgust. In the course of that evening the mayor sent me, through the town police station, a telephone message urging me to send a patrol to keep order in the town, as a great number of rowdies were causing alarm to the peaceable citizens. I had left but one constable in the station to attend to telephone messages, and him I directed to take my compliments to the mayor and say that the appearance of a Mounted Police patrol strong enough to take the rowdies into custody would be likely to cause more disturbance than then existed, and might possibly cause bloodshed. I emphatically declined, therefore, to provoke any such breach of the peace, and advised him to swear in special constables to deal with the situation. I concluded by saying, "The town will have to police itself to-night in any event."

After all, nothing happened. The reputable people were kept awake for some hours by the disreputable element, but the whole trouble had simmered down before the morning.

In the course of the forenoon I called my men together and said to them: "I told you not long ago that if you would go on doing your duty as you had done it up to that time you might easily become the best disciplined armed force in Canada. I can this morning go a deal further than that, and can say to you—after your magnificent exhibition of discipline on the athletic grounds yesterday afternoon, when, despite the fact that angry passions were aroused, and there was every prospect of a disastrous row, you answered the call of duty and left your traducers and assailants in contemptuous silence—I say to you that it rests only with yourselves to become the finest force of constabulary in the world; for you have shown to the North-West public that you can control yourselves. You have learned the discipline of the Royal Marines. I am proud of you, men, and I thank you for what you have done."

I was very much annoyed during the sitting of the Louis Riel Court when, one day, General Middleton's aide-de-camp handed me a half-sheet of note-paper on which was written, "The General will inspect the police at ten o'clock to-morrow morning. By order, etc."

We were not under the Militia Department (we were not engaged in military operations, seeing that we were in an Assize Court), and the Commissioner of the Mounted Police, a stipendiary magistrate, was, to my mind, entitled to at least a more courteous notification than this intimation handed to his adjutant by the General's aide, and my blood fairly boiled. I tried to get Colonel Irvine to object to this inspection, but could not succeed.

At 10 a.m. next day the parade was drawn up ready for inspection. The men were all "sized" according to the uniform that had been issued to them and irrespective of the stages of their training, and the General Officer Commanding the Militia rode up and down the rank, and then went off to inspect the tents, etc., in which the men lived. I told the Commissioner before his "High Mightiness" arrived that if the General should say anything about drill he would have to wait until the afternoon, as it would take some time to sort the men into their various drill squads and rides. As it happened nothing was said about drill, but the Lieutenant-Governor remarked to me afterwards: "The General was very pleased with the parade, but *there was no drill.*" "No," I replied, "I took good care of that; when I want General Middleton's assistance in training a force of constabulary I shall be quite sure to ask him for it."

Not long after this the Lieutenant-Governor went to Winnipeg, where a force of Mounted Infantry had been recently established. He had seen the men on a church parade, and came back full of their smartness, etc. Without in any way wishing to depreciate the Winnipeg men, I remarked, "My night guard of thirty men, or thereabouts, mounts every evening at seven o'clock. Of course, I know that that is an inconvenient hour for you, but it is a pity that you cannot take a look at them, because, if there is anything smarter to be seen in Canada I will apply for leave to go and see it."

Towards the close of the year 1885 I was told by a man who was "in the know" that the Government had decided to supersede Colonel Irvine in the following spring, and that there were three nominees for the position: first, Major (now Sir Edward) Hutton; Mr. Lawrence Herchmer; and myself. Mr. Lawrence Herchmer was a bosom friend of the Hon. Edgar Dewdney, and Mr. Dewdney had Sir John Macdonald's ear. Mr. Herchmer got the appointment. He was some five or six years older than myself; had served three or four years (it was understood) in a British infantry regiment; had tried the brewing business in Winnipeg, and then had been appointed an Inspector of Indian Agencies in the North-West. A place called Birtle, in Manitoba, was the home from which he migrated to us.

In 1887, when I was on recruiting duty in Ottawa, I took the trouble to ascertain, through the late Sir David MacPherson, then Minister of the Interior, and Mr. George Allen, then Speaker of the Senate, why these things were so. Sir David said that Mr. Herchmer's father had been an old friend of Sir John Macdonald, who felt bound to do something for the son.

Colonel Irvine had managed to acquire some very bitter enemies. One of these was Lieutenant-Governor Edgar Dewdney, another was the late Nicholas Flood Davin, editor of the *Regina Leader*, and to these General Middleton appeared at this stage to have added himself. At all events, his idea was to have the Mounted Police transferred from the Prime Minister's own particular care to that of the Militia Department, and his reports of the inefficiency of the Force were such that Sir John Macdonald at last resented them and decided to keep the police under his fatherly eye, and not to hand them over to the Militia Department.

An incident occurred some little time after Mr. Herchmer's accession to power. A staff-sergeant of the Force had found a woman whom he desired to marry, but the autocrat of the Mounted Police set his face steadily against matrimony among the non-commissioned officers and men, and he said to the staff-sergeant, "There is a commission coming to you if you remain single, but you will have to choose between the commission and a wife." "Thank you, sir," said the other, "I'll take the wife." When this story was repeated to Sir John, he said, "I like his spirit; he shall have the commission too," and he gave it to the bridegroom.

Colonel Irvine was subjected to a great deal of very unfair misrepresentation. I knew him for a gallant and honourable gentleman, who would never have stooped to soil his fingers with the looted furs which subsequently formed the subject of a conversation in the Canadian House of Commons.

CHAPTER IV

1886—88. REGINA

MR. LAWRENCE HERCHMER duly presented himself at the office of the Commissioner of the North-West Mounted Police on the morning of the 1st April, 1885. Colonel Irvine was not there to receive him, as he had started off two or three days previously to Macleod, without having said a word, even to me, about his supersession. I had, however, by that time become quite used to the eccentricities of the Mounted Police Force, and informed the new Commissioner that, in my opinion, he need not expect his predecessor to hand over his command in person.

Mr. Herchmer therefore sent telegrams to the officers commanding the various posts saying that he assumed the Commissionership from that day, and that in future all official correspondence should be addressed to himself at Regina. Having done that, he went back to Government House, where he was staying for the time being.

In the evening a farewell order was received by wire from Colonel Irvine, and was duly published in General Orders. Among the telegrams sent by Mr. Herchmer on his arrival was one to his brother, the superintendent in command at Calgary, desiring him to come to headquarters, for, as he said, "I don't know how my brother may take my appointment." The brother, however, could never have been fool enough to think that he was

THE MOUNTED POLICE BARRACKS, REGINA, 1885

A squad at skirmishing drill. The barrack water-cart drawing water from the "Pile of Bones" Creek otherwise known as the Wascana River

in the running for Colonel Irvine's vacancy, and so there need have been no anxiety on that score. He came readily enough in answer to the summons, and the first object to which they gave their minds was the breaking up of what they called "the Macleod clique." The officer commanding the Police Post at Macleod at the time, viz. Superintendent John Cotton, my predecessor in the adjutancy, had always objected to the transfer of the police head-quarters to Regina from Port Walsh, a point which was much farther westward, but had nothing to recommend it as far as I could see, beyond its old associations, etc. The climate was, it must be confessed, very much less severe than that of Regina, but the post itself was situated in a flat entirely at the mercy of rifle fire from surrounding hills. It was here that Sitting Bull, with his victorious band of Sioux Indians, had presented themselves after their massacre of the American troops under General Custer, and naturally some allowance might be made for the sake of old associations; but they could not necessarily be allowed to militate against the deliberate decision of the Government, which was to place the head-quarters of the Mounted Police at Regina, the capital of the North-West Territories, where, indeed, it would be most convenient. Regina, be it noted, was the choice of Lieutenant-Governor Dewdney, and was christened by the Princess Louise. Mr. Dewdney had been severely criticised for selecting such a spot for a capital, and I was shown an old American map wherein the settlement (for it was neither village nor municipality in those days) did unquestionably appear within the apex of a district, delineated on the map as "The Great American Desert." All I can say is that it is a pretty fortunate desert to have such soil as it has—deep, rich and heavy —which will be able to grow wheat and other cereals when less favoured localities will be played out, as some of them are now already. I know something of the Regina soil, for, with the exception of that at Government House, I made probably the first garden in the place. A good garden it was, too, though it was made within ten days in the spring of 1884. It is an historical fact that in 1886, when Sir John and Lady Macdonald paid their first visit to Western Canada, I sent to Government House in time for their breakfast a musk melon which, under glass, of course, happened to mature in the nick of time, and was certainly the first of its kind grown within many miles of the spot.

It is necessary here to explain that the officer commanding the Mounted Police at Macleod had, until the time of which I write, viz. A.D. 1886, acted also as Collector of Customs for the western country. This brought him a good round sum every year, as all the cattle, horses and other dutiable goods which entered the country from the south had to pay duty at Macleod, and the former occupant of the position, during his tenure thereof, had made about 25,000 dollars in addition to his police pay. At Macleod also was stationed Dr. George Kennedy, a great friend of Superintendent John Cotton's, who was the assistant surgeon in medical charge of the post and district, and the only practitioner in that neighbourhood. This was the combination that Herchmer used to call "the Macleod clique," and between him and it there was bitter enmity. It goes without saying, therefore, that when the Herchmer family came into power the first sign of attack on "the Macleod clique" showed itself in orders transferring "C" Division and its officers to Battleford, a post in the far north about five hundred miles from Macleod. Dr. Kennedy said he would not go, and resigned his commission; so that the division went without him, and was replaced by the division from Battleford.

William Herchmer elected to remain at Calgary,

where he was already stationed. The Customs appointment at Macleod was doomed to extinction, so far as the police were concerned, for there were many hungry politicians in the East looking for just that kind of job, and the gift was very soon bestowed upon a "stalwart" of the Conservative party in Ontario.

As soon as the newly appointed Commissioner had learnt, as he thought, enough of the rudiments of his new profession to qualify him for the attempt, he started off to make an official inspection of his brother's command at Calgary, by way of practising his 'prentice hand upon a division which might be expected not to be too critical of his academic methods. "E" Division fooled him to the top of his bent, and he was delighted with everything he saw; he liked the place, he liked the people, he liked the climate, and, as there were lots of trout in the Bow River at that time, some of the men got up early in the morning of his departure and caught some fish, which they packed in ice for him, and sent him home rejoicing. He was as pleased as a child with a new toy, and took an early opportunity after his arrival to unbosom himself to Lieutenant-Governor Edgar Dewdney, to whom he imparted his opinion that Calgary would be a preferable place to Regina for the capital of the North-West Territories. This was the first intimation that his Honour had that his quondam protégé was now able to sit up and take notice for himself.

Meanwhile life was none too pleasant for me, as Lawrence Herchmer lost no opportunity to vent his spite upon myself. One instance of his methods was exemplified at the time of his departure to make his first inspection at Calgary, as already mentioned. On the morning after he had gone, when I went out into the barrack square, I noticed that the flag was not flying, and meeting the sergeant-major (now Colonel R.

Belcher, C.M.G., of Strathcona's Horse) I inquired, "What has happened to the flag? Halyards broken?" "No, sir," replied he, "the Commissioner sent for me yesterday and gave me orders that the flag was not to fly when he was out of the Post." "Well," I remarked, "he said nothing to me about it, and I saw him last night before he started off for the station."

That was just the kind of thing that Mr. Lawrence Herchmer did, and there was a hoot of derision from all over the country at the new rule, which could not be kept secret.

I have said enough to show that he was quite an impossible man to work with. His appointments did not bespeak the welfare of the public service as the first consideration.

For about a year I fulfilled the duties of my office with scrupulous exactitude, and supplied the many deficiencies in the Commissioner's semi-military education, until on the morning of March 14, 1887, he overstepped the line of hard and fast demarcation which I had resolutely drawn, and I told him a little of what was in my mind regarding himself and his methods.

It happened that the Comptroller of the Force from Ottawa had arrived at Government House on the previous night, and stepped over to the barracks in the morning. He had occasion to pass through my office on his way to see the Commissioner, and as I greeted him I said, "The inevitable row has just occurred. Do not make up your mind until you have heard my side of the story." He nodded and passed on. In a few minutes he came out alone, stopped long enough to say, "Don't let that trouble you, Deane. I quite see how impossible your position is here. I will come over and see you this evening," and wended his way back to Government House.

He came to my house soon after ten that night,

and we had a private talk on the existing regime. Daily manifestations of injustice were producing grave discontent. For myself, he said that I had put in three years of hard work and should have a rest. He had decided to tell the Commissioner in the morning that I should go to the east on recruiting duty for some months, and that thereafter I should be given the command of a post somewhere, possibly at Calgary or Macleod.

In pursuance of this arrangement I left Regina on March 27 with my wife and family for Toronto, which we made our head-quarters for the ensuing four months, during which time we renewed acquaintance with many old friends there and in Ottawa.

On my return I found myself in Orders to take command of the Depot Division to which all recruits were posted, and to which all men at head-quarters belonged. This was very much more palatable than resuming my former position in the Commissioner's office. I had dry-nursed him for a full year and was heartily sick of the job.

During the autumn and winter months I organised a theatrical troupe, and we had considerable fun from our amateur attempts and from little dances that we occasionally gave. We beguiled the time as best we could, for the winter months were long and dreary. We had, of course, sleighing and snow-shoeing, but we had no covered skating rink, and it was too cold to skate out of doors. We were, moreover, two and a half miles from town, so that we had to be self-contained while the thermometer averaged 20° to 25° below zero, Fahrenheit, and occasionally dipped into the thirties and forties.

My family and I were always welcome visitors at Government House, for the late Mrs. Dewdney and my late wife were great friends, and we were in no way dependent upon the uncongenial society of the

Herchmers, between whom and Government House the "rift" was gradually but surely widening. It was well understood that the winter of 1887 would be my last in Regina, for the Commissioner had told me on my return from recruiting that I was to take "E" Division, from Calgary to Macleod, in the autumn, and, although that move had not come off, a transfer to some other post was ahead of me. It was customary at that time for the Commissioner to pay an annual visit to Ottawa during the session of Parliament, so that the Premier might obtain, at first hand, any information which might be required from the head of the Force as to police conditions in the West, and, incidentally, this gave the visitor an opportunity to do a little "lobbying" on his own account. *Inter alia,* movements of officers had to be discussed, and it was, therefore, without any feeling of surprise that I learned one afternoon from the Lieutenant-Governor that he had that morning "received a letter from Fred White," the Comptroller, who told him that it had been decided to transfer me to Prince Albert in the spring. Now, Prince Albert was, as I had always understood, a very charming place—a landmark in the country, long before either Regina or Calgary had been thought of. It was one of the old-time head-quarters of the Hudson's Bay Company, where a chief factor named Lawrence Clarke had his habitat, and was altogether a most desirable place to live in and work from. It could not, it was true, compete with Regina or Calgary as the metropolis of the North-West Territories, but what did that matter? I should be only too glad to go anywhere where my services were required. As to taking my family, that was quite another matter. My wife was inexperienced in prairie travel, so were her three younger children, and as there were roughly 300 miles of prairie to be negotiated in wagons in order to reach this delectable spot, it was quite out of the question for me to subject them to that long journey in weather which was as uncertain as the roads, and I decided to send them to Ottawa. In about a fortnight's time the Governor looked me up again, saying "That Prince Albert deal is off. I have had a letter from Fred White in which he says, 'We cannot have *her* here.'" I replied, "All right, your Honour, it is all the same to me. Fred White is not such a fool as you might think, is he?" He laughed. As my wife and I had spent some months altogether in Ottawa, we were not entirely friendless there.

When the Commissioner came home I learnt that we were to be sent to Lethbridge, so called after the president of the North-West Coal and Navigation Company, which company had been opened by Lord Lansdowne in 1885. The Police Post there had only been completed about a year previously, and the place was still shown on maps as "Coal Banks." I wrote to the officer commanding asking for measurements of his various rooms, etc., and he, poor chap, was quite cut up, for he said he had no previous intimation nor any reason to anticipate a move. He had, as a matter of fact, got into some hot water which had formed the subject of newspaper paragraphs all over the country, and he was moved to Macleod under a senior officer.

There was in force in those days a Dominion statute prohibiting the importation, sale and even the possession of intoxicants by any person within the North-West Territories, except by permission of the Lieutenant-Governor, and it was the duty of the Mounted Police to enforce this Act. When a permit was issued a notification was sent to the police, and they watched for every consignment, promptly took up each permit, and returned it to the Lieutenant-Governor's office. Permits were not altogether easy to obtain, and one uncancelled permit might be used to cover other importations.

The suspicion of a permit caused the "boys" to hang round the Dominion Express office, and wait and wait and watch, until at last, after a long time, the Express Company would be free to deliver the consignment. Then there would be a gathering of the eagles to the slaughter, and the wagon would be followed to its destination, at a discreet distance, by all the thirsty harpies who wanted to have a drink at the expense of someone else. If the owner happened to be away from home the visitors were out of luck, but if, on the other hand, he was there, the entire crowd would follow the keg in and stay with it as long as it contained a drop.

This course of action the present-day reader might think would have strained the ties of friendship to the breaking point, but it was not so at all. The generic question of liquor, licit or illicit, was governed by a code of honour all its own. Men, whose word in the ordinary transactions of life (always excepting a horse deal) one would accept without reserve, could not be trusted to speak "the truth and nothing but the truth" where a liquor prosecution was concerned.

The first elected Member of Parliament for the Dominion House, when he went north to canvass his constituents in the Edmonton section of Alberta, took with him a sleigh load of carcasses of hogs, and each carcass contained bladders full of whisky, contraband at that, for he never could have obtained permits to cover such an amount as there was, and it had all been smuggled into Macleod from Montana. The half-breed vote might easily be conciliated with whisky, and the candidate was triumphantly returned at the head of the poll.

There were, at this time, men who made their living by dealing in illicit whisky, playing poker, etc., and those who had the wit to take care of their money became well-to-do. Probably the most impudent theft on a large scale that came under my notice was that of whisky from a car-load of liquor which passed through the North-West Territories en route to British Columbia, where there was no prohibition law in force. This car was bonded and sealed until it arrived at its destination. It happened, however, that it was side-tracked for a day or two somewhere near Calgary, when the trans-continental train service was in its infancy. In some way the liquor-dealing miscreants had ascertained that the car contained (among the profusion of barrels, kegs and cases that it carried) a barrel of whisky, which stood at a certain spot at its rear end. So, with a long auger, a hole was bored clean through the bottom of the car into the bottom of the barrel, when the rest was easy. They drained the liquor into the receptacles which they had ready and drove off with the plunder. Obviously they would not waste time in trying to cover up the traces of their *modus operandi,* and no clue remained to enable the perpetrators to be identified.

When "Larry" (as he was popularly spoken of) returned from Ottawa in the spring of 1888 he was feeling, as the saying is, "pretty good," and, with the true Hohenzollern spirit, looked for other worlds to conquer. He had a fine new house waiting for him, a flag that was impatiently longing to fling itself to the breeze, and, taking it all in all, he had every reason to think that it was good to be alive. With the hearty co-operation of his *vis a tergo* (so christened by Dr. Jukes) he thought out a scheme of officially asking the Lieutenant-Governor not to issue any permits to members of the Mounted Police unless the applications were sent through and were recommended by himself. I had private information as to the receipt of this letter in the Governor's office, and knew also that the Governor took several days to consider the proposition. When he assented, which he finally did, a General Order was issued by the Commissioner to the Force throughout the country. I was then free to talk to the Governor about this order, and told him frankly that I considered it to be an infringement of the liberty of the subject, and calculated to bring into disrepute a body of officers without whose co-operation the existing prohibition law could not be enforced. From a personal point of view, I represented that I considered the order an insult. I said to him, "Your Honour is quite well aware that liquor is not abused in my household, whatever may be the case elsewhere." He understood the implication without any further enlargement, and said it was within his personal knowledge that, in some instances, it might not be inadvisable to have the order carried out, but that so far as I was concerned he should not think of setting a limit to his own discretion. I might rest assured that he would grant me a permit whenever I might think proper to ask for one. Upon this I simply "sat tight," and ignored Mr. Herchmer in the matter of my permits.

It was at this juncture that my family and I left Regina for Lethbridge, but it will be convenient to close up this controversy at this point. Every successive permit that was issued to me threw my domineering friend into a fresh paroxysm of rage, and while he lost his temper I placidly kept mine, and stood my ground. The end of it was that, after the lapse of some weeks, the Minister at Ottawa gave instructions that the offending General Order should be cancelled and a new one issued providing that intoxicating liquors should not be taken into police barracks without the consent of the Commissioner. As this was entirely *intra vires* of that officer, I cheerfully accepted the conditions during the few years that the prohibition law remained in force. The ramifications of this dispute brought about an entire rupture of the quondam friendship between the

Lieutenant-Governor and Mr. Herchmer, and they ceased to speak to one another. This was rendered the more easy, so far as the public service was concerned, as the Governor, on the expiration of his term of office in the Territories, carried the constituency of Moosomin, and entered the Cabinet at Ottawa as Minister of the Interior.

CHAPTER V

1888. LETHBRIDGE

On April 30, 1888, my fortieth birthday, the "Turkey Track" (so was the narrow gauge railway known) from the Canadian Pacific took me into Lethbridge, a village of about 500 or 600 people—many of them miners—a place where I was destined to spend fourteen happy years thenceforward. There my boys and girls grew up into men and women, and when the inevitable time of parting came, we were all sorry to sever our connection with the people we liked so much, and among whom we had lived so long. There was in those days a camaraderie about life in the North-West which is entirely lacking now, and life was a great deal more worth living. "Live and let live" was the principle upon which we conducted our business; we constituted a little oasis in a desert, and were as happy a little community as one could find on the broad prairies. I look back with great pleasure upon our theatrical entertainments, which were given always for a local charity, and also upon the little time of stress when our Church of England parson was laid up with a bad throat. I waited for him after the service one day and said, "I will read the lessons for you if it will be a relief." "It will be a great help," he said, and I did so for one Sunday. Then I said, "Better give yourself a chance. Let me read the prayers and you preach the sermon?" "I shall be so glad if you will," said he. This arrangement continued a while, but the poor chap had to give it up and go to a milder climate. So it was my lot to keep the church doors open and continue the service until a parson could be procured to take the job. In later years, when business had become more progressive and remunerative, and we had to find maintenance for a parson, or to dispense with him altogether, a young Englishman was allocated to our parish, and asked me to be his churchwarden. This was an honour which I had theretofore studiously declined, but at last I gave way. It was a case of the self-supporting rectorship at last, and the question before the vestry was the stipend which we could guarantee to pay. Twelve hundred dollars a year was the irreducible minimum, and I said that I thought we ought to be able to guarantee that much. The people's warden at this juncture was one J. H. Cavanah, and he disagreed with me. There are not many old-timers of that day left in the land of the living now, but such as are in the flesh will endorse what I say about him later on. At the vestry meeting I said: "I will find out what it is possible to do and report at the next meeting." All my exertions in the interim showed that we could not, in addition to church expenses, guarantee 1,200 dollars a year to the rector.

As a Government official, independent of business considerations, I was the only person in the community who could try the experiment of securing offers of monetary assistance. I admitted quite frankly to Cavanah that he knew more about it than I did. He was a successful business man in a small way; that is to say, he ran a very reputable grocery, etc., store, of which the stock was paid for before he began to retail it, and he was a man of sterling character. At the time of the miners' lock-out he was Grand Master of the Ancient Order of the United Workmen of Manitoba and the North-West Territories, and I was Master of the local Masonic lodge, No. 22. We had a good many ideas in common, and I often used to drop into his shop for a chat. He had a philanthropic disposition, and his death was a distinct loss. Almost the last that I knew of him was in 1902, when I returned to Lethbridge from the Customs round-up described in future pages. No sooner had I reached home than I was called to the telephone: "This is J. H. Cavanah. You were elected Worshipful Master at the last meeting, and old Fred Champness is in hospital, like to die. There is not much time to lose if you want to see him." I kicked off at once to the hospital to see the old chap, whose only expression was, "I'm *so* tired!" and I left him with the impression that I had better lose no time in memorising the Masonic ritual for the dead. It was well I did so, for three days later it fell to my lot, as the first act of my assumption of office, to lay to rest a worthy old brother Mason, who had been in Australia and New Zealand before coming to Canada, and whom, at the request of the Customs Department, I had nominated as local assistant collector of Customs at Regina in 1885.

It was after I left Lethbridge in 1902 that Cavanah was seized with appendicitis and died from it. Dr. Mewburn, who attended and operated on him, is a graduate of the McGill University of Montreal. He is the fifth of his family in the medical line, and he has for years been known as the first surgeon in the West. What he has done for me and my family I could not adequately tell. We had the benefit of unremitting care and attention and up-to-date skill, for "the little man" (as I speak of him to mutual friends and acquaintances) was nothing if not up to date, although we lived in a little oasis at the foot of the Rocky Mountains. I remember so well the beginning of our acquaintance. Mewburn was the only medical man in the place (naturally it would not have supported two!), and was both the acting assistant surgeon of Mounted Police and medical officer to the mining establishment. For our part we had, on the bank of the Belly River, a small building which had been erected as a hospital. This was about half a mile from the centre of the village, and contained room for two or three beds, a small kitchen, accommodation for the hospital orderly, and a very limited surgery.

It was obviously inconvenient to send every man who had a trivial complaint to attend the hospital parade at such a distance from the barracks; and within a few months of my arrival the hospital conveniences were brought within the four walls of the wire fencing enclosing our barracks.

But that little hospital on the bank of the river, while it lasted, answered Dr. Mewburn's purpose to the full. A chance Indian came to him one day, accompanied by a good many of his relations, and asked if any relief was possible. This case, if my memory serves me correctly, was that of a bad goitre, and "the little man" thought he could relieve that condition, with this proviso, as he put it to the patient and his assembled relatives, "I think I can do good, but I shall have to make a big cut. If I think right, and if you all do as I tell you after the cut is made, this man may get well, but I cannot tell for sure until I have made the big cut, and then, if he does not get well, and if he should die, you must not blame me. What do you say? Shall I make the big cut?" A chorus of "Ugh, ugh, ugh," came from the patient and his numerous satellites, and the operation was duly performed. It turned out successfully, and then "the little man's" fame began to grow. It spread from the Bloods to the Blackfeet, and severe cases would go to see the Lethbridge doctor.

The official medicos, be it observed, were paid liberal salaries by the Indian Department, but not a cent came to Dr. Mewburn, who undertook the work, not so much for the prestige which it gave him amongst the Indians, as for the experience which he gained for the benefit of the world at large. The Indians grew to have a blind faith in him, and brought him all sorts of cases. The enormous experience thus gained begot him the subsequent reputation of "the first surgeon in the West." In a few years' time the primitive conditions under which he had been compelled to work were replaced by an up-to-date little hospital, which the late Sir Alexander Galt built and presented to the company, of which he was president.

I never shall forget the night of my arrival at Lethbridge. There was only one hotel in the place, and one did not expect very much, but I sat down opposite my bed and for at least five minutes wondered how I could put in the night. There was a clean pillow-case on the bed, but this only served to intensify the mahogany colour of the sheets. In desperation, at last I wrapped myself up in my blue cavalry cloak, and was glad when the morning came. The Police Post at that time consisted of nothing more than a number of houses dumped upon the open prairie, forming the four sides of a sufficiently capacious square, with the guard-room and cells at one end and two stables, each capable of containing forty horses, at the opposite, the north end. The range cattle swarmed all over the place at their own sweet will, and at night they used to come and upset our slop barrels, and pick over the contents, making a horrible mess outside our back doors. As the months rolled on we overcame these difficulties by enclosing the barrack reserve within a stout wire net fence with top-rail, and by constructing a substantial corral for the 300 tons of hay which we intended to stack in the coming season. In connection with the stables I once had a bad scare. The commanding officer's house was the nearest to the stables and hay-corral, and about eleven o'clock, when I was in my little smoking-room, I heard the stable picket vault over the lower half doors, which were locked, and shout: "Fire!" Beyond a few patent extinguishers, we had in the barracks no means whatever of controlling a fire, and on this occasion I bolted out of my front door and ran like a hare into the stable which was nearest to me. At the far end in the centre aisle I saw the wooden floor ablaze. It was just behind the stalls of two very fine shire horses that we used for hauling water from the river. If I had not been too much preoccupied and anxious, I could have laughed at the quizzical expression on the faces of these beautiful creatures as they looked round, as much as to say: "What are you doing? This is bedtime; why don't you leave us alone?" I was just in time; the fire was on the point of reaching the bedding of one of them. In lying down, the horse had pushed some of the straw beyond his stall into the aisle, and I whipped off my coat and beat it away. That was all I could do single-handed, but the danger was past. I had barely saved the situation when my next-door neighbour, Inspector Moodie, ran in and helped. Then came Staff-Sergeant Charles Ross with an armful of blankets. He was on his way home, saw the flicker of light in the stable windows, and knew that there could be only one explanation thereof, and like the man he was, ran to the sergeant-major's store, gathered up an armful of blankets (which were always kept handy for transients) and came to the rescue.

In a jiffy, too, came the men from their beds with axes, etc.; in almost less time than it has taken me to write these lines a plank was chopped through and any remaining fire effectually smothered. Perhaps I should here explain the necessity for the blankets which Sergeant Ross brought. None knew better than himself that a horse will not face fire, and that in order to lead the animals out of their stalls it would be necessary to blindfold them. Happily, this was not necessary, and most of the horses did not bestir themselves. All's well that ends well, but I had a bad *quart d'heure* while I was keeping the flames under and while I was superintending the subsequent operations. "How in hell did this thing happen?" was the question running through my mind. As I subsequently learned, the stable picket had heard a horse loose in this particular stable, and, as was his duty, went in to tie him up in his stall. He had quietly coaxed the horse down to the eastern end of the stable, and just as he was about to lay hold of his halter the brute dashed by him, kicked at the lantern which the man was carrying, and smashed it to smithereens. The lighted oil ran down between the planks and set alight any inflammable dry rubbish that was there, and so spread.

The two horses that I speak of were used for nothing but to haul our water-tank, and they, and the teamster who was told off to look after them, were kept fully occupied. All water in the town had to be delivered by water-cart in those days, and used to cost ten cents per barrel. The year 1888 was the first of a dry period that lasted for seven years. Dry summers and hard winters went together, and each year became a little drier than its predecessor. Farming was out of the question, even if anyone had thought of it, which no one did. That would have been far too much like work. Riding long hours after cattle or horses on the prairie was not looked upon as work. There was a story told of an old-timer in the Macleod district who would not take a contract for digging a well because he could not do it on horseback. The country was intended by

Providence for stock-growing, and anybody connected with stock who was worth a second glance swore tremendous oaths, wore Mexican spurs and schappes, and possibly a buckskin shirt with a fringe. I myself did a lot of work which, if it was not hard, was steady, for I determined to have a garden at all costs. Experience taught me that the only way in which the seed could be induced to germinate was to make the necessary drills, saturate them with water, then sow the seed, cover it up and keep on watering. As I had about half an acre of garden and did the work myself, it used to keep my spare hours pretty well occupied. Now and again I used to get a prisoner out of the guard-room to help me. There was one to whom I used to give a "horn" of whisky the last thing. He was the cleverest and most successful horse-thief in the country. He was a B.A. of Dublin University, and lived with a squaw on the St. Mary's River. He had a bunch of 500 or 600 horses running at large on the prairie—most, if not all of them, stolen—and once or twice a year he would round them up, cut out some of the likely ones, and drive them across country into Manitoba, where he would sell or trade them for cattle. He had not only a merry life, but a long one, for it was years before we could get a clear case against him, and when at length he was convicted for the first time the judge gave him only six months in the guard-room.

It was during this temporary "retreat" that he "used to learn gardening from Captain Deane" (as I found he told his friends afterwards), and earned the little drop of "Oh! be joyful" which always sent him happy to bed. Poor "Pat," as he was known, did not profit by his experience, for at a later date he came under the notice of Chief Justice A. L. Sifton, who had no sympathy with horse thieves, and sent him to the Manitoba Penitentiary, where he died. I had no fewer than seven barrels, conveniently disposed round my garden fence, which the water-cart man used to keep filled from day to day, and that, to anyone unconnected with the Mounted Police, meant a daily expenditure of seventy cents. It was no wonder that people could not afford to have gardens in those days, for every little onion had an appreciable value, and my old wife's principal enjoyment in life was to drive about in her phaeton with a goodly basket of vegetables and give them to her friends. Of cucumbers I always had an abundance, and they were the first of the particular brand to be grown in that country. I had almost forgotten to mention my first tree-growing experiment which turned out so unfortunately. To the south and east there was, for many miles, nothing but a waterless wilderness, with no habitation whatever and without any semblance of a tree or even bush. Having prison labour and water facility at command, I obtained permission from the Coal Company to take seventy-five suitable saplings from their property in the river bottom and to transplant them on the barrack site. For each tree, I prepared a hole measuring, roughly, three feet each way, and loosened up the bottom with a little rubble for the sake of drainage. With the exception of about six inches of top soil the rest was clay, very hard to work, which was all taken away. With each tree I brought a cubic yard of the soil that it had been growing in, and, prior to planting the tree, the hole was kept full of water, with the idea of making the walls of clay more negotiable by the roots. I could not foretell that we were simply wasting our time, but so it turned out. As each successive year became a little drier than the last, so the clay subsoil became more and more impervious. Some of the trees lasted one year, some two, some three, but, in spite of the water that we gave them, they succumbed one by one, and of all the seventy-five saplings that I set out in 1889 and nursed assiduously there is only one alive to-day. It stands at the turnstile entrance to the barracks in a slight hollow, where the snow gathered in the winter and the rain drained at other times, and as the subsoil was thus kept moist the roots were able to take hold. That experience, however disheartening, is one which the pioneer in a new country has to put up with.

CHAPTER VI

1888—89. LETHBRIDGE

THE Commissioner had told me before I left Regina that he was trying to find some solution of the water problem at Lethbridge, in order to obviate the expense of having a pair of horses and a man do nothing all the year round but fill and haul and empty the water-tank, and to that end had made an arrangement with a local contractor to bore an artesian well at a spot within the barracks which he had designated. This spot was between my house and No. 1 stable, and until I got to know the run of the prevailing winds I used, with some apprehension, to watch the sparks from the gentleman's engine. The contractor had not bored more than about 325 feet when, his troubles with his tools and his tubing multiplied every day, he had at length to admit that he was beaten. He had not quite reached the level of the Belly River, and his tools were not good enough to carry him any farther.

Then, of course, he wanted to be compensated for his loss of time, labour and wages of his engine driver, and that opened up a quarrel with Mr. Commissioner Herchmer with which I do not propose to worry my readers.

In connection with the ineffectual boring of this well an interesting incident occurred some twelve years later.

Mr. Charles A. Magrath, Dominion Topographical Surveyor, pointed out, within a mile to the north and east of Spring Coulee, a remarkable feature of the North American continent. This is a gentle swell on the prairie, accurately ascertained by survey to be only eighteen inches above the general surface level. Horses drawing a wagon over it would hardly feel any tightening of the traces, and it measured no more than 299 feet across. Yet, standing on the crest of the swell, he said that it was certain that water falling to the north-east would drain eventually into a water-shed falling into Hudson Bay; and to the south-east water would drain into the Missouri River and finally reach the Gulf of Mexico. It was probably ignorance of these facts which accounted for the unsuccessful boring for an artesian well at the Lethbridge barracks.

My division in 1888 consisted of 100 men and about 110 horses and pack ponies. We had, in addition, a Blood Indian interpreter and a couple of Indian scouts. The Milk River was about fifty-five miles to the south of us running eastward, and on its banks, when I took over the division, I found three camps of about five men each, with a non-commissioned officer, established. Midway between the barracks and the camp at Milk River Ridge there was another camp, in a place called Kipp's Coulee. It was mainly there because our loaded teams, hauling supplies to the Milk River, required a half-way house of call. Four horses could not haul a heavy load fifty miles in one day, and Kipp's Coulee was the only spot where there was water. It was a pestilential spot, and no teamster stayed there after three o'clock in the morning, for mosquitoes were a veritable pest. A "coulee," I should explain, is equivalent to what in Australia is called a "gully," and Kipp's Coulee (so christened by an old-timer named Kipp who had camped there) was a waterway in the prehistoric times, when Milk River was a very much bigger stream than it is to-day.

In 1889 the Kipp's Coulee water was not fit to drink, and the camp was not sent thither. We found, as it happened, a very excellent spring at a hill which was about fifteen miles from the village, which we called "the Fifteen-mile Butte." (A "butte" is the same thing as a South African "kopje.") We boxed this spring and took great care of it. Although we put a good substantial cover on it, careless travellers did not always close it, and one day we found a dead fox in the water. We established a camp there instead of at Kipp's Coulee, and then we found that the place abounded in skunks, so much so that we had to build a little lattice-work fence round each tent, for if one inmate thereof had inadvertently scared one of these brutes which had inquisitively gone in, he would have created a stench that would have saturated the tent and everything in it for months. These are the gentle creatures that supply ladies with the "Alaska sables" which are so becoming. They are good to wear and desirable in all ways but one—don't get them wet, for if you do you will find that "the scent of the roses will cling to it still."

The first of my detachments to obtain winter quarters was that stationed at Milk River Ridge, and good accommodation for about eight men, with a non-commissioned officer and twelve horses, was built by a local contractor in the autumn of 1889. All the other detachments had to come into barracks for the winter. At a small butte, some nine miles to the north of the Ridge detachment, a patrol had the good fortune to find another excellent spring, and this settled for us the difficulty of watering our work teams when hauling supplies for the detachments. A couple of mounted men were installed in camp here, and the senior constructed three capital reservoirs with the help of stones and some lime that he asked for. The first was for drinking water for the men, the second for the horses, and the third for bathing purposes. Each reservoir overflowed into the next, and the conjunction of the whole was as clever a contrivance as ever I saw. This meant that a loaded team from the barracks would spend half a day in travelling to the first stopping place, one long day in covering the thirty-nine miles to the Nine-mile Butte, and from thence an easy half-day into Milk River Ridge. Everything had to be so hauled—rations, forage, coal, coal oil, and equipment of every sort. By the time I had my Milk River outposts built and supplied in 1889 for the coming winter, it meant a round trip of 230 miles to reach the farthest detachment. We had good horses, good transport, good harness (that much is due to Mr. Commissioner Herchmer) and, what was a still greater asset, good teamsters. We had four four-horse teams doing nothing but hauling supplies, and it required a capable man to put in nine or ten months of such work out of a year, driving and caring for four horses, picketing them at night, cooking for himself, etc. etc., delivering his load safely and keeping his horses fit. There was no division in the Force that had such long haulage work as we did. In 1889 I was empowered to spend the sum of eleven hundred dollars in constructing three sets of detachment buildings, two on the Milk River and one on the St. Mary's River. This provided for the roofing and, so far as the money would go, sheathing of the buildings. They themselves were composed of logs from twelve to eighteen inches thick, but these we had first to find in convenient coulees and then cut and haul. All this work was done by the division, supervised by a Sergeant Keenan, who was for the time being detached from elsewhere.

The establishment of permanent outposts meant that hay had to be provided for winter use, and there was no one to cut it but ourselves. This necessitated a haying party with mower, rake, rack, etc., and as the prairie dried up more and more, year by year from 1888 onwards it was a very difficult matter to find a sufficient supply. Mr. Herchmer asked me once how many tons of hay we cut to the acre. I replied, "You've got the boot on the wrong foot; you mean how many acres do we travel over to cut a ton of hay?"

One year the grass was so scanty that at Writing-on-Stone detachment, twenty-five miles east of Milk River Ridge, we were reduced to cutting and stacking some reeds which grew in a few small lakes some ten miles distant.

From the year 1889 onwards our barrack supply of hay came from the Milk River Ridge, and was hauled about forty-five miles before we got it. This was invariably done by local contractors at a price per ton stacked.

The first year I went to Lethbridge I called for tenders for 300 tons of hay. The only offers I received were from twenty-two to twenty-five dollars per ton. This price being exorbitant, I purchased the amount at five dollars per ton at Pincher Creek, sixty miles west of Lethbridge; the haulage by I. G. Baker and Co. brought the price to twenty-two dollars per ton. As a consequence no further cornering for hay was attempted at Lethbridge.

Before I leave the subject of detachments, including one which I established at the junction of the Little Bow and Belly rivers, about twenty miles north-east of our barracks, I should not omit to mention an historic old place where I quartered a couple of mounted men, and which has now passed into oblivion. It was known as "Fort Whoop-up" (a characteristic name), and was the principal stronghold of the whisky smugglers, whom in 1874 the Mounted Police were sent to suppress. With a strong palisade all round it, and substantially built of stout logs, it withstood in the early days many an attack by Indians who had become maddened by "fire-water." It may interest my readers to know that the price of the Winchester rifle in those days was determined by the length of the weapon. The butt was placed on the ground and became the property of the purchaser when he had piled up on the floor sufficient skins, laid out flat, to reach the height of the muzzle. In my day the fort had fallen into bad repair. A good deal of the material had been used for firewood, and the property had passed into the hands of one Dave Akers, one of the old-time smugglers, who made a precarious living by illicit means and by growing a little honest produce. His holding was situated in the river bottom of the St. Mary's, where the soil was fairly good and moist, and he used to grow the best cabbages in those parts by utilising the numerous empty tin cans to be found in the neighbourhood. He would melt the bottoms off these at his leisure in the winter time, and when he set out his plants he would protect each by pressing a can round it into the soil to the depth of something less than an inch. This would keep the winds and the cut-worms away from his young cabbages, and when they wanted water he used to fill up the cans by hand. This ensured the water sinking down to the roots, where it would do most good. I adopted this plan myself, until I found that a paper cone around the stem answered the same purpose, and did not look quite so unsightly.

For a monthly consideration Dave Akers was able to give us accommodation for a couple of men and horses, and they remained with him until the old place caught fire, from some unexplained reason, and the men were burnt out of their lodgings. We then bought twenty sound logs of what were left and used them for our buildings on the St. Mary's. At a dollar apiece they were not a bad buy—sixteen to eighteen feet long and from eighteen to twenty inches through.

I had my own cows (generally two in milk) and chickens, and the two messes had their cows, so that we had an abundance of milk and cream in the barracks.

When the Coal Company built their narrow gauge railway into the thriving and picturesque town of Great Falls in Montana we were relieved of our long southward haul of supplies, but we still had to continue our annual making of hay for the outposts. In 1896 the rainy seasons had begun again and business advanced by leaps and bounds. Travellers from the south wondered at the beautiful green grass on our prairie, and began to think of investing in so promising a country. To all those (not a few) with whom I came in contact who asked my advice I made the one reply: "If you are thinking of taking up a holding do not go far away from water. Stick either to the irrigation ditch or to the rivers so far as your means will allow, but do not go blindly out on to the bald-headed prairie and expect to find water, because you must bear in mind the time-honoured injunction, 'Blessed are they who expect nothing, for verily they shall get it.'"

In course of time Lethbridge became incorporated, and rejoiced in a mayor and councillors. We continued to police the place as of yore from an office in town, where one man was stationed, and he had telephonic communication with the barracks, so that if, as generally happened, a Hungarian or Slav wedding was on the *tapis,* and the inevitable drunken row ensued, he could always get assistance at a few minutes' notice from the barracks. What was called "The Red Light District" used to cause a disturbance now and then, but, as a rule, one capable man could easily handle that and any other spasmodic trouble.

It was in the year 1891 that Mr. Commissioner

Herchmer communicated with this infant town, and demanded that the municipality should pay the rent of fifteen dollars a month for the building occupied by the Mounted Police, and alternatively threatened to remove the men of his Force from the town. It was pointed out to him that people from all parts of the district congregated there; that it was there, so far as intoxicants were concerned, that all dealings were carried on, and that it was there that the police were able to secure information and ascertain facts in regard to breaches of the law (either actual or contemplated), and that without the facility of an office in town the police would not be able to keep themselves informed of what was going on. The town intimated quite plainly that it was not their business to pay the rent of an office, and I reported that without such a facility I should be unable efficiently to police the district. This, of course, gave Herchmer the chance he was waiting for, and he promptly sent orders for my transfer to Battleford, a point about 200 miles north of the main line of the Canadian Pacific. The Lethbridge people, however, would not hear of it. They got up a numerously signed petition and sent it to the Premier. I dutifully began to pack my goods and chattels, and wrote to my cousin, T. C. Patteson, who was postmaster at Toronto, telling him the circumstances. He wired to the Premier: "Re Deane transfer—Lethbridge to Battleford, Vox Populi Supreme-Lex." He did more: he took the next day's train to Ottawa and saw Sir John Abbott, who promised that no change should be made until after the Herchmer Commission had made its inquiries. So I unpacked my stuff again and "sat tight."

The name T. C. Patteson is barely known to the present generation, but it was a name to conjure with thirty-five years ago. He was the man who, when the Conservative party was in its deepest depths after the

"Pacific Scandal," which hurled Sir John Macdonald's Government from power, was entreated by the leading men of the Conservative party to undertake the editing of *The Mail,* the principal organ of the party published in Toronto. Patteson was nothing if not thorough, and with characteristic thoroughness he devoted his whole energy to the task before him. An old Montreal millionaire, Henry Judah by name, with whom I stayed a few days in 1882, said of him: "That man can write more and write better than any man in Canada, and I have always been opposed to his giving up the paper." I replied that Patteson's point of view was, that after he had written the Conservative party into power, as had been freely remarked to me by all sorts and conditions of men since my arrival in Canada, and had possibly shortened his life by the unstinted labour which he had given to the call of duty, he was entitled to his rest, and to his reward in the haven of the Toronto Postmastership. The old gentleman admitted all that, but thought it was a pity notwithstanding.

Patteson's connection with me was this: His mother was my father's sister, and when I first went to Canada (which was at his own suggestion, when the Winnipeg boom was in full blast), he said, "I will do all I can for you, because I shall so be pleasing my dear dead mother." That was the sole bond of connection between us, and he lived up to his end of the bond. This was the only time in my career that I ever invoked his aid, but, as he said, "You know where to find me." I have often thought that while it was Sir John Macdonald's voice that spoke, it was T. C. Patteson's brain that conceived. His brother-in-law told me that Lord Dufferin often used to ask him to go to Rideau Hall (the viceregal residence in Ottawa) to discuss some knotty problem during the troublous days. I am confirmed in my belief by an appreciation of T. C. Patteson published in *The News*, Toronto, on September 21, 1907, just after he had passed away at the age of seventy-one. The writer says, *inter alia*, "Anyone who looks back over the files of *The Mail* of thirty or thirty-five years ago will find editorial writing of unusual power and of great felicity and dignity. . . . We have had no better editorial writing in Canada, and Mr. Patteson had the genius to preserve the unity of the page, no matter by how many hands the work was done. We cannot penetrate the secrets of that time. *We know, however* [the italics are mine], *that it was in* THE MAIL *office that the movement for protection was organised,* and if Mr. Patteson had ever told all he knew possibly some great figures would be diminished in stature and some considerable adjustment effected. But he did not speak, and the story must wait." Many of the prominent Englishmen of the day were his contemporaries, either at Eton or Oxford, and (to quote the aforesaid "appreciation" once more) "He was in intimate touch with the Governors-General of Ottawa for a generation." Patteson it was who, in 1882, at the behest of the Canadian Pacific Syndicate, wrote a pamphlet introducing the railway to the English public, and telling them that the presidency of the road was held by George Stephen, who, having begun life as a journeyman carpenter, had worked himself up until he had become president of the Bank of Montreal. It was easy for a man like Patteson to get me enrolled as an extra clerk during the Parliamentary session of 1883 in the office of the Marquis of Lorne, the Governor-General, and thither I went at a dollar and a half a day for some months.

In Ottawa, during that time, my late wife and I met a good many of the Ministers and other prominent people in the social life of the capital. It was not easy, however, to get speech of Sir John Macdonald. Fred

White, now Colonel, C.M.G., retired, Comptroller of the Mounted Police, had been Sir John's secretary during the dark days of the party, and was still his chief political agent. I am very much beholden to him for his keen sympathy and assistance, and he said to me one day, "I want to introduce you to Sir John." I got a "hurry message" from him one morning, and went to his office. "Sir John is, by the doctor's orders, confined to his house at Earnscliffe—you know it—take this note for Pope (private secretary), and be as quick as you can." As luck would have it, I was the only visitor at the time. Mr. Pope read the note, ushered me into Sir John's study, announced "Captain Deane," and retired, shutting the door behind him. I was not exactly a stranger to Sir John, because my wife and I had been to a dance at Earnscliffe, and Lady Macdonald had very kindly made a point of introducing me to her husband. However, I now had the opportunity of having a "pow-wow" with the old gentleman, and told him that I was seeking an inspectorship in the Mounted Police, and that my qualifications were so-and-so. His manner was very nice and attentive, but he was entirely non-committal, which was no more than I had expected. It seemed to me that there was something in the old man's mind to which he did not give expression, and I found out, a day or two later, what the hindrance was from a note from Fred White, the gist of which was, "Why did you leave the Service?" I had already explained that stagnation of promotion had driven me out of the Service, but now I wrote a full explanation.

In 1866 I joined the Royal Marines, a non-purchase corps, with the belief that if my life were spared and I was not invalided or tried by court-martial, I was bound to become a general officer. In 1867 Mr. Childers, the First Lord of the Admiralty, reduced the strength of the corps by abolishing the Woolwich Division, some 3,500 officers and men, and as a result, with no adequate provision for supernumerary officers, for four years and ten months no single promotion took place from the lieutenants' to the captains' list. I was a subaltern of fifteen years, and at the date of my promotion to captain I was nearly five years too old for my place in the seniority list.

When I was retired from the Royal Marines in 1882 I was 34 years of age, and if I had continued to serve in the corps I was due to be compulsorily retired, if I was then still a captain, on attaining the age of 42, on a pension of £225 a year. As this was not enough to provide for a family, I "cut the painter" and went to Canada. I may add that from 1876 I was adjutant of the Chatham Division, and retired with the rank of captain in 1882.

That was as much as it concerned the Canadian Department to know, but I may here tell my readers how it was that I brought about an amelioration of the conditions prevailing in my old corps before I left. In the year 1881 the Lords Commissioners of the Admiralty inspected the Chatham Division of the Royal Marines, of which division I was adjutant, and of which corps I was the senior subaltern. I interviewed their Lordships and handed them a memorial which I had drawn up. Lord Northbrook (First Lord), Lord Brassey, and Sir Cooper Key (First Sea Lord) were the principal personages, and very attentive they were. I expatiated on the points which I have previously summarised herein, and Lord Northbrook at length said, "I think, Mr. Deane, we shall all be agreed that you have a grievance. Have you any remedy to suggest?" "I have, your Lordships," I replied, "and it is this: Give us the same opportunities of retirement while we are young that are open to the two big seniority corps of the Army

—the Royal Artillery and Engineers." Legislation to this effect was passed into law, and I was one of the first officers to take advantage of it, and retire with £1,600 to the good. Having followed the drum for so long, I hated to leave it, but what could I do? Warm and well-meaning friends tried to dissuade me from my purpose, but to each one I replied: "This bed is for me and mine. Shall I not have the making of it myself?"

My interview with Sir John Macdonald had no immediate result, and I left Ottawa at the close of the Parliamentary session with the idea of going into a new railway proposition which had been suggested to me, for I could not afford to remain idle. I dropped into Patteson's office in Toronto to report progress, and he, without saying a word, wrote a short letter, which he read to me and signed "T. C. P." He added, as he stamped the envelope with the official stamp, "I think you will hear something within a week." So I did, for within that limit I received a letter from the Comptroller directing me to report myself at the head-quarters of the Mounted Police at Regina, and enclosing with the necessary credentials a cheque for a hundred dollars to pay my expenses. So began my career in the Mounted Police, and now, after thirty-one years and nine months' service in that Force, I became a pensioner of Canada from April 1, 1915. Looking back, it hardly seems possible that I can have served upwards of forty-seven years, as I may say, with the colours, that is, as a regimental officer. I am curious to know how many officers there were on the active list of the Royal Navy on March 31, 1915, who can say that they learned the handspike gun drill which was in vogue at the time of Nelson, and how many Army officers there are now on the active list who bit off the end of the cartridge before ramming the powder and bullet down the muzzle of the rifle. Both handspike and ramrods were in the curriculum when I learned my drills. I trust my readers will pardon my being so extremely discursive, and that I may now be permitted to recur to the Premier of Canada whom, in 1891, T. C. Patteson interviewed on my behalf. Sir John Abbott had been formerly the legal adviser of the Canadian Pacific, and had been called upon to take the helm of Government after the tragic death at Windsor Castle of Sir John Thompson, of whom the late Nicholas Flood Davin, "the silver-tongued orator of the Western prairie," wrote, that the man who, at birth, was laid in a three-and-sixpenny cradle, had his requiem boomed by the cannon of an Empire.

Sir John Abbott had promised that the question of my transfer should remain in abeyance until after the Herchmer Commission. The Government had, very reluctantly, and after long deliberation, consented to appoint a judge of the Supreme Court to act as a commission of inquiry into the many complaints against this officer which had been made in the Press and otherwise. Mr. Justice Wetmore held sessions at Regina and Macleod, and I was called upon to attend at both places. I said what I had to say without fear or favour, and as a result my Commissioner treated me thereafter with respect, although we had no greater affection for each other than before.

One fact became apparent, and that was that sundry officers who had instigated newspaper-men to publish attacks against the Police Commissioner lacked the moral courage to go into the witness-box and under oath to substantiate their former statements. It was a pitiable exposé, but it had the effect of clearing the air. My transfer to Battleford was no longer a moot point, and the rent of the office in Lethbridge continued to be paid from police funds.

CHAPTER VII

1890—97. LETHBRIDGE

No history of the Great Lone Land in these latter days would be complete without some mention of the late Lieutenant-Colonel James Farquharson Macleod, C.M.G. He first went West with the Wolseley Expedition of 1870, and subsequently succeeded Sir George French as Commissioner of the Mounted Police. Later, when Lieutenant-Colonel A. G. Irvine was appointed Commissioner, Colonel Macleod became stipendiary magistrate for the North-West Territories. His head-quarters at first were at Pincher Creek, where he had a nice place, of which he was very proud. He was also very proud of his charming wife and family, most of it daughters, who, I believe, are all well and happily married. After the stipendiary magistrate blossomed into the Supreme Court dignitary, Colonel Macleod went to live in Macleod. From there he would come down upon us when Lethbridge wanted a gaol delivery, or when there was anything special to try, and on such occasions he would cover the thirty-two miles of road either by means of a convenient police team or he would mount the box of the tri-weekly stage coach, take the reins from "Polly," the stage-driver (his name being Pollinger, an old-timer), and drive the four horses himself. We used to have to hold Court in any convenient place in those days; sometimes, for the convenience possibly of witnesses, etc., it might be held in a room at the hotel, but generally in the barracks.

1890–97. Lethbridge

After a time the Coal Company built a very pretentious building, the lower part of which was designed as a theatre, with stage, proscenium, drop curtain, etc., while the second story was divided up into rooms which could be, and sometimes were, rented. The lower story came in conveniently, too, for concerts, dances and political meetings. I opened this theatre, by the same token, with a play which I got up for the purpose. When Court was to be held I always used to call at the hotel with my carriage for the judge. When I first congratulated him on being able to sign himself J.S.C. (Judge Supreme Court), he said, "For God's sake, Deane, don't call me Judge." "All right, Kurnell," I replied, and so it was ever after. I used to call for the Colonel at the hotel and drive him to the Court room. I always carried with me a little pig-skin bag, which he christened "*amicus curiæ,*" which contained a small glass, a corkscrew, a bottle of soda water, a little wee drop of the "cratur," a pouch of tobacco, my own pipe and some matches. We knew that the place to which we were going was desolate, and that we must provide our own creature comforts. The judge sat on the stage, the barristers' table was just across the footlights in the pit, the dock and the escort were a little beyond, and the Court had a comprehensive view of all that went on within the limit of its vision. I used to do all the J.P. work of the place, and I remember being told of a remark made by one woman whose evidence was necessary in a certain case if she would consent to give it. There was the rub. A summons would have been no use; she would, in the witness-box, have been more dumb than the traditional oyster. So it was delicately intimated to her that Captain Deane would be very sorry if she would not help him to get at the bottom of the business. She retorted: "I've never been in a P.'lice Court in me life, but I would as lief go up to thim barricks in front of Captain Deane and tell him what I know as I'd go to me church." So that difficulty was overcome.

Colonel Macleod always insisted on my sitting beside him. "Don't you hate a conscientious witness," he whispered to me one day after we had been bored to death, for the best part of the morning, by an eminently respectable citizen who would go into minute particulars and would prayerfully submit to correction at the hands of cross-examining counsel. "How would a smoke go?" "Just the thing we want to sustain us both, Colonel," I replied, and this was his dictum: "Gentlemen, the Court adjourns for ten minutes," and we slid off behind the wings to try and forget our boredom.

It was my good fortune once to uphold my own conviction in the Court of Appeal—a case of dealing in illicit whisky. After hearing the arguments *pro* and *con,* the judge decided not to quash my conviction, and in furtherance of his decision, rose from his seat and beckoned me towards the wings.

"What shall we give this fellow?" he said. I replied, "Well, Colonel, as you have upheld my conviction, I have not much more interest in the matter. If you think proper to let him go on suspended sentence you will not hear a whimper from me." "All right," said the judge, "we'll settle it that way, and then we'll have a smoke, eh?" The appellant in this case, Pete S——, never appeared before me again—he went to the Yukon at the outbreak of the gold rush, and was killed in a brawl there.

Colonel Macleod had grown up with the country, did substantial justice in his decisions, and was an exceptionally good man for the job. If he had had a crooked streak in him he could have made lots of money, but he had neither a crooked nor a mean streak, and that was why he was generally held in favour. He had the most extraordinary capacity for whisky, and was never known to show any effects of it. An amusing story is told about his going on one occasion to Fort Assiniboine on some business or other. This was an American military post in Montana, a few miles across the International boundary line, where there were usually stationed a squadron or so of cavalry and some companies of infantry. The American officers had heard of the Colonel's reputation and of his capacity, and determined to make a comprehensive test of the latter. It was even said that they had one or two relays of officers who were to keep their guest company until he was finally disposed of. As the evening wore on, and the bottle circulated freely, man after man disappeared, either under the table or into an arm-chair or some other seclusion, and when Colonel Macleod assisted the one solitary survivor up the stairs to his bed, the latter stopped short on the first landing and said, "By God (hic), Colonel, w-here d'you put it?"

We had a little piece of excitement now and again. One was when it was reported that coal oil had been found in the Kootenay country, and a miniature boom started. It was kept as much a secret as possible, but there were comparatively few people in the country then, and it was a long way to go. I had a capacious four-horse wagon which would comfortably hold half a dozen men and their equipment, and a party of us, which included a surveyor, drove for two long days (seventy-five or eighty miles) to the scene of action. We duly located our respective claims, paid the Dominion Lands Office the fees due thereupon, and engaged a man who had the tools to go out and drill holes. He had everything comfortably settled, derrick erected and ready for operation, when the structure took fire, and as he had no means of coping with a violent blaze, "bang went" our scheme, and we were "out" the fees that we had paid.

It was in this neighbourhood that there dwelt in the foothills of the Rocky Mountains an old fellow who chose to live the life of a hermit. He had cattle on the range, and was well enough to do. He used to employ an ex-mounted policeman to gather his cattle and to attend the spring round-up for him, so that the calves might be branded, etc., and in the autumn the hired man would cut out any beef cattle that might be fit for the market, but otherwise the old chap lived alone.

Somebody put it to him one day: "I don't see what you do and how you put in the time during the long winter months when there is no occupation for you out of doors. What do you do?"

"Oh, well," said the hermit, "sometimes I sets and thinks, and sometimes I—just—sets!"

A mining craze struck Southern Alberta not long after. Pioneers in a new country must have faith or they are no good. We had faith, and we backed our faith with good dollar bills, which we had far better have kept in our pockets. A banker calculated that a sum of at least one hundred thousand dollars had been withdrawn from circulation in Macleod and Lethbridge. Superintendent Sam Steele, who was then in command of the Mounted Police at Macleod, was the mainspring of the movement, and that was a guarantee that the conduct of the business was at least honest. My friend Dr. Mewburn, and I, and a mutual friend, invested a thousand dollars between us in this venture, but with no result.

The next speculation I went into was the Dundee Mine at Ymir, in British Columbia. This was a gold mine, and, unless the reports were all falsified, a good investment. I bought 100 shares (of one dollar par value) at thirty cents per share, and never had any sort of run for my money. I was by no means the only investor in Lethbridge, many of whose prominent citizens put their money into it. The local manager of the Bank of Montreal was one, the manager of the Coal Company was another, and so on. The bank manager said to me one day, "By such a date I expect to see those shares selling in the market for fifty cents." The shares did not advance in value, and the directorate at last wondered why no profits were accruing and called in an expert. He pointed out a large dump which had been dug out of the bowels of the earth and said, "Gentlemen, your profits are there; the wind is blowing them away." Think of it! The management knew no more about managing a gold mine than they knew about making boots, and even that was not the worst of it. The directors quarrelled amongst themselves, and matters went from bad to worse. Finally, *without the knowledge or consent of the shareholders,* they borrowed twenty thousand dollars from some British Columbia bank (God knows what became of the money), and when the money was not repaid the bank took the mine!

Readers who have had the patience to follow me through these details will admit that my experience in oil wells and mines had been unfortunate, and will not wonder that when an oil boom broke out in the Calgary neighbourhood in the year 1913 I resolutely refused to have anything to do with it. There was in 1913 and 1914 a wild craze amongst all classes for speculating in oil. I do know this, though, that in spite of all my preaching, the devil whispered to me that, if there were anything worth buying in the entire outfit, it was the "Dome" Company's shares. The heart of man, besides being "desperately wicked," dearly loves a gamble, and I reasoned with myself that a hundred dollars would neither make nor break me, and, for the sake of a "flutter" I bought 100 shares at ninety cents apiece.

They were of the par value of a dollar. They went gradually down until, about a fortnight after I had bought them, I found them quoted at fifteen, sixteen and seventeen cents. I had had by that time so much domestic affliction that I was glad to find something that amused me, and I stood opposite a bulletin board and laughed until the passers-by came to see what I was laughing at! From that moment I forgot all about the "Dome" Oil Company until after I had arrived in England, when a marked Calgary paper reached me giving an account of a judicial proceeding, from which it appeared that the "Dome" Oil Company had been sued in the Supreme Court for breach of contract and had been ordered to pay 250 dollars and costs. "A fool and his money, etc."

Early in January, 1898, Superintendent Steele was sent to the Yukon from Macleod, and I was ordered to take over his command and run it in conjunction with my own. This meant that I had a lateral front of about 600 miles to police. The Canadian Pacific were then building a line through the Crow's Nest Pass into British Columbia, and the Mounted Police had been placed in police charge of the line under construction from the eastern boundary of the Province of British Columbia as far as Kootenay Landing. This was 400 miles. In order to familiarise myself with the British Columbia locale, etc., it was obviously necessary that I should go and see for myself. I therefore drove along what was called the "tote" road for about 200 miles, in March, 1898, and, as construction had not then begun beyond Cranbrook, it seemed to me that I had better get home and attend to business. Mr. Assistant Commissioner McIllree had been sent to Macleod to take my place while I was away. It was quite a change from our windswept prairies to drive into the British Columbian forest. The "tote" road was just a passage cleared of trees, etc., to admit of the passage of wagons, etc., hauling supplies for the various contractors' camps, and was pretty rough going. Amidst all the wealth of trees there was not a single twitter of a bird. The only live creatures to interest one were innumerable little black squirrels. We had outposts of Mounted Police dotted at convenient intervals along the line of construction, and I had fortunately a capable officer to supervise them; he went to South Africa with the Mounted Police contingent at the time of the Boer War, and returned as Lieutenant-Colonel G. E. Sanders, D.S.O. He is now police magistrate at Calgary under the Provincial Government, having retired on pension from the Dominion Force. Our red coats carried as much weight in British Columbia as they had done since the opening up of the Western prairies, and our troubles were only of an ephemeral nature.

I used to spend four days out of each week at Macleod and three at my house at Lethbridge. I had at my disposal a four-horse team at each place, which were not diverted from my personal purposes, and, as a rule, at nine o'clock on Tuesday morning I stepped into my wagon at Lethbridge and the team started. The routine was the same winter or summer, except that in winter, when sufficient snow was on the ground, the vehicle was a sleigh. The distance to Macleod was thirty-two miles, and at about the thirteenth milestone the Old Man's River crossed the road. There, on the far side, was a small police reserve, with appropriate buildings, wherein a small detachment of two or three men and horses were accommodated. This was an appanage of the Macleod district, and it frequently happened that it meant a saving of horseflesh to have a Macleod team there waiting for me. There were times and seasons when it was not possible for a team to ford the river, and occasionally, when the stream was in flood, or when slush ice was running down, I had to cross to the opposite bank by means of a flat-bottomed boat. When the river was frozen over the crossing was, of course, easy, and then one was often glad of a twenty-minute interlude at Kipp to thaw out and warm up with a cup of hot tea.

My pet team belonged to Lethbridge, and consisted of four good trotting horses that were a delight to the eye. Two of them had been sired by a well-known trotting horse named Combination, and they had all been bought from what was known as the "Frank Strong ranche," situated near Kipp. They were driven by a half-breed named Harry Taylor, whose father was an old-time white man who owned the Macleod Hotel, and his mother was an Indian woman. Old Taylor had done his duty by his son, for he had sent him to an excellent school at Port Hope, in Ontario, and young Harry had had a capital education. He was employed by us as an interpreter, but as his services in that respect were not very much in demand, he was given charge of the team I speak of. I first found what his capabilities were in that line when he drove me along the "tote" road in British Columbia. One instance will suffice to exemplify his capacity as a "whip."

In 1898 Sir Roderick Cameron, a wealthy New Yorker, who had some years previously bought and fenced a township of land, thirty-six square miles, on the Bow River, within the confines of the Lethbridge district, asked me if I could give him a passage to Macleod. I was only too glad to have his company, and I had arranged to take my team right through from Lethbridge.

The team was not its normal self on that day, for the off-wheeler had been found to be a little off colour, and Harry Taylor, in conjunction with the sergeant-major, had chosen another horse to take its place. This substitute was a bright chestnut, a good, capable horse, well able to hold his own, but hot-headed, like a good many of his colour. He had, too, a habit of swishing his tail about, which was rather annoying. However, we had got to within about a mile of Kipp, and had made good time so far, when this brute of a horse swished his tail over the rein and would not part with it. Our wagons, I should explain, were not built like English vehicles, from the box-seat of which the driver looks down upon his horses. Harry Taylor's seat was very little above the level of the horses' backs, and in such a case the driver was at a very considerable disadvantage. The fact that the horse was able to gather the rein under his tail shows this. Taylor made several attempts to free the rein without success, and the chestnut began at last to plunge and kick. This very unusual disturbance communicated itself to the other horses, who had not been accustomed to this kind of thing, and they started off on the dead run. They swept off the beaten trail and, being beyond Taylor's control, headed for a point about a quarter of a mile distant, where the current of the "Old Man" had washed out what is known as a "cut bank," an almost perpendicular precipice cut out of the bank by the stream. Sir Roderick Cameron was a horseman, and had no lack of nerve, but I realised that he was over seventy years of age. The old gentleman said, "They're off!" Instead of replying I moved up to the front seat and said to Taylor, "Give me the leaders or the wheelers, whichever you think best." "Wait a minute, sir," said he, "I'll have one try," and with that he slacked up all the reins and shouted to his horses: "Whoa!"

There was no more surprised man in Southern Alberta that day than Sir Roderick Cameron, Kt., when the maddened horses heard their master's voice and "whoa-ed," came to a standstill, and allowed me to jump out and free the rein from the chestnut's tail!

I have seen runaways—I was in one only myself—but I never saw such a triumph of mind over matter as I saw on the occasion just described. If the horses had not known the man and had not answered his call as they did, it might have been "Kingdom Come" for some of us. We continued our journey as if nothing had happened, and arrived at Macleod in due time. There was nothing in the demeanour of my septuagenarian companion to denote that his pulse had quickened, but mine had on his account, although I treated the matter as a common incident of prairie life.

CHAPTER VIII

1898—1902. LETHBRIDGE AND MACLEOD

At Macleod I had to live in the buildings known as "the Officers' Mess-house," which happened to be bare of occupants, as all the Macleod officers were married. It was a comfortless, barn-like place, but I had to make the best of it, and was fortunate in being able to secure, as a special constable, a Chinaman of middle-age, named Ling, who was quite a good cook and very faithful and attentive to my wants. Particularly so after I had, in one of my cold, blizzardy drives, picked up a bad attack of bronchitis, and was obliged to spend my week-end at Macleod instead of in my comfortable home. Trains were running, but I had not time to go by train whenever it was possible to avoid it. My teams called at my door at five minutes to the hour, and, as the clock struck, the sleigh bells began to jingle and we were off. I knew that within four hours I should reach my destination, but, with a train, one might waste an appreciable slice of one's life in waiting about stations for overdue trains and the like.

With a white mantle of snow covering the ground, and no trail visible, we had to be guided by distant landmarks. If they happened to be obscured a compass came in handy. Of the bronchitis that I acquired in that winter of 1898-9, recurrences stayed with me, fitfully, to my great annoyance, for a period of about twelve years, and then I got rid of it for good. And all by a very simple method, which I do not recommend to anyone whose bellows are not sound. I used at odd times, preferably in the winter, or when a cold wind was blowing, to take a long, deep breath, give it time to distribute itself in the lungs, where it could be felt, hold it there until the coolness had worn off, and then let it quietly emerge from mouth and nostrils. By the inhalation of the cold air in this process I unwittingly cured a weakness in the throat which had at times (as Dr. Mewburn knows) given me trouble.

Ling remained with me until one fine day in the spring; he awoke me early and said he had terrible pains in his inward parts and would have to leave at once. The greater part of his life had been spent at sea, and I had an idea that the ocean was calling him. He had answered my purpose well, and I made no objection. It was not difficult to replace him, as the work was easy and the pay good. But I was not quite so complacent subsequently in the case of a namesake of his, a young man, whom I engaged for my family at Lethbridge. The worst feature of Chinamen was that they would suddenly say that they wanted to leave, "quit," they called it, and off they would go at a minute's notice. This was generally after their month's wages had been paid. One afternoon I was in my Lethbridge office and got a "rush" message from my house, which was only a few yards away: "Ling says he is going to quit, right away. Can you come?" I was very much absorbed in a troublesome case, and it made me as mad as a wet hen to have my attention diverted, but the least said is soonest mended, and in I went to my kitchen. "Well, Ling! You quit, eh? All light (a Chinaman pronounces his "r's" like "l's"). Good-bye. You get no money. Good-bye. You know Corp'l Louey? I tell him to wait for you in town, he bling you up to guard-loom.

Good-bye!" and back to my work I went. I found when I went in to dinner that Ling had thought better of it. "Corp'l Louey," as the Chinamen called him, was a Corporal Lewis, on town duty, who was a terror to the evildoer, and I 'phoned him instructions, in case Ling should quit, to lay before a town J.P. complaint under the Master and Servant Ordinance against him for absenting himself from his employment without leave, and to act accordingly.

One of the functions at Macleod was an annual "pow-wow" with the chief and representative head-man of the Blood Indians. The Indians of the Canadian North-West had a childlike faith in the honesty of purpose and sense of justice of the Mounted Police, who had never deceived them, and had always looked after the Indians' interests and upheld them as well as they could. The Indians were in charge of a department of the Government known as "the Indian Department," which had sole and whole control of these wards of the nation and their affairs. The Indians had the Mounted Police always with them, but the self-assertive officials of the Indian Department they had not always. They had their local agents, of course, who were supreme (subject to the orders from the department), and were left no sort of discretion where dollars and cents were concerned. Poor devils! They had a hard row to hoe! Their arm-chair critics would come round and cut off a little bit here, and a morsel there, until the poor local men, who had to do the actual economising with aborigines, of whose language they were very imperfectly informed, did not know what they were at. And then the Redskins used to come to us to find out the why and the wherefore. "As it was in the beginning, is now, and ever shall be," the politician or employee whose intellect is devoted to problems of economy will always gain a substantial hearing, and generally make his way. "Economy" is such a catch-word that efficiency or even convenience of the public is a minor consideration. One such severe economist retired from the Indian Department when the Liberals came into power in 1896, and was elected secretary of a Montreal club. I was in the company of a member of that club "somewhere in Western Canada" when the announcement of the appointment was made in the papers, and, after reading it, my friend closed up the paper and said, "That means three pieces of toast, instead of four, for breakfast." The same severe spirit of economy manifested itself in 1908, wherein I became sixty years of age, and married a second wife, the dear mother of my children having died in 1906. In the course of a modest little honeymoon, we made our first stop at Banff, in the Rocky Mountains, where the Canadian Pacific has a very pretentious hotel. Our accommodation had been bespoken beforehand, so that we had no difficulty in that respect, but the place was swarming with German Jews and other tourists, and at dinner on the evening of our arrival I ordered some sherry. Two glasses were brought to us, and I at once disposed of mine. My wife, however, took only a sip of hers, and, after a little while, I noticed that her glass contained a good deal of sediment, which had settled at the bottom. I pointed this out to her and sent for the head waiter, who was shocked beyond measure at the occurrence. He carried off the glass, saying that he would "look into this" and would bring us some more, but time went on, and he did not reappear. We went on with our dinner, and presently I coaxed a waiter into coming to me for a parley, and he, after considerable hesitation, said, "Well, sir, that was the last bottle of sherry in the house, and you had the end of it. But (with an anxious glance around) don't give me away." "I will not," I replied; "thank you for telling me." The head waiter did not enter the dining-room again that evening while I was in it, and I forgave him. Later, at Lake Louise, west of Banff, we could not get any lager beer. The best substitute the waiter could give us was pints of stout, and we had therewith to be content.

It is almost unthinkable, from a business money-making point of view, that a very large hotel system, stretching across a continent, should run even a risk of being reduced to such straits as I have described, but such are the effects of the spirit of economy when placed in the hands of its devotees. In "The Crooked Lakes Affair," hereinafter described (page 140), the selfsame economy was brought face to face with *ultima ratio*.

The management of the C.P.R. system became aware of these shortcomings on the part of their staff, as I judged from a visit paid shortly after our return to our home at Calgary by an old Regina friend of mine, who was in the C.P.R. hotel business, dropping in to see me unexpectedly. At the time of his visit to me he was supposed, to some extent, to control the liquor supply of the hotel system, and I knew quite well that he had casually dropped in to see if I had anything to say on the subject. I, however, said never a word. I did not choose to backbite an unhappy manager when I shrewdly suspected that he was very little to blame.

I seem to have wandered away somehow from the Blood Indians and their "pow-wow." Their chief at that time was Red Crow, a fine old fellow, who said that the faith of his fathers was good enough for him, and who lived up to it.

There was no "forked tongue" about old Red Crow, who realised that the Mounted Police always "played the game," and frankly came to them to say what was in his mind.

On the occasion of which I now write, he and his following came to talk about the "Sun dance," which the Indian Department had prohibited. I may say here that I had a very strong objection to this dance, which, having once seen in the early days, I never wanted to see again. It was a brutal and senseless proceeding, from a white man's point of view. I saw a large ring enclosed, and partly covered by boughs of trees and the like, in the centre of which was a tall pole, from the crest whereof depended a number of ropes, according to the number of débutants. Each débutant was secured to the end of his rope by a skewer passed laterally through the flesh of each breast, and it devolved upon him to dance at full pressure round this pole until he fainted from exhaustion or until the continuous strain should compel the flesh of his breast to tear open and set him free. This process constituted the making of a "brave." The unhappy "brave" had a whistle, or something of the kind, put into his mouth, and round that pole the wretched creature jumped sideways (as in a "giant stride"), always at full tension until, as I have said, his flesh or his endurance gave out. The audience consisted of a circle of closely packed natives, with voice and tom-toms encouraging their representative to hold out to the end. This went on for hours, while the poor victims were struggling with pain and, with their painted faces, were blowing their whistles and trying to show that they were putting some heart into their performance. Then the "braves" who had successfully passed through the ordeal in former years would be recounting their stories of successful horse-thieving and scalp-taking expeditions, and would exhibit, all to the sound of the tom-tom, their search for and finding of the enemy's trail, the stealthy advance, the crash of the tomahawk into the victim, and then the triumphant war-whoop.

All such exhibitions as this could only have the effect of keeping alive the primeval homicidal and criminal instincts of the native, and my sympathies were wholly with the endeavours of the Indian Department, but I never allowed my sympathies to show themselves.

However, old Red Crow made a long speech to set forth the views of his followers, and here it was very helpful to have an interpreter like Harry Taylor, who could interpret finer shades of thought than could the ordinary man. My office at Macleod was unusually large, and with all the windows open could accommodate quite a number of Indian visitors sitting cross-legged on the floor.

When the old chap had done, he subsided into an office arm-chair, and within two minutes was sound asleep. The burden of his song was that the Bloods wanted to have a Sun dance, which was forbidden to them by the Indian Department. He represented that the dance was a part of the Indians' religious belief, and was to them (as my interpreter explained it) in some sort a sacrament. That was the sum total of the representations made by a great number of Indian orators who "spread themselves" during a long summer afternoon.

In reply, apart from a long preamble and eulogistic comments upon the habits of the Indians generally, in my district, I could only ask the question: "When the Indian Department says 'No,' how is it possible for a humble individual of the Mounted Police like myself to say 'Yes'?" Old Red Crow had by this time been awakened by his attendant squaws, and admitted that that was a difficulty which seemed to be insuperable. We all parted the best of friends, and an issue of tea and tobacco cemented the compact.

In September, 1898, I thought I was entitled to a holiday, seeing that I had not had one since my appointment in 1883, and took my family to Victoria, B.C., for a month. The Canadian Pacific had always treated us liberally in the matter of travel, and gave us free transportation to and fro. In visiting a place some 800 miles distant this was a very substantial concession. Our old friends the Dewdneys were living in Victoria. He had served a term of five years as Lieutenant-Governor of the Province of British Columbia, after giving up the portfolio of the Ministry of the Interior, and at his house we met Admiral Palliser, who was then in command of the Pacific Station. His Flag Captain happened to be Captain T. Adair, an old shipmate of mine, who was a sub-lieutenant in the *Warrior* when I joined her in May, 1869. Since that year I had never come across him.

While on the subject of H.M.S. *Warrior,* I may here say that I had the honour of being a shipmate also of the illustrious Field-Marshal who commanded the British army in the early stages of the war. I have not seen him since the ship paid off in 1871. He was a midshipman in her. In 1910 Sir John French came to Calgary to inspect the militia during the month of June, and that happened to be the very month that I had selected to spend on the Pacific Coast, and I was not, therefore, privileged to see him.

I left a note for him, offering my own trooper, Johnny, for his use in riding about the country, but he replied that his wants in that respect had been supplied from Winnipeg, and he could not, naturally, interfere with the arrangements that had been made for his convenience.

Admiral Palliser was very kind and hospitable. He invited us to luncheon one day, and sent his galley to the wharf to take us off. We took our seats, and the coxswain asked me to take the tiller while he pulled the stroke oar. We had a most enjoyable time from first to last, and to me it was a great treat to be associated again with the inimitable spick-and-span Jack Tar. I was particularly curious to know what my daughter thought of it all, and gave her plenty of time to digest all that she had seen before I asked her what had impressed her most. "Oh, Father," she said, hesitatingly, "I think—the men—and the boat." I had an idea that that would probably be her reply. We had paid our visit to the coast a month too late in the year, and were all of us glad to be at home again when we resumed the even tenor of our respective ways until the Mounted Police were invited to volunteer for the Boer War, and to form a unit under Mr. Lawrence Herchmer. Officers and men volunteered freely. For myself, I officially reported that I was ashamed of not having joined the ranks, but that, as I had joined the Queen's service a year earlier than Sir Edward Hutton, the General commanding the Canadian Forces, and had commanded a company of Royal Marines in the Naval Brigade under Commodore Hewitt, V.C., in Ashanti in 1874, I did not feel called upon to serve with the relative rank of captain in the Canadian Militia. This was the reason I gave officially, but, apart from that, it was to me unthinkable that I should go on active service under a man whom I considered to be unfit for the responsibility he was seeking, and so I stayed at home. A very short interval in South Africa was sufficient to prove the truth of my contention, and Lieutenant-Col. Herchmer was quietly laid on the shelf. On his return to Canada, he found that his subordinate had served him in the same manner that he had Colonel Irvine, and had gained the Commissionership of the Mounted Police by the exercise of political influence. I had no sympathy to spare for Lieutenant-Col. Herchmer, who had camped on my trail for many a long year, and I can dismiss him from my reflections with the assertion, that if his doing so had amused him it had not hurt me. The completion of the Crow's Nest railway relieved me of my British Columbia responsibilities, and it was well that it was so, for I had plenty to do near home. I filled up the blanks in my command as much as possible by means of recruits, but these men had to be trained, and I had no one but myself to take the riding school at each post, so that I had few idle moments.

In addition to this, I formulated a new system of crime reports, which was badly needed by the Force at large. I did this at Mr. Commissioner Perry's request, and copies of my specimen reports were circulated for the guidance of officers commanding other divisions. This system has been in vogue ever since.

A spell of bad weather was responsible for an untoward contretemps when the Governor-General and Lady Minto came West. They had been invited by Mr. Elliot Galt, president of the Coal Company, to pay him a visit, and to go out to a new settlement named Magrath, about twenty-two miles from Lethbridge. It was settled by Mormons, who had announced their intention of making the country blossom like the rose. Their Excellencies were coming to us from the Pacific Coast, and Mr. Commissioner Perry and I met their train at Fernie, which had been known as "Coal Creek" when I had spent a night or two there in the "tote" road days. The new name was given to it after that of the original settler. Our first objective was Lethbridge, where rain was threatening. The programme for the morrow was this: Eighteen miles out from Lethbridge on the south-bound railway was the village of Stirling, which was the name of its first Mormon bishop, and there we had placed a temporary camp of half-a-dozen men, with saddle horses for the family and suite of the viceregal party who might wish to ride, and light spring wagons for the convenience of others. It came on to rain heavily that night, and the next morning was so wet that I went to ask Mr. Galt what the programme was to be. He replied, "Oh! I think you'll find they'll go," and so it was. We all took the special train which had been provided as far as Stirling, and there we naturally found everything sopping wet. It only remained to pack the ladies into a spring wagon with oil sheets, etc.; the gentlemen elected to ride, and we galloped over the twenty-mile prairie road to Magrath. We duly arrived at our destination in good spirits and with good appetites, but a little later than we had intended.

It was, therefore, somewhat disconcerting to find that the Magrath people had come to the conclusion that even English men and women would not be crazy enough to travel in such weather, and had *eaten the luncheon* provided for their guests. Their Excellencies, as might be expected of English nobility, took the whole matter so good-naturedly and unconcernedly that the situation was in no way uncomfortable. It was not long, however, before a very nice, satisfying mid-day meal was served to make up for our long fast. In the unsatisfactory state of the weather there was little else to be done but to talk and speechify, and that came quite easy to Mormon apostles, so that as soon as the weather cleared a little we started on our twenty-two mile run to Lethbridge.

We had ahead of us a similar jaunt on the following day to the Blood Reserve from Macleod, and to facilitate this operation we loaded our horses into a box-car and attached it to the viceregal train. We then went out to the Blood Reserve, and had luncheon, and saw what was to be seen, being guests there of Mr. W. Wilson, the Indian Agent. Lady Minto told the Indians that she was descended from a famous Indian princess, Pocahontas. They were not at all impressed by the circumstance, and as a matter of fact did not believe the story. An Indian is loath to believe what he cannot see. In the early days a bunch of them came to Regina. Colonel Irvine left Red Crow and some of them with me in my office, and took Crowfoot and the rest to his quarters. Then we set them talking to one another over the telephone, and their delight was great, but when they went home to their Reserve and told their kith and kin of their experience they frankly thought that the travellers were telling them lies! On returning to Macleod, Her Excellency was kind enough to ask me to join their family party at dinner in their car, and that was the last time I saw Lord Minto, whose visits were always welcome. He did pay a later visit to the North-West for some duck-shooting, but did not then come into Southern Alberta.

Being Governor-General of the Dominion, he quietly effaced himself when their Royal Highnesses the Duke and Duchess of York visited the country. We then gathered up, from all surrounding districts, a force of about 250 officers and men, formed them into a camp at Calgary, and had the honour of being there reviewed by the Heir to the British Crown. After the review, the Royal party went to a hill adjoining the city, where a large number of Blackfeet and other Indians were encamped. Mounted braves in all the extravagances of their native costume lined the road of approach on either side for about a mile, and at the summit their chiefs and head men, under the ægis of the Indian Department, were permitted to see and speak to their future King. This ceremony being completed, their Royal Highnesses and suite took luncheon at the barracks as guests of the officers of the Mounted Police. The mess-room of "E" Division was a capacious and handy room for the purpose, and the walls were decorated with a large number of well-preserved animals' heads, which had been lent to us for the purpose by owners scattered over a great extent of territory.

His Royal Highness was observed to take particular notice of these heads with the eye of a sportsman. The officers had all been presented to their Royal Highnesses before luncheon, and after that function a smart travelling escort, under command of the late Inspector Montague Baker, conducted the Royal visitors to their train.

We had already entrained an escort for duty on the Pacific Coast, and of this, as being by many years senior superintendent of the Force, it was my birthright to go in command, but I had got mixed up with a criminal prosecution in Montana, which was to be tried in Great Falls within a few days, and, as it was necessary that I should attend the trial, I was perforce compelled to abandon the trip to the coast.

Soon after the occurrences just described, His Royal Highness was graciously pleased to ordain that the Force should be known as the Royal North-West Mounted Police.

The necessity for my attendance at Great Falls had occurred in this wise. A Swedish settler in Southern Alberta had had twenty-seven head of horses stolen from him by an American citizen, and I had for months been engaged in working up the case, so as to bring the thief and his coadjutors to justice. This could easily be done, as a State law was in force in Montana making it felonious to take into that State property which had been stolen in another country. The Montana authorities and I used to work this to our mutual advantage, as we had a similar law on our side. The twenty-seven horses had been stolen in Canada and taken into Montana, where they had all been disposed of to different customers.

The United States Collector of Customs at that time was Mr. David Brown, to whom I am under obligation for many international courtesies, and he and his chief deputy, Mr. Ernest Ringwald, were at all times anxious to help me to keep our mutual frontier free from crooks of all kinds. They took up this horse thieving instance with great earnestness. They found out where the thief had disposed of each animal, and had obtained a promise from each purchaser that, if necessary, he would give up his property to the original owner. There could be no greater expression of goodwill than such a course as this, and it was obviously my duty to live up to it. These attentions, be it observed, were mainly of a personal and reciprocal nature, and had been of prolonged and steady growth.

My Swedish friend was a capable, hard-working man, who had a wife as hard working as himself. The Government paid his expenses to Great Falls, and I duly accompanied him there. I was in dread lest he should not keep sober enough to appear as a witness, but he gave excellent evidence at the trial. What seemed to impress the jury a good deal was what a reporter called "his audible thinking." He began by holding up his left hand and by ticking it off finger by finger with appropriate commentaries as each horse floated past his mind's eye, then he resorted to the other hand, and so on, obviously in dead earnest, and thinking out each item with childlike simplicity.

The judge (good judge, too) charged the jury very shortly, and they retired to consider their verdict and sentence. I learned then, for the first time, that, in case of conviction, the jury had the right to assess the punishment, if it was their will to exercise that right. This jury brought in a verdict of guilty and a sentence of ten years in the penitentiary.

I had, when the jury retired, gone out into the street to have a cigarette, and had lighted a second one, when a newspaper reporter passed me with a rush, gasping as he went, "Prisoner committed suicide." It transpired that, after the jury had fulfilled their part of the programme, the prisoner asked to be taken to the lavatory. While there he swallowed a pellet of cyanide of potassium, which he was said to have kept in his waistcoat pocket, and then told his guard what he had done. The resources of medical science were, of course, immediately available, and were successfully applied. The prisoner, however, happened to have a foster father who was unusually well-to-do, and who was very much wrapped up in the boy whom he had adopted. He left no stone unturned to obtain the young man's release, and succeeded after he had undergone four years at the penitentiary. Not long after these occurrences I undertook the prosecution of a case of "wholesale cattle smuggling," the particulars of which are fully described in the chapter under that heading.*

As a result of my successful engineering of a round-up party, terminating in the capture of 596 head of cattle, smuggled into Canada by bosom friends of an influential member of the Dominion Cabinet, I was ordered to be transferred to Maple Creek, a very small municipality in the Province, then known as Assiniboia, but since then re-christened Saskatchewan. A prominent member of the Lethbridge Liberal Association came to ask me the question, "Can't we do something to stop this?" (meaning the move). I said, "I should prefer that you do not interfere." The Minister in question was then in the plenitude of his power, and did as he liked, but there came a day, a year or so later, when he was hurled from his seat by an exposé in the Calgary *Eye Opener,* and took refuge in "the tall timber."

The end of it all was that my wife and I transferred ourselves, our Lares and Penates, to Maple Creek,

* See p. 154.

where it happened that our eldest son was successfully practising medicine. We were Darby and Joan, so to speak, for our two daughters were happily married, and, of our other two sons, one was dying of consumption in California, and one was in the Bank of Montreal in British Columbia. The people of Lethbridge gave effect to their sentiments in the following resolution, in an illuminated form, which unexpectedly reached me soon after I had established myself in my new post:

"To

"CAPTAIN R. B. DEANE,

"*Superintendent, N.W. Mounted Police.*

"The Lethbridge Town Council and Board of Trade, representing the Town of Lethbridge and surrounding district, sincerely regret your recent removal from this district.

"You have had charge of all police matters, in the large territory adjoining the Montana boundary, for the past fourteen years, practically since Lethbridge came into existence.

"For several years your Department has almost annually disturbed us with threatened rumours of your removal to other points of the North-West, and on each occasion every effort at our command was put forth to retain you.

"The Government of a country is much stronger than a small portion of that country, and recognising that truth on this last occasion when you were called away, we decided to lodge our usual protest and then quietly submit.

"The North-West Mounted Police Force is a credit to Canada, and in our opinion that Force is deeply indebted to you, as wherever you are stationed law and order will be firmly established and the police respected.

"It is unnecessary to recount your services to this district. Being a soldier and a gentleman, you did your duty. We know you always performed it with honour to your country and credit to yourself. Your work has not been in vain.

"The universal regret throughout the district occasioned by your departure is evidence of the esteem and respect in which you are held by the general public, and after so many years of service it is certainly indicative of a record of which any public man should be proud.

"Please assure your estimable wife that she has carried away the deep regard of our people, and we trust you will both look back with pleasure upon your many years' residence in Lethbridge.

"We ask you to accept the accompanying present, as a slight token of the warm appreciation that prevails throughout the district for Mrs. Deane and yourself.

"*Dated at Lethbridge, in the district of Alberta, this 15th day of October,* 1902.

"THE MUNICIPALITY OF THE TOWN OF LETHBRIDGE.

"(*Sd.*) WILLIAM OLIVER, *Mayor.*
"(*Sd.*) C. B. BOWMAN, *Secy. Treasurer.*

"THE LETHBRIDGE AND DISTRICT BOARD OF TRADE.

"(*Sd.*) M. BARFORD, *President,*
"(*Sd.*) C. B. BOWMAN, *Secy. Treasurer.*"

"The accompanying present" consisted of a handsome gold watch, chain and locket. The locket I gave to my wife, the watch and chain I have used ever since.

The Western Stock Growers' Association was also pleased to send me a memento in the subjoined form :

[*COPY*]

President:
W. F. Cochrane, Macleod.

1st Vice-President:
D. Warmock, Livingstone.

WESTERN STOCK GROWERS' ASSOCIATION

Secretary-Treasurer:
R. G. Mathews, Macleod.

2nd Vice-President:
Henry Smith, High River.

Office of the Secretary-Treasurer.

Macleod, Alberta,
"*10th October*, 1902.

"Supt. R. B. Deane,
"*Commander N.W.M. Police,*
"*Maple Creek.*

"Dear Sir,—At a meeting of the Executive Committee of this Association, held in Macleod on the 8th instant, the following resolution, a copy of which I was instructed to forward to you, was unanimously adopted, viz.:—

"Moved by Howell Harris.

"Seconded by A. R. Springett.

"'This Committee recognising the energy and ability shown by Captain Deane, N.W.M. Police, in the discharge of his duties as Superintendent of the Lethbridge District, desires to record its appreciation of the services rendered the Live Stock Interests of Southern Alberta.'

"I have much pleasure in carrying out my instructions.—Yours very truly,

"(*Signed*) R. G. Mathews,
"*Secretary.*"

It is needless for me to say that such remembrances as these cannot fail to be dear to the heart of a public servant.

CHAPTER IX

1902—6. MAPLE CREEK

I SPENT four years at Maple Creek. It was a funny little Methodist-ridden place, containing from four to five hundred people. I was there called upon to resume my clerical duties, which had fallen into abeyance during a term of years. The Church of England had a church there, and a limited vicarage, which some hard-working devotees of the village and its surroundings had managed to raise money enough to build. It was a poor enough living for the incumbent, who had to administer one or two outside parishes, and when he was called away on sundry Sundays during the year he fell back upon me to hold the fort in the Creek. I was very willing to do what I could in that respect, and, although I never presumed to fill the absent gentleman's pulpit, I read the service and gave contributors an opportunity of placing their offerings in the plate. A parson has been called an "incumbent," a "padre," a "sky-pilot," and I do not know how many more names, but, as far as my knowledge goes, it remained for a cow-boy of the Western prairie to christen him the "Devil-dodger!"

The barracks at Maple Creek were about two and a half miles from the embryo town, and I am quite free to confess that I sometimes found it hard to put in the time. I used to ride two and three horses a day for the sake of keeping them exercised, and I have now and again ridden into the town to see if I could find someone to exchange a word with. I had a friend in the manager of the Merchants' Bank, named E. W. McMullen, and while he was there I was sure of finding somebody, but after he was promoted to a larger branch I have often ridden home disappointed. It was a stock country, and there were no idle men in it. What police business there was was mainly in connection with theft of cattle and horses, and the smuggling of animals on the hoof across the imaginary boundary line. The feed on the American side of that line had become depleted, and American owners were in the habit of ranging their cattle and sheep on the Canadian side, where they would fatten them for the Chicago market. The Canadian Customs protested that for this privilege duty should be paid on these animals, and a special officer of Customs was appointed to protect Canadian interests in this behalf. To carry out his instructions he was naturally wholly and solely dependent on the Mounted Police, and we worked with him very cordially, for he, the late Mr. F. Stumden, always "played the game." He was assigned the duty immediately after my successful seizure of smuggled cattle, and seemed to be in communication with the Premier, because he told me one day that he had received a letter wherein Sir Wilfrid said he was very glad to find that his relations with the Mounted Police were so happy.

The Department of Customs, however, did not always "play the game." They did not do it with me, and to-day they owe me $430 on account of the Spencer seizure in 1902. When Mr. J. Bourinot was sent from Ottawa in that year to co-operate with me in the matter, particulars of which had been reported through the ordinary official police channels, he brought with him and showed me the then prevailing Customs regulation in print, to the effect that, in case of a seizure of smuggled goods, one-half of the value thereof became the property of the Crown, the other half was to be divided between the informant and the Customs officer making the seizure. The amount of the penalty in that case, approved by the Exchequer Court, and, on appeal, by the Supreme Court of Canada, was six thousand dollars. Bourinot was therefore entitled to fifteen hundred, and I, as the informant, who had by my own unassisted efforts worked up the case and carried it successfully through two courts of law, was entitled to a like sum. Whatever may have been done since, the case was unique in Customs annals at that time. After the Supreme Court had affirmed the judgment of the Exchequer Court, refusing to set aside the penalty of $6,000, I received on November 25, 1907 (five and a half years after the seizure had been made), a Customs cheque for $550. I represented that considerably more money was due to me on this account, and, on February 4, 1908, received another cheque for $575, making a total of $1,070, and leaving due a balance of $430. By advice of the legal adviser of the Merchants' Bank at Calgary I accepted the cheque "under protest."

It was sent to me through the Collector of Customs at Calgary, by an Inspector of Customs at Toronto. I told him the circumstances, and he said that a somewhat similar fate had befallen him, as, in a seizure which he had made, he had been paid only a percentage of what was due to him. The Inspector of Customs at Toronto who sent me the $575 cheque told me to apply to the collector at Calgary, and to *give him a receipt,* and also said that he did not know who the informer was. It was never clear to me why *he should know,* or why he should have had anything to do with a matter in which the Province of Ontario could not possibly be concerned, for it appertained exclusively to the North-West Territories. I then made inquiries, from the result of which I gathered the conclusion that what was known as the "Inside" service of the Customs Department expected to levy a toll upon the work of the "Outside" service—that is to say, the "Outside" people did the work and the "Inside" people surreptitiously shared the "rake off." Against this there seemed to be no appeal. I wrote a letter of protest addressed to Sir Wilfrid Laurier, the Prime Minister, and sent it through the Commissioner of the Mounted Police.

Whatever was done with the letter, I can only say that I never received even the passing civility of a reply to it, and I presume that it never reached Sir Wilfrid's hands. It was open to me, of course, to pull political strings, but I thought that would be "too small potatoes."

At Maple Creek I was responsible for the protection of about two hundred miles of the main line of the Canadian Pacific Railway, and I studied very deeply the possibility of a train being held up and robbed within the limits of my district. Arrangements had therefore to be made to meet such a contingency, and more than once I talked to the Commissioner about it, but the details would neither interest the public nor be good for the public service.

Suffice it to say, that if such a thing had happened in my district and I had not been able to account for the thieves, I should have considered it an indelible disgrace upon my name; more than that, the public among whom I lived and worked would have thought so too. Although my division numbered something less than fifty officers, non-commissioned officers and men, someone would have been sure to ask what the Mounted Police were maintained in the country for.

In 1906 a Canadian Pacific train was held up and robbed in British Columbia, and, at the request of the

British Columbian Government, a posse of Mounted Police were rushed into the mountains, where they captured the robbers. The ringleader, a hardened old ruffian named Bill Miner, was sentenced to a long term of imprisonment, but was permitted to escape from the penitentiary at New Westminster, B.C. "What we have we hold" did not apply in that discreditable instance.

When, if ever, the Mounted Police are withdrawn from duty in Saskatchewan and Alberta, the public, not only of those provinces, but the travelling public of the Dominion, must make up its mind to face the probability of train robbery.

The Mounted Police system appears to be doomed to extinction in Saskatchewan, as, had it not been for the outbreak of the war, that province would have denounced the existing agreement with the Dominion on April 1, 1915. As the head-quarters of the Force are in Saskatchewan, and as the Alberta Government have intimated their desire to continue the present arrangement, there are indications that new barracks will be built at Calgary on some land which is still the property of the Dominion Government, on the banks of the Bow River.

These changes were foreshadowed in 1905 when the provincial autonomy celebrations were held at Regina and Edmonton respectively. A couple of squadrons of Mounted Police attended, and as they travelled from one capital to another it was openly remarked amongst themselves that, "we are going to attend our own funeral and are going to make as brilliant a flash in the pan as we can."

In the spring of 1904 a syndicate of cattle-men imported, from the East, a number of "stockers," as they are called—that is, young cattle—which they turned out on the range to grow. It happened that, after these poor little creatures had been turned loose, the weather became very bad; a snowstorm, which subsequently turned to rain, set in and soaked and chilled the poor animals through and through. A range-bred yearling will, to some extent, know how to rustle for itself, but these imported beasts knew nothing of the conditions of life on the bald-headed prairie, and they consequently died by the score of exposure and starvation. I never had any sympathy with the syndicate, for they deserved to lose the money which they plentifully lost, and were lucky to escape being prosecuted for cruelty to animals, because that was what their greedy policy amounted to. It transpired, as time went on, that some of the young pilgrims were in process of being stolen by sundry ranchers, and into that complaint it became my duty severely to inquire. In two cases the theft by a prominent and well-to-do rancher of the neighbourhood was abundantly proved, and the judge at the trial, Chief Justice A. L. Sifton, awarded a sentence of two years in the Manitoba penitentiary. The verdict was hardly expected by the general community, and came as a kind of shock to its nerves. The first comment that came to my ears, after pronouncement of the sentence, was a conversation between two ranchers as follows:

"Well, Joe, what do you think of this?"

"It would have done more good, Pete, if it had happened fifteen years ago."

That epitomised the general opinion of the neighbouring stock-owners, who had lost "here a calf, there a calf, here and there a calf," and had never been able to obtain redress. The convict, in this instance, was a pillar of a Nonconformist church and a man of means, who was very assiduous in his religious attendance and duties. After a few months' confinement in the penitentiary, he was suddenly released by order of the Minister of Justice, and took up his former abode as if nothing had happened. The train that conveyed him westward towards his home carried also the Chief Justice who had tried and sentenced him, and of the latter queried a passenger:

"Do you know that —— is in this train going home? He says he is not on ticket of leave, and seems to have been given a pardon. Have you heard anything about it?"

"No," said the Chief Justice, "and, what's more, I don't believe it."

The passenger's statement was, however, true enough, the convict had simply been released, and the local authorities had no information on the subject. It had for some time been no secret that the minister of the nonconforming church in question had been very active in making supplication to the Government to quash the righteous sentence, and the result showed that he had not laboured in vain.

It was a very different proposition, however, a few months later when the same reverend gentleman came to us to complain that his son, a young man, who had recently started a ranch of his own, had had some half-dozen bags of oats stolen from his stable while the owner was absent. The theft was traced to another young rancher, who was trying to earn a living for himself, and then nothing would content the minister of the gospel but his pound of flesh. He insisted on prosecuting the thief, who was convicted in a court of summary jurisdiction and sentenced to imprisonment. It makes all the difference whose ox is gored.

In 1906 I was officially asked if I would like to go to Calgary, the command of which post had been vacant for some months, and on my replying in the affirmative I was transferred thither. It was whispered to me, with how much truth I know not, that the new Minister of the Interior, to wit, Hon. John Oliver, was responsible for this amelioration in my condition. He had said that he would not stand by and see an officer persecuted for having done his duty, and, being in the Cabinet, it was within his power to rectify a wrong if he chose to do so. Anyway, to Calgary I went, and my Maple Creek friends, on the eve of my departure, very kindly presented me with a short appreciative address and a gold-headed walking stick, both of which I value very much.

CHAPTER X

1906—14. CALGARY

WHEN I went to Calgary in July, 1906, the population there was about 15,000 souls, and in the five or six following years it mounted up to 65,000 or thereabouts. In the barracks the commanding officer's quarters had been torn down, having been declared uninhabitable on account of age. They were a little over thirty years old. The Barrack Reserve consisted of rather more than thirty-five acres, situate on the north side of the Bow, at its confluence with the Elbow River, which latter bounded the reserve on its eastern side, and along the northern boundary ran the Canadian Pacific Railway. I was instructed that I might build myself a house on the site of the old one, which had been prettily situated, and the sum of 5,000 dollars was appropriated for the purpose. A suitable plan was soon obtained, and the work was put in hand without delay in August. The excavation of the basement was made by prisoners from the guard-room. The supervision of the work was entrusted to our Division carpenter, named Joseph, who was a most capable mechanic, and who left us soon after to go into business for himself at Okotoks. I said to my staff, "Give the working party all the meat they want to eat, and charge the excess ration to me, but tell them also that I want to be living in that house by Christmas." The consequence was that the men worked willingly and well, and gave no sort of trouble. It happened just at that time that the Carpenters' Union took it into their heads that their wages should be increased by ten cents per hour, and at the increased rate of fifty-five cents the cost of my house exceeded the estimate by $1,200. No exception, however, was taken to that at Ottawa. There was nothing mean about the Police Department so long as Sir Wilfrid Laurier was at the head of it. He is the best friend that the Mounted Police have ever had. He gave them their Pension Bill and took a personal interest in the Force. Any money Bill affecting the Mounted Police passed through the House of Commons without a murmur—to wit, the vote of $35,000 to defray the expenses of the Mounted Police contingent attending the King's Coronation.

My house (it was finished early in December, 1906) was certainly the best house in Mounted Police occupancy at that date, albeit it was a lone house for me to go into, as the dear mother of my children, whom I had been obliged to send for treatment to the Pacific Coast, died there on the day before Christmas Eve, 1906, and my Christmas Day was spent in travelling thither to bring back her remains for burial at Lethbridge.

My house had a twelve-foot wide veranda on the south and east sides, and this came in very handy in the summer of 1907 when it became a question of entertaining H.R.H. Prince Fushimi of Japan. That nobleman had been to England on his royal master's business to the King of all the Britons, and was on his way home. Some angel of light had suggested to him that he should see Calgary on his way through the Rocky Mountains. The problem for me was that the royal foreigner desired to spend half a day in Calgary, and what could be done for his entertainment? In reply to the official letter, I said that I should be glad to entertain the Prince and his suite to luncheon, and it would go hard if I could not, in the interval, devise some sort of amusement to attract his interest. To a man who had commanded an army of 100,000 men in the Russo-Japanese war, it was idle to think of anything in the nature of a military display.

My reply as to the luncheon brought a prompt answer from Comptroller Fred White at Ottawa, "I shall be glad to foot the bill"; and upon me then descended Mr. Commissioner Perry.

The programme that we arranged between us was that a travelling escort should meet the train on its arrival, with a four-horse wagon for the Prince and pair-horse carriages for his staff, and that the visitors should be shown as much of Calgary as was possible in a thirty-minute drive. This drive was to terminate at the barracks, where the party were to be transferred to motor-cars and taken into the country some ten or twelve miles to see a horse ranch of repute, the owners of which were going out of business, and were making preparations to sell their stock, etc., by auction in the very near future. The party was then to be brought back to the city to witness an exhibition game of polo, which the Calgary Club had genially offered to get up for the Prince's edification, and after that he and his suite were to be given luncheon at my house. The Prince's west-bound special train was timed to leave at three o'clock in the afternoon, and every member of my command appreciated the nicety of my life-long dictum that three o'clock meant exactly sixty minutes after two. In order to see how we could most profitably fill in the thirty minutes that we had to start with, I went out one afternoon with the team that was to drive the Prince and drove at a good smart trot round the roads which would show the most prominent points of interest, and timed the drive by my watch. I was unexpectedly delayed at the principal fire quarters by the chief of the Fire

Brigade, who said that they had just had a new electric plant installed, and would I, could I, arrange to get the Prince to open the new addition by stopping on the way for one moment, opposite the Fire Hall, on his road to the railway station from the barracks, and ask him to press the necessary button?

I thought then, as I think still, that Calgary's Fire Brigade, under its competent chief, commonly called "Cappie Smart," is Calgary's greatest asset, and I readily assented. "But show me," I bargained, "where the carriage is to stop, where the string will be hanging that is to carry the button, and mark the spot where the escort is to halt." It happened that the stopping place was across the road from the Fire Hall, so that the Prince and his suite would be well out of the way, they would have a good view of the proceedings, and their journey would not be interfered with. That was all satisfactorily settled, and I took out my watch to time my return to the barracks.

In turning up a street from the avenue in question, when the horses had got well into their stride, we crossed a blind drain which had been insufficiently filled in, and as the hind wheels of my spring wagon crossed it they bumped into the soft depression, which was not noticeable from the road, and I was shot up into the air for something like six inches. When I came down upon the seat I suffered the most excruciating pain that I ever felt in my life. I made noise enough to stop the driver, and was then no more than able to whisper to him to call at Dr. Sanson's house, which we had to pass. The doctor was fortunately at home, he climbed into the wagon with me, and the horses walked very gingerly home. The doctor undressed me, and put me to bed, and went away saying, "I'll send you a nurse; you require massage for that injury to your spine."

It will fit in here, as well as anywhere, to say that

my nurse was a daughter of Captain Barry Valentine Dennehy, once of the 12th Royal Lancers, and subsequently Governor of Kilmainham Gaol, wherein the late Mr. Charles Stewart Parnell was incarcerated. Captain Dennehy, on retirement from the Irish Prison Service, at seventy years of age or over, went to Western Canada and died in Calgary. His daughter graduated in nursing at Victoria, British Columbia, had all sorts of experiences in San Francisco at the time of the earthquake there, and had, at the time of which I write, gravitated back to Calgary, where her father's remains were resting with those of others of her family.

As there was nothing for me to do but to be massaged twice a day and to lie on my back for the rest of the time, my nurse had to act as my eyes and ears and an intelligence department generally, and well she did it. I had a competent working housekeeper, who was quite equal to the occasion of cooking a good luncheon for the party, and I had no misgivings on that account, but there was shopping to be done, every conceivable arrangement to be thought out, and I could only do the thinking while my nurse did the rest, and it kept her busy.

There were twelve persons, all told, in the Prince's suite, and they, with Mr. Commissioner Perry, my two subalterns, Inspectors Duffus and Shaw, and myself completed two tables of eight each: one table in the dining-room and the other in the drawing-room. My next-door neighbour, Mrs. Duffus, as good a neighbour as a man ever had, had undertaken to provide the cut glass, silver, cutlery, etc., for one table, and this relieved me of a great anxiety, for my household had not been designed to provide for more than a dozen people at the outside. The menu I selected was well within my housekeeper's ample capabilities, and I studied "The Times Cookery Book," which I had recently bought, for etceteras. The book had been compiled by a famous ex-chef of Delmonico's, in New York, and would bear quite a lot of study. In it I found a "Sauce Tartare," which was new to me and which I determined to have. I had, as a matter of fact, outlined all the arrangements before I was hurt. I had engaged a Mr. Augade, a French musician, to make himself responsible for the small string band required.

I had seen the florist about table decorations, and a decorative screen of shrubs, &c., for the front of the balcony, where the band was to be ensconced. The florist was also to provide the word "Banzai," in smilax letters, for the veranda at the front door entrance, and the superintendent of the Canadian Pacific dining-car system had undertaken to provide four waiters for the mid-day in question. The sergeant-major had written instructions as to the hauling up and down of the Japanese flag, and I had, humanly speaking, left nothing to chance. My trouble at the time of which I write consisted in seeing that all my arrangements should be properly carried out.

When the eventful day arrived everything passed off according to schedule. The travelling escort, under Inspector Shaw, was fully up to the Mounted Police level, which had been fully established on the occasion of H.R.H. the Duke of York's visit, and the carriages (being spring-seated wagons) were good enough.

When the special train hurtled into the station every horse of the escort stood on his hind legs and pawed the air with his front feet, but, as a newspaper report subsequently said, "The Riders of the Plains quickly got them in hand again," and when His Highness emerged from his car they all stood stock still in their rank. The prescribed drive round Calgary was taken, and at barracks the members of the party were transferred to motor-cars, which were all in readiness. Inspector Duffus drove Prince Fushimi in his own car, and led the procession. At the ranch there was a good lot of horses to be seen, and one His Highness pronounced to be the finest horse he had ever seen in his life. Back to town, to the polo ground, travelled the party, and thence to the barracks, where they sat down to lunch at two o'clock. The dining-room was under the room which I was occupying. Commissioner Perry ran in to me for one moment to say that everything had gone like clockwork, and that there had been no hitch anywhere. I reminded him that the escort and carriages were ordered for a quarter to three. Just before that in came Inspector Shaw to say that the Under-Secretary of State objected to any change in the programme, meaning the opening of the Fire Hall.

I replied, "The Under-Secretary of State has had nothing to do with the programme, and is not going to be allowed to interfere now. You have got your orders, Shaw?" "Yes, sir." "Carry them out to the letter—you know where the carriage is to stop?" "Yes, sir." "Say nothing to anybody, just carry out your instructions, and deliver the party at the station by three o'clock."

Away went Shaw and away went my guests. A slight delay occurred at the Fire Hall, as nothing would induce the Prince to press the necessary button. One of his staff, however, did it eventually: the Fire Hall doors flew open, the fire horses jumped into their collars and out galloped the Fire Brigade in a very gratifying style.

My outfit went on its way rejoicing, and delivered its passengers on the railway platform at sixty minutes after two o'clock.

The viceregal party were then bound for Banff, where they were timed to stay a day or two, and where the Prince hoped to get some fishing. It happened that there was stationed there at that time, in charge of the Mounted Police detachment at Bankhead, a Corporal (now Inspector) Townsend, who was an enthusiastic and knowledgeable fisherman. He was instructed to take Prince Fushimi under his wing, and he accordingly took him out in a boat on one of the lakes where fish were abundant. It so happened that at his first cast the Prince caught two fish on one hook, and was so delighted that he laughed heartily. His staff said it was the first time he had laughed since leaving Montreal! We had done the best we could for him, and there was nothing more to be said.

My nurse stayed with me in all for eleven days, and after she had left I found that life was insupportable without her bright eyes, cheery manner and Irish wit, and, to cut a long story short, I haunted her in a quite persistent fashion until she consented to marry me.

We were married by Father Jan, Roman Catholic priest, at Calgary, on April 22, 1908. This was the year in which, on April 30, I attained my sixtieth birthday, and Mounted Police Regulations provided that, unless an officer married before he became sixty years of age there would be no pension accruing to his widow. As my bride-elect was fifteen years younger than myself, I did not think it prudent to take any unnecessary chances in that direction, and we were thus married a little earlier than we proposed.

On September 20 ("When the Alma's heights were won"), 1911, my dear wife was ordered to hospital for treatment, suffering from pneumonia. That night pleurisy set in, and as a complication her foot had to be amputated. This was a terrible loss to the patient, as she had always been such a very active woman. Even after that she nearly lost her life in the month of December in the same year, having to undergo an operation for empyema. So little a flicker of life remained in her

THE MOUNTED POLICE BARRACKS, REGINA, 1885

The central building across the square is the Guard-room, which had been recently enlarged, as shown by the dark stripe on the roof

after the operation that she could not be moved from the operation table for four hours, and she unquestionably owed her life to the surgical skill of my eldest son, who was practising in Calgary, and who was her medical attendant from first to last.

We tided over Christmas Day, and the outlook was very hopeful. For the first time in twenty-eight years, the Mounted Police did not give their annual ball in 1911, nor since. E Division had always, from the days of barbarism, given a New Year's Eve ball, and old-timers never failed to attend it when possible, but in 1911 the subject was never mooted, and I was too sick at heart to raise it. As the weeks rolled into months we dispensed first with the night nurse, and after a time with the day nurse, and substituted a lady companion, without whom, after some months, we found that we could do. In November, 1913, my wife gave an afternoon tea-party, not in her own house, where the "racket" would have been too great for her, but in a Calgary restaurant, where they had just "caught on" to that idea of so attracting custom, and she was like her old self, and her many guests were glad to be welcomed by her genial smile.

As the year 1913 drew to a close, I began to feel less satisfied with my wife's condition, and talked to my son about it. He reminded me that he had always been apprehensive, and had warned me (as he had) of the possibility of tuberculosis intervening in her medical history, and he had had, more than once, analyses made of the patient's sputum.

On March 27, 1914, I received information verifying the diagnosis, while we were in process of packing up to vacate the barracks, for the benefit of the Grand Trunk Pacific Railway. As a matter of fact we turned out of our quarters into a house in Calgary which the Government had rented for us on April 1. The guard-room was not emptied of its prisoners, nor were the buildings occupied by our men and horses vacated until some days later, but I, personally, did not choose to be under an obligation to the Grand Trunk Pacific Railway, and moved myself and my belongings off their premises on the date stated. I was then in a position to talk to them, and the opportunity soon arose. As I have previously indicated, the lawn and gardens surrounding my official quarters were made by my own self. I had, for instance, a caragana hedge, to which I had devoted a good deal of time and thought and some money. I had watched over it for seven or eight years, and had sworn loudly and coherently when some maniacal cricketer now and then had dashed through it in pursuit of his ball, when he might have gone round. But that has nothing to do with this point. The management of the Calgary Cricket Club always used to protect my garden and its surroundings as far as they could, and, if a light of my cucumber or melon frame was broken by a stray ball I did not mind, but I had a rooted objection to anyone running through my hedge.

The hedge which I had planted I had taken up and given to an old lady friend, who had just moved to a new house. One afternoon, soon after, I was called up by telephone in respect of this action by Mr. Zimmermann, solicitor of the Grand Trunk Pacific Railway, which had purchased this land. I explained sweetly that I had only been giving away my own property.

"We'll see about that," he thundered. "You need not worry," I rejoined, "I have seen about it, the last load has just gone." And herewith I hung up the telephone and left him talking.

CHAPTER XI

1906—14. CALGARY (*continued*)

In giving now an account of the work of the Calgary Division, I may say the Police District extended from the eastern boundary of British Columbia to the fourth meridian, a distance averaging roughly about three hundred miles, with a longitudinal width of about one hundred. To administer this expanse of country we had detachments, varying in number from twenty-two to twenty-five, dotted over the area. There were in the Rocky Mountains and the foot-hills coal mines that depended on us for police protection, and on the whole we had, comparatively speaking, very little trouble with the workmen. It is true that at one time there was a general strike of miners almost throughout the Province of Alberta, and coal had even to be imported from outside sources. The elaborate Governmental arrangements for arbitrating such disputes turned out to be a fizzle, cost the country money as a matter of course, and did no good at all. My clients, as I called them—that is, owners along the main line of the Canadian Pacific—used to come in and see me sometimes, but I always threw cold water upon anything in the nature of agitation.

The directorate of one of the companies came one day and said that a considerable number of their workmen had acquired some rights on the company's town site by having erected buildings thereon for their own occupation, and those men would not go to work themselves and had generally a bad influence upon the mining community at large. Obviously some legal process was necessary in order to make these malcontents vacate the company's property, and that always took time. The owners, of course, acting under legal advice, had taken their troubles to the courts, which had issued all manner of injunctions to the trouble-makers to do so and so.

It was in this half-way stage that one manager in particular came to me with a view to police protection.

I said, "I have not a man to give you, and if I had, he would simply be wasting his time. If you could spend the inside of a week with me, and realise how sometimes I am puzzled to find a single man for any duty whatever—when the courts are going full blast, and escorts and orderlies have to be found for them, lunatics and convicted prisoners have to be conducted to their respective destinations, horses in the Post have to be groomed and fed, even if they are turned out into the corral to exercise themselves—do you realise that if I had not prisoners here the horses would never be groomed at all, for there would be no one to do it, and one escort cannot look after more than five prisoners in a gang at a time? I should like you to realise that my division consists of sixty officers and men all told; and if I withdraw a man from a detachment elsewhere and send him to you, some other place suffers, and what do you gain? An additional red coat in your community will simply irritate your men and provoke them to breaches of the peace. That is the very thing you want to avoid. Do nothing to irritate them if you can help it.

"You tell me that all the necessary process of law has been served to enable your company to rid itself of the objectionable persons now encumbering your property? There is no necessity for the Mounted Police to butt into that proposition, and they have no right to do so. When the time comes, the order of the Court will be issued to its own officers, sheriffs, bailiffs, etc., and if those officers find that they cannot execute the orders of the Court, reference will unquestionably be made to us. . It will then be for me to decide whether I can enforce the decree of the Court, or whether I have to apply for assistance. In the last resort, you understand, of course, that the militia might have to be called out.

"All that you have to do, my friend, is to sit tight and let the machine work. Don't let your men think you're worrying—be as genial to them as you can, and you may avert a great deal of damage to your works."

The manager in question, when he left me, said, "Captain Deane, it does me good to come and talk to you—I feel like a different man."

"Well," I replied, "it is an inexpensive form of entertainment, and you are quite welcome to any comfort that I can give you whenever you choose to come for it. But I bar visiting that village of yours. Goodbye!" and with a laugh we parted.

I have more than once mentioned prisoners in connection with Calgary. The guard-room there contained more prisoners than any other guard-room of the Mounted Police except at Dawson City in the Yukon.

The only gaol for females in the Province of Alberta was situated in our grounds, and was in our charge.

I found it necessary to make a change after I had a few weeks' experience of Calgary, and imported a matron of my own selection from Maple Creek, and a great help and comfort she was to me. Sarah Stuttaford was the widow of a staff sergeant of Royal Engineers, who had served with his regiment in India and South Africa, and had ridden in a baggage wagon over many a weary mile.

When I first met her in 1902 at Maple Creek she had lost her husband, was over sixty years old, and had then been nursing maternity and other cases for twenty years.

Some of the cases that we had to deal with were heart-breaking. That is where old Sarah Stuttaford shone. Without any apparent desire to do more than pass the time of day if her patient were sufficiently affable for that much civility, she would unobtrusively get to the bottom of the trouble, and was thus better enabled to deal with the sufferer, who never failed to meet sympathy with confidence. One poor woman, I remember, had had, I think, fourteen children in a very short space of time, and was literally "played out." She was done to death with motherhood, babyhood, and hard manual labour. No change, no relief from the monotony of the bald-headed prairie with its dismal outlook, day after day, week after week, month after month, year after year, and after that "the Beyond." Father has got his work to do, there is in it some change, and it is not so bad for him. The children have their fun at school or elsewhere, but when or where does poor Mother get any relief? Has she a neighbour with whom she can exchange a word once a week? In that country of illimitable distances it is most likely that she has not. The poor woman that I have been speaking of went to the asylum, and I have not heard of her since.

Another case of a woman, just as sad, lingers in my memory. It happened in the country, and when the police report came in I wrote a marginal note on it: "The saddest story I have ever read in my life." Briefly it was this: An inquest had been held on the body of a woman who had taken her own life, and a letter which she had written to her children was put in as an exhibit. The substance of it was that she loved her children as much as ever and grieved to be parted from them, but the conditions of her life were intolerable, and she was therefore driven to deliver herself from her thraldom by the poison route. Her husband was apparently a Shylock who must have his pound of flesh, and by the time her conjugal duties in that respect had been performed, and she had done to her family the manifold and ever-increasing duties of a mother and a housekeeper, there was no time left in this world for a space to breathe, and she frankly admitted that she could not continue the fight. Hence the inquest.

We did not take coroner's inquests very seriously in Western Canada, as a coroner's warrant there will not suffice to place a man upon trial for homicide; but, in every instance, the Mounted Police used to collect all the available evidence and place it upon record. It not infrequently happened that a body which had been buried by virtue of a coroner's order had to be exhumed, and the cause of death investigated in a magistrate's court.

There is, on the other hand, a danger of going to the other extreme if the ancient "Crowner's quest" is too lightly set aside. I had one notable instance of this in the early days at Lethbridge. What was known as the "Yard engine," in the course of its daily perambulations up and down a stretch of a mile and a half or so, while shunting coal and other cars, and making up trains, had imperceptibly become the vehicle whereby school children had thought that they might "have a free ride" between their homes and their school, etc. A kind-hearted engine driver was always complaisant, and he allowed them to climb into his cab in order to let them have their "ride," and was always careful to take good care of them. But this practice was fraught with possibilities which might render the railway authorities ultimately responsible for a violent death; and, when their attention was called to it, they issued a peremptory order that no person, other than one of their own recognised employees, should take unauthorised passages by such trains.

Unhappily it befell that, notwithstanding the driver's care, a boy was killed.

I rang up the coroner and insisted on an inquest. He replied that "this was obviously an accident, and the boy had no business to be there."

I agreed with all that, but represented that the boy had come to a violent end, that something or somebody was responsible for the accident, and that it was the coroner's business to inquire into the particulars.

At the inquest these were thoroughly thrashed out, and the storekeeper of the company deposed that he had been visiting an extensive coal-shed and, on his way back to his office, had crossed the railway lines in the neighbourhood of the accident, had noticed the switch in question, and, as he passed by, thoughtlessly pushed it over, with the result that the flat cars were deflected from their proper line of rails on to the line whereon some loaded cars were standing, and a boy died a violent death in consequence. "Accidental death" was the jury's verdict, and there was nothing more to be done.

To return to Mrs. Stuttaford, the manner in which she controlled her various ward women of all nationalities, and lunatics, amply justified my selection of a matron. As time went on, we had to get a night matron, and then an assistant. With all the help which I did not stint to give her, it was difficult to keep the old woman from working herself to death. The number of prisoners that she looked after frequently ran from twenty to twenty-four, in accommodation that was supposed to provide for ten or twelve at the outside.

It was just as bad on the male side. On one occasion I had ninety-six prisoners, all told, in my custody, in premises which were intended to receive only about fifty-five men, women, and lunatics. That was an exceptional occasion, when a bunch of prisoners for stealing rides on the railway was brought in when my back happened to be turned, and the Provost very properly did not refuse to receive them, as I would have done had I been on the spot. I resolutely refused to receive more prisoners than I could reasonably provide for. The cells in both guard-rooms were always full, and, beyond that, it became a matter for my consideration. As a rule, I allowed that we could find room for about seventy without unpleasant overcrowding, but "ructions" sometimes threatened.

The situation once became particularly strained. We had, some months previously, had a half-breed prisoner named Moses Brown, committed for a term of imprisonment from the city. We knew Moses and his attractions quite well. He was suffering from a loathsome disease and was a nuisance to everybody whom he approached. On the day of his arrival I instructed the Provost to give him a pair of the cheap garden shears, and to conduct him to the limit of the police reserve on the banks of the river and invite him to cut as much of the wire grass growing there as he felt disposed. If he should get tired in the course of the afternoon he would be welcome to rest.

When at locking-up time the guard went round to look for Moses he was not to be found, and the weeks ran into months before we heard of him again. We did not want to hear, be it observed, and I did not offer any reward for his recapture.

Moses could not, however, apparently go away to his

relations and friends on the prairie, and give them the exclusive benefit of his society, but he must gravitate again towards Calgary and there fall foul of the City Police. His return came to my notice when the Provost handed me a warrant of commitment, and said, "Moses Brown is back." "How did he come?" said I. "By the City Black Maria, sir." "Tell the Black Maria to give my compliments to the Chief of the City Police, and to say that we have no accommodation here for Moses Brown."

A day or two later the Deputy Attorney-General at Edmonton rang me up: "Good morning, etc. etc. What is the difficulty between you and the City Police magistrate?"

"Is there any?" I inquired. "I was not aware of it."

"Well," he rejoined, "I have here a letter from him which leads me to think that there must be considerable trouble between you."

"Is that so?" I retorted. "I don't think you need worry. The young gentleman perhaps is under the impression that he is running my guard-room as well as his own office; and if you will believe me, he is not doing anything of the kind. At the same time I would say, send me that letter. It will amuse me to answer it. Good-bye." That settled that.

Our guard-rooms were, I should not omit to remark, places of execution, and although we had only two death sentences actually to carry out, we had several other prisoners under sentence for whom we had to provide the "death watch," and an intolerable nuisance it was, until the sentences were commuted for one cause or another.

A man named John Fisk, whose crime, etc., is described under the heading of the "Tucker Peach Murder,"* was the first to go. While he was awaiting

* Page 234.

the due process of the law, a man came to see me one afternoon, just as I was stepping off my veranda steps into my garden—a fine big man he was, with the eye of a religious enthusiast. He wanted to see John Fisk to convert him from the error of his ways before it was too late, and I explained to him very patiently and quietly that the convict was being attended daily by the spiritual pastor of his own choosing, and that, even if I wished, I could not admit a stranger to the exercise of that holy office. It would not be fair to the Methodist minister who was looking after the prisoner's spiritual welfare. My visitor, as I found, was not open to any sort of reason; he had a wild eye; he was as big a man as myself, and was probably fifty pounds heavier.

When he finally realised that he was not to have the entrée of the prison, he said, "I summon you to the bar of God for refusing to allow me to see the condemned prisoner." I replied, "I'll be there! I'll meet you, but in the meantime you cannot see John Fisk." Then he raised his voice and began to rant, and I heard an upstair window softly open, and pictured to myself an anxious little face looking out, so I walked quietly up to him and said, "If you brawl here I will have you locked up." He glared at me for a moment, and I did not know what he might do, but suddenly, without a word, he turned on his heel, and I did not see him for dust.

The other condemned convict was an American citizen, who had brutally murdered the employer who had brought him into Canada from the United States, and he gave us quite a bit of extra and unnecessary trouble.

His name was Jasper Collins, a native of Missouri, U.S.A., and the story of his crime is related under the heading of "The Benson Murder and Arson."* This young man started a hunger strike. He would not take

* Page 250.

any nourishment, so we had to feed him forcibly. He would not speak or help himself in any way, so a constable was told off to nurse him. This was in addition to the "death watch," who sat in a chair in the guard-room and gave his undivided attention to the occupant of the condemned cell. He thus brought himself to a very weak state—had to be assisted up the steps to the scaffold, and was sitting in a chair when the drop fell.

I cannot omit to mention the loyal and devoted service which our prisoners used to receive from the Salvation Army. Every Sunday morning of their lives they held services on both sides of the guard-room, by men on the male side, by lasses on the other, and both sexes were always welcome. "Rain, hail, shine or snow," "the Army" never failed to keep watch and ward, and their one most persistent question to every poor creature who showed any reciprocity to their persuasions was, "What can we do for you when you come out?" They would take an expectant mother into their fold, nurse her through her confinement, and take every tender care of her and her baby until they could make some permanent provision for both. And all this for the sake of the faith that was in them. No other denomination troubled itself to do the like.

One of the Roman Catholic priesthood always made a point of holding a short service in the guard-room every Sunday afternoon, and the women gladly listened to him, whether they were members of his flock or not. When a Roman Catholic bishop was appointed to the See of Calgary the Oblate Fathers of the Immaculate Mary ("O.M.I." they signed themselves) were generally withdrawn from the city parishes and their places were taken by English-speaking clergy. The Oblate Fathers had spent their lives on the Western prairie, and had helped to open up the country, witness the Venerable Father Lacombe, without whose incomparable influence among the Blood Indians the Canadian Pacific Railway would not have been constructed without trouble in 1882. The then General Manager of the C.P.R. (the late Sir William Van Horne) recognised this when he sent to the Reverend Father a life pass on the railway "as a charm against conductors!" In his latter years Father Lacombe conceived the idea of immortalising himself by the erection of a "Lacombe Home," for the old and destitute pilgrims among whom he had spent so many years of his life.

All sorts of stories are told of his begging faculty. He had literally nothing himself.

There was a very nice property, of about two hundred acres, situate on Fish Creek, about ten miles distant from Calgary, and Father Lacombe had his eye on this. For various reasons Pat Burns, the "Cattle King," did not respond to invitations in this direction, and drove the old father to several other locations whereof he could take his choice, but he was quite irresponsive, and was in no way to be diverted from Fish Creek.

When it came to the final point the old father said, "You give me dat, or you give me not'ing."

Fish Creek is the site of his Home, to which I paid almost my last visit in Calgary, to say good-bye to my old friend, then in the very late eighties, and feeble.

I can never forget his coming to see me in 1902, when I was in hospital at Lethbridge, worn out both mentally and physically, and having been obliged to send my wife to the Pacific Coast for change of air and treatment.

CHAPTER XII

THE PASSING OF THE CALGARY BARRACKS. 1914

It was in 1907, the year after I took up my abode in my new house at Calgary, that the agitation began which eventually resulted in the site of the Calgary Barracks being handed over to the Grand Trunk Pacific Railway Company. In the course of that summer a man, whom I knew very well, dropped into my office, and said he was the agent of a syndicate which had placed considerable sums at his disposal for the purchase of property in the immediate vicinity of the barracks. He interviewed the Divisional tailor, and offered him 15,000 dollars, spot cash, for a house and 25 foot lot which he owned near the barracks. The tailor, being a man of singular domesticity, said that he must consult his wife, and did so at the noon-day recess.

On receipt of his conjugal instructions, however, he found that the aforesaid agent was no longer looking for him. When he discovered the agent, and said that he was willing to sell, the agent replied, "Oh! my dear fellow, that money has been invested elsewhere; you did not accept my offer, my people would not wait, and I bought another property. The money is now all gone, so that you see you are out of luck."

The syndicate that I have mentioned was composed of Liberal politicians (possessed of inside information as to the tentative negotiations that had then begun) who were interested in exploiting the public domain to their own advantage. A year or so later I was instructed to have the barracks painted, and a contract of about 700 dollars was let for that purpose. Before the work had commenced I met a prominent lawyer, one of the inner circle, in the barrack grounds one day, who said, "Captain Deane, within three months you will see the Grand Trunk Pacific men in possession of these grounds, removing the buildings and levelling the site, preparatory to constructing a big union station here." The union station was intended to accommodate the Canadian Northern and Grand Trunk Pacific Railways, both of which desired a foothold in Calgary in opposition to the Canadian Pacific. I said to my friend, "Do you know that we have just let a contract to paint all these buildings here?" "Waste of money," he somewhat angrily replied, and I retorted, "That may be so, but the indications are that your dream is not going to be immediately realised."

Year after year rolled on, and there were no results in sight.

The Grand Trunk Pacific may be said to have been Sir Wilfrid Laurier's foundling. His desire was to go down to history as the promoter of a trans-continental line which should worthily compete with the Canadian Pacific, and the railway authorities thought that they could acquire a parcel of something over thirty-five acres from the Dominion Government for a song.

But they reckoned without their host, for Sir Wilfrid had no idea of throwing away an important asset like that for nothing, and he stipulated that the price should be one million dollars. That was a hopeless proposition to the G.T.P., as they are called, but there are more ways of killing a cat than by choking it with cream. When Mr. (now Sir Robert) Borden, then in opposition, toured the country prior to the General Election of 1911, and held a very large meeting at the Calgary rink, the then member for Calgary cast reflections at the Dominion Government for "holding up" the Grand Trunk for a million dollars in the case of a property worth "say a hundred and fifty thousand."

Although we were both ardent Conservatives, my wife and I were so disgusted at this statement that we abandoned our seats on the platform and went home.

This statement, which was uncontradicted, lighted a fresh spark of hope in the hearts of the before-mentioned Liberal syndicate. "My God!" said they, "we may come through with it after all." And the irony of it was, that the chance came to them through their political opponents, who were bound to be "agin the Government" whether it was right or wrong.

Eventually a committee of Calgary men was deputed to look over the site and form an estimate of its value.

The only map apparently extant used to hang in my office, and the Comptroller, R.N.W.M.P., in an early stage of the conference, asked permission to carry it off to Ottawa, as he had none. My recollection is that the map showed the site to consist of thirty-seven acres and a fraction. Be that as it may, it came to be spoken of as embracing about thirty-five acres.

The committee of townsmen assumed the site to consist of thirty-five acres, and calculated that each acre would cut up into ten lots, making 35,000 lots of 25 foot width. These they assessed at $1,000 a lot, with one dissentient member, a Mr. Diamond, a Calgary jeweller, who considered that the lots were worth $5,000 apiece.

After the Borden Government came into power, the Assistant Judge of the Exchequer Court was sent to make inquiries on the spot and to assess the value. He held an informal sort of inquiry, and eventually fixed upon $225,000 as the figure. It was essentially an inquiry designed to popularise the award with the party in power, but even then the amount was regarded at

Ottawa as being inadequate, for it was raised by Mr. Borden to $250,000. Certain witnesses, most of them interested, tendered their evidence, but the judge failed to call the one disinterested witness, namely, the city assessor, who could have told him that the 25-foot lots adjoining the barracks enclosure on its western side were valued, for city taxation purposes, at $20,000 each, and that those on the eastern boundary, across the Elbow River, on the same avenue, were valued at $5,000 each. A mean estimate between the two would have been a business-like proposition, and would have supported Sir Wilfrid Laurier's estimate, but that was the last thing that the party in power had in their minds, so it came about that the Grand Trunk Pacific, for the payment of a quarter of a million dollars, obtained a very desirable slice of the public domain which was worth at least four times that sum.

It was not until St. Valentine's Day that I received official notice that the barracks had to be vacated by April 1 following, which was a fair sample of maladministration on the part of the Dominion Government. Mr. Borden had had two years and a half wherein to consider whether or not, and at what price, he would sell the barracks site to the Railway Company, and, after all that, the departments concerned were allowed six weeks wherein to make arrangements which it was not possible to make in the time.

That was where one of the pleasantries of opposing politics came in. It was the duty of the Provincial Government to make provision for the prisoners, and they had done nothing of the kind, so that, in effect, the Dominion Government's order to us to vacate the barracks by April 1 was an absurdity.

Until provision had been made elsewhere for the prisoners they were obliged to stay where they were, and so long as the prisoners had to be looked after, our men could not be moved, so that it was not until the last day of the month of April that we sent away to Macleod, in a special train, forty male and nineteen female prisoners, with two matrons and a suitable escort. I saw Mrs. Stuttaford then for the last time, as she was going to inaugurate the women's prison in Macleod.

Quarters in the city had been provided for our men and horses, and we moved into them within a day or two after the departure of the prisoners.

The once pretty site soon became unrecognisable, the shrubs and trees were removed, the buildings torn down, and the only house left intact was the one that I had vacated, and that was moved to the opposite end of the enclosure for occupation by the station agent.

Personally, I had no particular regrets. My wife and I had agreed that we would leave Western Canada at the end of June, to seek out some little spot in England where the Maréchal Niel rose will grow out of doors, and to that end, early in the year 1914, I had bespoken our passages to Liverpool, to leave New York by a ship sailing on July 11.

We moved off the Grand Trunk property on April 1, and settled in a house which I rented in West Calgary. There the best that I could do was to establish my patient in comfortable surroundings under canvas at the back of the house, with electric light, bells, heat and fan, for the weather was so variable that the fan and hose-pipe spray were required in the daytime to keep the tent cool, and at night the heater had to be turned on to keep it warm.

Comfortably housed in a double-roofed tent, with two excellent nurses to wait upon her by day and by night, my dear wife spent her last days, and passed away peacefully and painlessly on the early morning of July 22.

I laid her to rest by the side of her old father

in the Roman Catholic Cemetery at Calgary, had a suitable headstone erected, and then, having had only two months' leave in my thirty-one years of service, I applied for six months' leave from the ensuing October 1, to be retired on pension at the expiration thereof.

My department was generous enough to assent to every request that I made, and Commissioner Perry was very considerate. He pressed me to consider myself quite free from office obligations during my stay in the West, and to devote my attention to regaining my own health and strength. I took him largely at his word, and on the night of September 30 I bade farewell to Calgary, the associations of which, despite the sympathy of kind friends, had become unendurable.

CHAPTER XIII

MOUNTED POLICE LAW

THE *raison d'être* of the subject-matter of the following chapter is to be found in the circumstances that, at the date of which I speak, the relations of the Mounted Police Courts to the ordinary Courts of Law stood as an unknown quantity. There was an undefined feeling that they were subject to the control and supervision of the Supreme Court, but the question had never been raised in a concrete form, and neither Bench nor Bar was interested in the abstract question. I had on one or two occasions noticed on the part of young, aggressive lawyers indications which led me to think that some day the question might be raised in a manner that would call for a pronouncement thereupon by some competent authority, but so far there had been no clash. In the month of November, 1898, however, the monster raised his head in such an uncompromising fashion that something had to be done to settle the dispute for all time. As it happened, it fell to my lot to take the self-assertive monster in hand, and, as it also happened, perhaps fortunately, it had fallen to my lot to learn in my old corps some military law which no other officer in, or connected with, the Mounted Police had had occasion or opportunity to learn.

The difficulty came to a head in this wise: In November, 1898, I was in command of the division at Macleod as well as of that at Lethbridge, and used to spend four days of each week at the former place. Belonging to one of the detachments of the Macleod Division was a constable named B. O. Nettleship. It happened that on November 29 this constable would complete the term of service for which he had engaged, and would be entitled to claim his discharge. He had recently come into a legacy of a few hundred dollars, and intended to settle in British Columbia. He was a man of whom I, personally, knew nothing, but his record was good; he had been a handy-man in his detachment, and was a fairly good axe-man, etc., and I felt quite kindly disposed to him. When, therefore, he appeared before me on the morning of November 23, and asked me to give him leave of absence until the end of his term, and to allow him to "sign off," as it was called, before he left, so that he would not have to come back on the 29th to complete his discharge papers, I cordially agreed.

I convened the usual Board of Officers to carry out the regulations in such a case, namely, to verify and record the particulars of the man's service, to adjust his accounts, and to ascertain whether or not he had any claim against the Government in connection with his past service. This was all a pure matter of form, usual in every disciplinary community of which I have any knowledge, and was designed not only to protect the Government in the future, but to see that the person about to be discharged was in process of receiving all dues that were properly coming to him.

During my weekly visit to Macleod I had to compress about a week's work into four days, and was naturally kept pretty busy. That afternoon, while in my office, the door between that and the clerk's office being open, I was very much annoyed by the strident tones of a man's voice which seemed to have a great deal more to say than was necessary, and at last it worked so much upon my nerves that I called to the chief clerk and asked who the man was and why he was talking so much. The sergeant replied that the man was Constable Nettleship, whose discharge papers were being made out by the Board of Officers, and that he was under the influence of liquor. I said, "Send him out of the office at once to return to duty. His pass is cancelled. Let the sergeant-major know."

This was the only alternative to placing the man under arrest on a charge of "Intoxication, however slight," according to the wording of the Mounted Police Act. I thought that in all probability he would reappear next morning, say he was sorry, and renew his application for leave. I had it vaguely in my mind that if he should do so I would give him his leave and let him go.

This, however, proved to be the last thing that Nettleship intended to do; for in the course of the same afternoon he deserted. He went to stay with some friends of his in Macleod who kept him perdu for a couple of days or so at great risk to themselves, and then he developed diphtheria. The Health Officer promptly isolated him in the "Pest House," and applied to me "to make the necessary arrangements for his medical attendance, nursing, and maintenance." I replied that a man of the name he mentioned was then in a state of desertion from the N.W.M.P., and I declined to accept any responsibility for his medical attendance, etc. I added that he was quite able to pay his own expenses.

There was at that time living and practising in Macleod a very clever lawyer. To him Nettleship applied for advice in his dilemma. The proposition made was quite simple: Nettleship had money which was burning a hole in his pocket, and his legal adviser was quite willing to relieve him of any inconvenient surplus.

The lawyer advised his client that he was no longer a member of the Police Force, and he may, for aught I know, have honestly believed that the advice he was giving was good. I made no secret of my intention to hold Nettleship accountable for his act of desertion as soon as he should be released from quarantine, and the lawyer then made application to a judge of the Supreme Court, sitting in Calgary, for a Writ of Prohibition.

The affidavits upon which this application was based bristled with falsehoods, and I made a trip to Calgary with material to contradict them.

While at Calgary I spent Sunday afternoon with an old Regina friend, Mr. Justice D. L. Scott, and to him I confided my troubles. He listened patiently for a time, and at last said, "Deane, do you mean to tell me that I cannot issue a Writ of Prohibition to prevent you from doing something that I think you ought not to do?"

I replied, "That's exactly what I do mean. So long as I do not exceed my jurisdiction, you have no lawful right whatever to interfere with me."

In general terms I explained the situation as I asserted it to be, and he finally said, "Well, if what you say is correct, I suppose there is something in your contention." I had applied to head-quarters, prior to my visit to Calgary, for authority to employ Mr. C. C. McCaul, a Calgary lawyer, to represent the Mounted Police in this matter, being well assured that he would, at all events, have taken some trouble to look into the matter. But he was what the Grits called "a Tory," and my application found no favour. The Liberal party was then in power, and wanted every visible fragment of the loaves and fishes. The North-West Territories were a sort of private game reserve operated principally in the interests of the Sifton family, the prominent member of which was the Minister of the

Interior in the Dominion Cabinet. I was therefore in no way surprised when I received instructions to employ Mr. A. L. Sifton, who was the Calgary Crown Prosecutor at the time. This gentleman had, in his official capacity, previously mishandled an excellent case for me, so I hardened my heart, left my case in his hands, and returned to my command to work up the case myself.

In course of time the case came up for argument in chambers at Calgary, and a lawyer who was present remarked to me afterwards, "If I had not known that Sifton was representing the police, I should have thought he was appearing for the other side."

It was no wonder, then, that the rule nisi was issued, and I was prohibited from dealing with Nettleship. The prejudice of the learned judge obtruded in every line. He set up a man of straw and battered him out of all recognition, to the admiration and delight of counsel on both sides.

In the meanwhile I had laid a charge of perjury against Nettleship on one of the many false statements in his numerous affidavits, and instructed the Crown Prosecutor at Lethbridge, Mr. C. F. P. Conybeare, K.C., to appear for the Crown. The charge was fully proved by the only two witnesses, besides Nettleship, who knew the facts, who positively contradicted the accused, but the judge showed his bias again, took the case from the jury, and directed them to return a verdict of "Not guilty," which they did. Then Mr. Conybeare, as instructed by myself, gave notice of appeal to the Court in Banco against the Writ of Prohibition.

We had got on to a business footing at last, and the ball was with me.

My friend Conybeare had a most excellent law library, which he placed unreservedly at my disposal, and during the ensuing weeks I made full use of it, and burnt many gallons of midnight oil in preparing that which would effectively "call" my opponent's "bluff."

On March 10, 1899, I was ready for the fray, for on that day I dated to the Commissioner of the Mounted Police a letter which epitomised the result of my labours and researches. This letter, I knew, would be referred to the Department of Justice at Ottawa, and from there it was forwarded to Mr. A. L. Sifton at Calgary to prosecute the appeal.

That gentleman could not, without breach of professional etiquette, take out of Mr. Conybeare's hands the action which the latter had initiated, and so, fortunately, we were able to travel still along business lines. The letter contained a good deal of interesting matter, dicta of eminent English judges, and so forth, known to an extremely limited circle of professional men in the North-West; but as the text is by far too long to be here reproduced in extenso, I shall here mention only that, after having marshalled my evidence, I concluded by saying:

"I submit that the N.W.M. Police, if not a military body, are as nearly military as it is possible for an armed body of Constabulary to be; that the Statute by virtue of which they exist enjoins and provides for the maintenance of discipline, and that their discipline is essentially of a military character. Their regulations respecting the grant of an indulgence of a pass, and the form of pass itself, are adopted from those in vogue in the British Army. They are purely matters affecting the interior economy and discipline of the N.W.M. Police. Similarly the regulations and customs affecting the grant of discharge from the Force are a question of interior economy and discipline.

"The question of the pass is the crux of the whole

matter, for, apart from that, the question of the discharge would never have been raised.

"It is clear from the learned Judge's minutes of judgment that the questions of 'Pass' and 'Discharge' must stand or fall together.

"This being so, I am entitled to contend, on the lines of Chief Baron Kelly's judgment, that the issue and subsequent cancellation of Constable Nettleship's pass affected a Police indulgence, granted by a Police Officer, in his capacity of Commanding Officer of Police, to a Police Constable, admittedly under his Command: and that the question being thus purely of a Police character, involving a question of Police discipline alone, is cognisable only by a Police tribunal, and not by a Court of law."

An eminent Grit lawyer and politician in Macleod, Mr. Malcolm McKenzie, to whom I showed my letter, remarked as he handed it back to me: "If your counsel does nothing more than take that letter into court and read it, he cannot lose his case. It is not a brief, it is a complete argument."

The case for the Mounted Police was very ably presented by Mr. Conybeare to the Court in Banco at Regina. One of the judges, Mr. Justice Maguire, had apparently heard Judge Rouleau's side of the story, and interjected so many interruptions to Mr. Conybeare while he was speaking, that, to use the expression of a lawyer who was present and told me afterwards, he almost "heckled" him. However, Mr. Conybeare withstood the ordeal with unshaken imperturbability, and the end of it was that Mr. Justice Maguire, after Judge Wetmore had written the judgment of the Court, added a judgment of his own giving reasons additional to those given by the Court why the Writ of Prohibition should be quashed. It would be too tedious to set forth these judgments at length. The judgment of the Court, as rendered by Judge Wetmore, concluded in the following words:

"This being so, we must find that the order of Mr. Justice Rouleau was granted incautiously, and, in view of what appears above, it is not considered necessary to allude to any other questions raised in the appeal.

"The judgment of the Court is: That the order granted by the learned judge be rescinded, and the Writ of Prohibition issued thereon and all proceedings thereunder set aside, with costs to be paid by the Respondent."

When Nettleship's counsel was subsequently notified of this issue, all that he had to say was, "Oh, well, I got all that I wanted out of it." His advocacy was said to have netted him from $1,200 to $1,300. He had the money and Nettleship had the experience. Previously it had been the other way about.

To arrest Nettleship and prosecute him for his desertion would, I thought, have looked like persecution. So I took no steps to carry into effect the logical sequence of the full Court's dicta. I looked at Nettleship in a quite impersonal light. What I was wholly and solely concerned with was to place the Mounted Police Courts on a solid footing, and I think most readers will agree with me that some such step was imperatively necessary.

CHAPTER XIV

AN UNRECORDED INCIDENT OF MOUNTED POLICE HISTORY: THE CROOKED LAKES AFFAIR

On the evening of February 20, 1884, I was requested to go to the Commanding Officer's quarters, and there I met Mr. Hayter Reed in conference with Superintendent Herchmer. The Lieutenant-Governor of the North-West Territories, who was also Commissioner of Indian Affairs, had gone away on leave and had appointed Mr. Hayter Reed, the Assistant Commissioner of Indian Affairs, to be administrator during his absence. Mr. Reed had been Indian Agent at Battleford in the days when Superintendent Herchmer had been stationed there in command of the Mounted Police post, and a close friendship had sprung up between them. Mr. Reed was thus at this time administering the affairs of the country, and his word was law.

On the line of the Canadian Pacific Railway, about eighty miles east of Regina, is a place called Broadview, and about ten miles north of the village, as it was then, was an Indian Reserve. A report from the local Indian Department officials had just been received by the administrator that about sixty or seventy Indians had broken into the Government storehouse, had threatened the life of the farm instructor, a Mr. Keith, and had stolen some sixty or seventy bags of flour and bacon. Mr. Reed's mission was to ask that a posse of police be sent to the spot to look into the matter. It

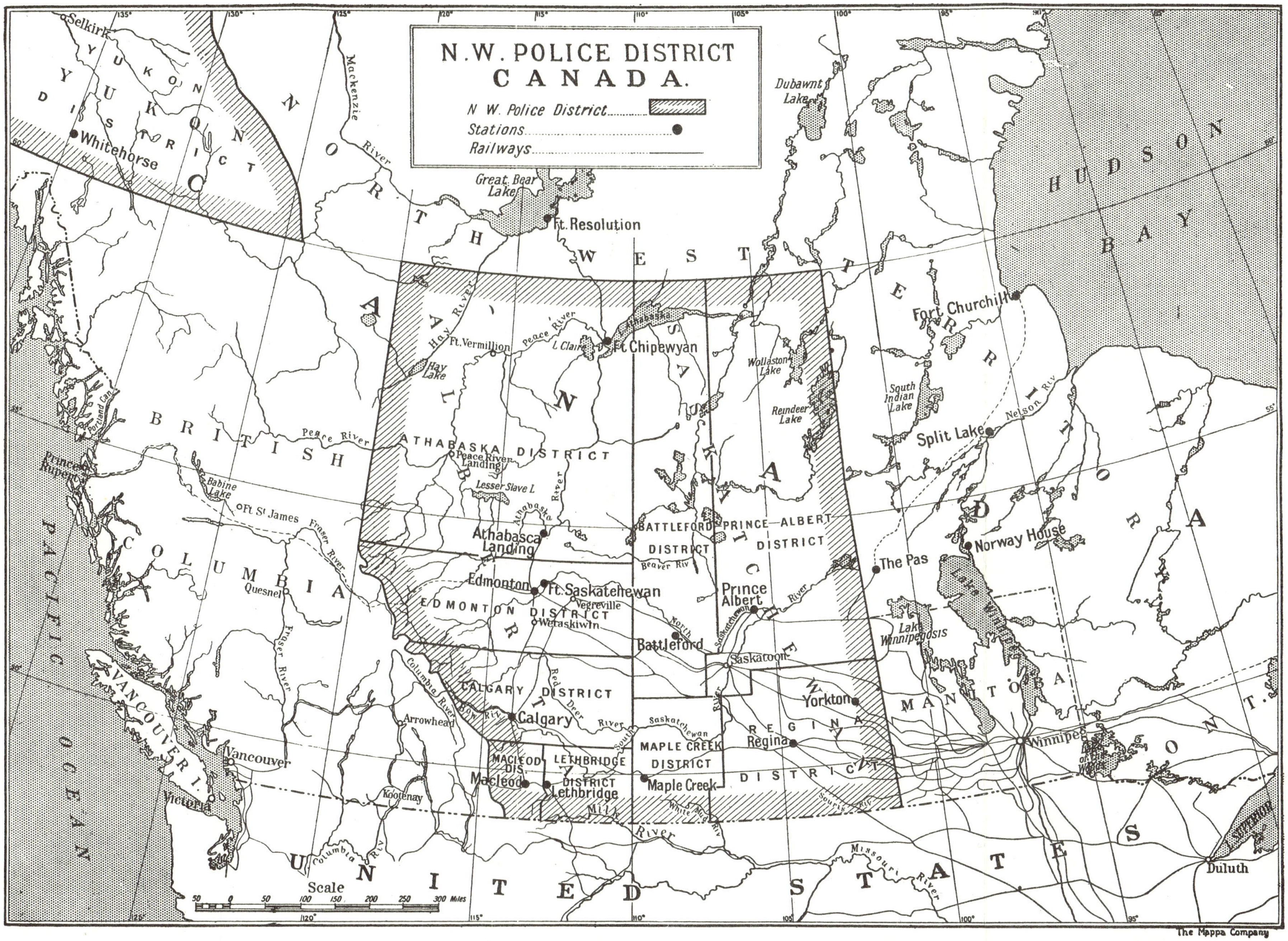
N.W. POLICE DISTRICT
CANADA.
N. W. Police District
Stations
Railways
YUKON DISTRICT
NORTH WEST TERRITORIES
HUDSON BAY
BRITISH COLUMBIA
ALBERTA
SASKATCHEWAN
MANITOBA
ONT.
UNITED STATES
PACIFIC OCEAN
VANCOUVER I.
ATHABASKA DISTRICT
BATTLEFORD DISTRICT
PRINCE ALBERT DISTRICT
EDMONTON DISTRICT
CALGARY DISTRICT
MACLEOD DIS.
LETHBRIDGE DISTRICT
MAPLE CREEK DISTRICT
REGINA DISTRICT
Selkirk
Whitehorse
Great Bear Lake
Ft. Resolution
Dubawnt Lake
Fort Churchill
Ft. Vermillion
Ft. Chipewyan
Hay Lake
Wollaston Lake
Reindeer Lake
South Indian Lake
Split Lake
Peace River Landing
Lesser Slave L.
Prince Rupert
Babine Lake
Ft. St James
Athabasca Landing
Norway House
The Pas
Edmonton
Ft. Saskatchewan
Vegreville
Wetaskiwin
Quesnel
Prince Albert
Battleford
Saskatoon
Lake Winnipegosis
Lake Winnipeg
Yorkton
Calgary
Arrowhead
Regina
Winnipeg
Lake of the Woods
Vancouver
Victoria
Macleod
Lethbridge
Maple Creek
Kootenay
Duluth
L. Superior
Mackenzie River
Peace River
Hay River
Fraser River
Athabaska River
Beaver Riv.
North Saskatchewan River
Red Deer River
Bow Riv.
South Saskatchewan
Columbia River
Milk River
White Mud Riv.
Souris Riv.
Missouri River
Nelson Riv.
Scale
50 0 50 100 150 200 250 300 Miles
The Mappa Company

was finally settled that I should go in charge of ten men, who were not to take their arms. They would take their side-arms, of course, but not their carbines.

A freight train was due to pass Regina at 9.45 o'clock next morning, and we went to the station to catch it, but it did not come in until 3 P.M., and it was 9 P.M. when we reached Broadview. We had had very "sketchy" meals during the day, so supper was the first consideration, and teams and bobsleighs were ordered for 10.30 P.M.

I then went to see Dr. Dodd, who was the resident J.P., and had a chat with him. He was very pessimistic, and advised me not to go out to the Reserve with so few men, but I said it was my duty to go, and that I should assuredly do so. It seemed that Mr. Keith had been in Broadview, expecting us to arrive earlier in the day, but had grown tired of waiting and had gone back to the Reserve. He left a message with Dr. Dodd to the effect that the matter was very serious —that the Indians were armed and had sworn to shoot the first man who attempted to arrest one of them. He quoted Mr. McKenzie, a trader living on the Reserve and doing business for the Hudson's Bay Company, as saying that the Indians were "uglier" than any Indians he had seen.

We were fated not to reach the Reserve that night, for it presently transpired that the only procurable horses were tired after a day's work which they had already done, and that the guide who was to show us the way to the farm buildings was by no means sure of the road. Considering that Mr. Keith had not thought it necessary to wait for us, I concluded that there was perhaps no desperate need of haste, and ordered the teams for 7.30 the next morning. Before going to bed I wired an epitome of the local opinion to Superintendent Herchmer.

It was clear and calm when we started the next morning, with the snow rather deep and the thermometer about thirty degrees below zero. Travelling was slow, and we did not reach the farm until 9.30 A.M. Mr. Keith then secured some "jumpers" for the further progress of the party on account of the deep snow, and it was half-past ten before we got fairly under way. We were, of course, entirely in Mr. Keith's hands, and his idea was to visit each of the minor chiefs and to ascertain where his Indians were to be found. Fortunately he had provided a very competent interpreter, a full-blooded Indian, named Gaddy, who had the reputation of being honest enough and independent enough to interpret correctly without fear or favour. He could, moreover, understand and interpret good English. The first minor chief that we visited was named Little Child, and was at home. He was almost blind, and had no taste for frivolities. He said he was sorry the young men would go in for dancing instead of working. His good example seemed to have impressed the rest of his band, for only one of them was implicated in the current disturbances. We had here to wait for a guide to be procured, because we had to break our own trail, and it was necessary in the few hours of daylight to make as many short cuts as possible. We made a meal on some grub that we had brought with us, and then headed for Yellow-Calf's house. He was the chief of the combination, had raised a fairly good crop, and was supposed to be loyal. We found his flag flying, but no one at home save squaws. From thence we proceeded to Acouse's, whose squaws were at home but no one else. At 5 P.M. we went down to the valley, and in course of time came to the house of a half-breed named Jacob Bear. There we came across the most astute Indian of the whole tribe, named Osoup. It was uncertain how far he gave the other Indians the assistance of his sympathy, but no overt act had ever been traced to him. He was in fairly good circumstances, dressed respectably, was a good hunter, and talked intelligible English. From him we learned that the Indians, some sixty or seventy in number, were in a house close to the river; also he offered to take us to the place. I asked him if he would tell the Indians that I was there and should like to have a talk with them, and that I should like to take with me Mr. Keith, Sergeant Bliss, and the interpreter. He returned with a message that the Indians were willing that I should do as I had proposed, and I then sent the rest of my men back to the farm. We had driven about twenty-five miles in the jumpers, and it was seven o'clock, time for a meal if there had been one in sight, which there wasn't.

The house which we were about to enter was a substantially built log house, with one door facing the east, and one small window facing the south—a one-roomed house, measuring about thirty feet by eighteen feet. An oblong excavation from eighteen inches to two feet deep had been made in the centre, and Indians were sitting around this oblong with others standing behind them. The place was literally packed with Indians, and it was as much as we could do to find standing room. However, we eventually did so, and I stood at the northwest corner of the "dug-out," which was a convenient place for speaking from. When I first went in at the door I stepped, of course, into the excavation, not being able to see it and not knowing it was there, and very nearly came a cropper, at which there was a general guffaw. Without wasting any time, however, I told the Indians that I was very glad to have the opportunity of talking to them—that complaint had been made that a large number of Indians had broken into the Government warehouse, had threatened the life of the farm instructor, and had stolen a great many bags of flour and bacon, and that the Great White Mother had sent me to ask them what they had to say about it. I said, "The Great White Mother is very sorry to hear that her Indian children have done this wicked thing. She keeps a store of food on the Reserve so that her Indian children shall not starve. She gives them of this food every two or three days, and expects that they will be content with what she gives them without money and without price. She feels quite sure that her Indian children would not have stolen her goods unless some bad men had put bad thoughts into their hearts, and she expects that those Indians who led the others in this bad act will give themselves up to be tried in her Court in the same way as white men are tried when they break the Queen's law."

That, and much more to the same effect, through more than two weary hours. Each sentence was interpreted as it was uttered; and, while the interpreter was doing his part, I was thinking out the next sentence in words of one syllable as nearly as possible. Three Indians replied in speeches of some length, and said that promises had been made to them by the Indian Commissioner which had not been kept, and that the Assistant Indian Commissioner had cut down their rations in a manner which constituted a breach of faith. They argued also that they helped themselves to the flour and bacon because they were hungry. I thought a good deal more of the Indians' complaint then than I do now, for the burden of the Red Man's song is always "Grub, grub, more grub." These rascals had been "dancing" for thirteen days straight on end, and had neglected even to go and draw their rations. Hence the occasion for the theft. I told them that I would tell the Indian Department what they said, and advised them, if they seriously intended to attempt to explain their conduct by the representation that they were hungry, to show their good faith by giving up the leaders of the raid to be tried by the Courts.

They replied that they would talk it over, and if I would stay there over night they would give me an answer in the morning. There was no place that I knew of wherein I could stay for the night, and having had nothing to eat since mid-day, I decided that I had better go back to the farm. So I told them there might be some messages there for me which might require an answer, and that it was necessary that I should go.

The Indians were perfectly respectful and friendly from first to last.

There was one, and only one, who meant to be offensive. He asked me as I was going out of the door what the police were going to do about his horses which he had lost some time previously. His tone and manner were distinctly impertinent, and I made him answer a good many questions, asking finally if he had reported to the police that he had lost his horses. He said, "No," and I retorted, "How did you expect the police to know that your horses were lost if you did not tell them?" An approving "Ugh" behind me indicated that at least one of my hearers had a logical mind, and under cover of it I went out into the night. We had talked from 7 to 9.15 P.M., and it was eleven o'clock before we reached the farm.

I found there a telegram from Herchmer to say that he and ten more men were on the way.

He arrived the next day in the forenoon, having brought no arms, and about one o'clock we all started for the house in the valley. Colonel McDonald, Indian Agent, also arrived in his own cutter and preceded us. The Indians, of course, were watching us, and knew exactly what was going on. When we came in sight of the house we could see that there were a number of armed

Indians round about it. Some had shot guns and some had Winchester rifles, but every Indian present had a firearm of some sort. As Colonel McDonald was driving up to the door the men who were standing there sternly waved him off. They made the same signs to us, but we took no notice of them, and the entire party got out of their respective sleighs. Herchmer was very impatient. Colonel McDonald, who had not spoken to the Indians at all, wanted to talk, but Herchmer would have none of it. He told me to fall the men in, and I did so. Then he said, "You'd better draw pistols," and I gave that order also. Instantly the heel of a butt was applied to the window sash, which fell out with a crash, and the cavity bristled with muzzles. Indians simultaneously appeared around the corners of the house, all having arms, and all being ready to shoot. Finding remonstrance useless, Colonel McDonald whipped up his horse and drove off, saying, "I'll have nothing to do with it." Herchmer and I were two or three paces between our line of men and the house when, without warning me of what he proposed to do, Herchmer suddenly said, "Well, I suppose we'd better go right in," and started off by himself.

Everyone who knew "Billy" Herchmer knew that, whatever his failings were, lack of courage was not one of them, and he presumed that "bluff" would carry the day, as it had previously answered his purpose in the North. He had not made allowance for a band of Indians who were strangers to him, and were, as Mr. McKenzie had told me, "Very determined." In the North he had been accustomed to deal with Crees; but the Indians with whom we were now dealing were Saulteaux, who were always looked upon as a rather superior race.

A young fellow named Jim Holford, consumed with curiosity, had, as we learned afterwards, followed our sleighs on horseback into the valley, but an Indian had warned him to go back, saying if there was going to be any fighting he would be killed with the rest of us. He took the advice and went.

Herchmer had taken no more than a couple of paces toward the door when a big, fine-looking and determined Indian, who was guarding the door, presented his double-barrelled shot gun full in his face at a distance of something like two feet. Herchmer stopped dead, as in my opinion he was well advised to do, for there was certain murder in the dusky ruffian's eye. The other Indians followed his example, and we were all covered. A movement on the part of any one of us would have precipitated a climax. As the seconds passed without any ulterior act, it became evident that it remained with ourselves to force the situation or not.

I do not know what Herchmer proposed to do in the house even supposing the Indians had admitted us all. We had no warrant to arrest anyone—no information had been laid, and neither of us knew who the guilty parties were. Thus, from a criminal point of view, we had no *locus standi* whatever. We were, in effect, provoking the Indians to commit wilful murder by threatening to thrust ourselves into premises into which we had no right to force our way without the Queen's Warrant.

If disaster had befallen us, as for two or three seconds seemed extremely probable, our blood would have been upon our own heads.

Presently Herchmer called for Yellow Calf, the chief, who persuaded the big Indian to lower his gun, and "talk" became once more the order of the day. The big Indian was not easily appeased. His blood was up, and he wanted to pull the trigger at some one of the men. I could not tell which one, nor why he wanted to shoot, but I thought he would do some mischief, and Yellow Calf thought so, too, for he held on to the gun for some little time. It is to be remembered that up to this time no shot had ever been fired in anger between the police and the Indians, and a very grave responsibility would thus rest upon any person who should initiate hostilities.

At this juncture the Indian Agent reappeared, and an adjournment was made to Osoup's house, a little way off, where a prolonged "pow-wow" was held. The Indians, however, were no longer in the complaisant mood of the evening before—they had hardened their hearts, and resolutely refused to give up the offenders. An arrangement was made providing that the administrator should be sent for, and we wended our way back to the farm, where we arrived about 8 p.m.

Hayter Reed arrived on the following afternoon, and the Indian Agent was dispatched to invite the Indians to a conference at the farm next morning. He stayed with them all that night, and eventually succeeded in inducing them to come and talk matters over.

At about 9 A.M. on February 25 Osoup, Yellow Calf, and some others, escorted by armed and mounted braves in full war-paint, duly arrived, and the whole forenoon was spent in talk. The administrator said, after a time, that he would like to talk to some of the young men themselves, and, after some difficulty, they were persuaded to come—very nervous and fearful of treachery. Late in the afternoon, after an eloquent speech from Osoup (Interpreter Gaddy said it was the finest speech he had ever heard an Indian make), four Indians named Yellow Calf, Kanawos, Möise, and Penni-pa-kē-sis consented to go to Regina for trial, and we all took the night train thither.

The trial took place on February 28, before Colonel Richardson, stipendiary magistrate, and Kanawos, Möise and Penni-pa-kē-sis were charged with larceny. Yellow Calf was not included in the indictment, as he was not concerned in the raid, and had, moreover, kept the peace on the previous day.

Mr. A. E. Forget (now Senator), clerk of the Legislative Assembly, appeared on behalf of the accused, who pleaded guilty, and made a strong plea for mercy on account of the Indians' ignorance of the white men's laws. The Indians were convicted, and discharged on suspended sentence. It was practically understood from the first that this was to be the outcome of the trial.

When the Court rose, Colonel Richardson called Herchmer and me into his room and said, "What were you gentlemen doing there without a warrant?" My answer was easy. "I simply obeyed orders which I received from my superior officer." Herchmer's answer was not so easy, and he said nothing.

All this, looked at from any point of view, was a very unfortunate occurrence. The police had made a *faux pas,* and had lost in a great measure their most valuable asset, their prestige. The story was naturally noised abroad among the Indians, and there is no doubt that it contributed somewhat to the turbulent spirit which manifested itself among the Battleford Indians later in the same year.

So far as the Government was concerned, the matter was promptly hushed up. Herchmer never made any allusion to it in any of his reports. I wrote the report which Hayter Reed sent to his department, and he struck out of it all reference to the complaints made by the Indians that they were starving. There were, in those days, only four newspapers in the whole of the North-West Territories, viz. *The Leader* at Regina, *Fort Macleod Gazette* at Macleod, *The Saskatchewan Herald* at Battleford, and *The Bulletin* at Edmonton.

I never saw any account of the trouble in any of these papers until in October, 1887, the Edmonton *Bulletin* published an editorial on the subject. It was used as a vehicle to attack the Lieutenant-Governor, the Assistant Indian Commissioner, Herchmer himself, and his brother, who had been in 1886 appointed to the Commissionership of the Mounted Police. Thus it will be seen that the story took rather more than three years and a half to filter through to Edmonton from Broadview. The Indian Department in those days had some very persistent critics in Parliament, who did not think it necessary by any means to confine themselves to the truth in making virulent attacks upon the departmental officials. It may be imagined, therefore, how careful the latter were to conceal anything which could be used to their discredit by their unscrupulous enemies in the opposition. The editorial to which I have alluded closed in the following words:

"Bad management has been succeeded by worse, and bad precedent by still worse, until the Force, which was the pride of Canada and the safety of the North-West, has been made a laughing-stock for the very men who a few years ago held it most in respect."

I could, if I chose, write a great deal on the subject from this aspect, but as I have set out to write nothing of which I have not a personal knowledge I refrain. I can only say that in the interval between October 1, 1887, and the time at which these lines are written, "*Nous avons changé tout cela.*"

There is now living only one white man who knows all the particulars attending the émeute at Crooked Lakes—Mr. McKenzie, to whom I have referred. He kept a small trading establishment on the reserve, and was in the confidence of the Indians.

It was suggested to me that I should submit my narrative to Mr. McKenzie, and ask him whether his recollections agreed with mine. I judged it highly expedient to do so, knowing how often I myself had grown tired of hearing tales current in the North-West which were more or less figments of the imaginations of the narrators. I received in return from Mr. McKenzie a long letter, and afterwards a very kind intimation, "You are at liberty to make any use of my letter that you see fit."

The following is an excerpt from the letter referred to:

"I have a very vivid recollection of that very regrettable and unwarranted disturbance at Crooked Lakes in 1884. Your story and review of all the details is most complete, faithfully portrayed, and in accordance with the facts as they actually took place.

"I was in charge of the Hudson's Bay Company's Trading Post on the Crooked Lakes Reserve continuously some years prior and subsequent to the 1884 trouble. I grew up with all those young men implicated, knew every soul on all the Reserves personally, spoke the language, and was conversant with the daily circumstances of each individual family. It is a long story, with which you are no doubt conversant, how the plains Indians were being gathered together at, and prior to, that time by the Government, and being placed on different reservations; Crooked Lakes being one of the largest, received the greatest number of Indians, and, of course, in those days had to be fed regularly or rationed regularly.

"The reducing of these rations from time to time to practically nothing in the hard winter of 1884, when there were no rabbits or anything else to hunt for food, brought these Indians face to face with actual starvation. In some cases children died of starvation during that month, their mothers not being able to suckle them from their weakened condition, from lack of even partial nourishment at this critical period. Mr. Reed further instructed Mr. H. Keith to reduce the rations still lower. I asked Mr. Keith for God's sake not to reduce their rations any lower, or there would certainly be trouble. He carried out Mr. Reed's instructions, a few more died, the Indians came and asked for grub, which they were denied, broke into the Government store-house, threw out as much flour and bacon as they wanted, and threw Keith out on the top of it. I ran up from my store in time to save Keith's life, took him away from them, and told him what a foolish mistake he had made. Before I got him to my store he took one of his fits which he was subject to, and remained unconscious for fully an hour. In the meantime the Indians were loading up their jumpers with flour and bacon, and making a general distribution to those present, and sending flour and bacon on to those who were too feeble to come after it, while the air was about 30 degrees below zero that morning. After they divided up the flour and bacon, they all came to my store, all, of course, very excited, but offered me no violence, only some of my best friends among them said in a jocular way that they had come in to clean out my store also, as they wanted tea, tobacco, sugar, rice and currants, so that they would have one good feed before they all died of starvation. I told them not to touch anything, that I had been helping many of them a good deal all the winter, and was very sorry for what they had done in a moment of excitement, through the foolhardiness of one of their young men—for which all the Indians would now be held responsible by the Government—whose name was Big Ben Kitchie, Osoup's son. I gave them what they wanted, and they all went their way to prepare the feast, having plenty of grub for the time being for themselves and families, after which the young warriors repaired to the house in the valley in which you found them, and it was very lucky for the M.P. that day that the Indians had

had a good feed, so that their tempers were somewhat cooled off by their stomachs being full, or there would not one of you ever have come out of that valley alive, hampered as you were with your buffalo coats, deep snow, and with only side arms. I shudder yet when I think of what would have occurred had a shot been fired even by accident. There is many a slip betwixt the cup and the lip, and anyway, that great tragedy was averted by a bloodless battle. I am the only living white man to-day that was on the ground, and was intimately and personally acquainted with all the details of this affair, which I reported to my Company at the time, and received their thanks for the way I handled the Indians and prevented them from looting our stores by providing them gratuitously with a small amount of provisions on that deplorable and critical occasion. They were supplied with a more liberal ration after that time, and there was no further trouble on that score until the following spring, in March, 1885, when the rebellion broke out at Duck Lake."

CHAPTER XV

WHOLESALE CATTLE SMUGGLING

In the month of November, 1901, the Collector of United States Customs at Great Falls, in the State of Montana, a place about 140 miles south of Lethbridge, wrote to me to ask what brands the firm of Spencer Brothers were using in Canada, and whether they had any cattle branded with the double rowlock.

I was aware that these people were American citizens, who had recently leased from the Dominion Government a large quantity of land. They were reputed to be wealthy, and to have a great number of very fine cattle. Beyond that my attention had not been particularly directed to them.

I now learned that the firm consisted of two brothers, Samuel and John; that they were intensely unpopular in the State of Montana, and that they had conceived the brilliant idea of coming to North-West Canada and leasing a large quantity of land, at two cents an acre, in the immediate proximity of the international boundary.

William Taylor, their manager, is my authority for the statement that a sum of money had been set down in the Canadian estimates for the year 1902 for the purpose of building a fence along the international boundary line. The project was not carried into effect, but that such a ridiculous proposition had even been taken into serious consideration shows what influence the Spencer Brothers had with the Government at Ottawa.

Wholesale Cattle Smuggling

The diagram herewith shows a plan of the lease, namely, Townships No. 1 in Ranges 5 and 6, and Townships No. 2 in Ranges 6, 7 and 8. As each township measures six miles north and south by six miles east and west, and consists of thirty-six square miles, it follows that the firm had 180 square miles of the public domain under lease. But this was not all the advantage they derived, for a glance at the map will show how

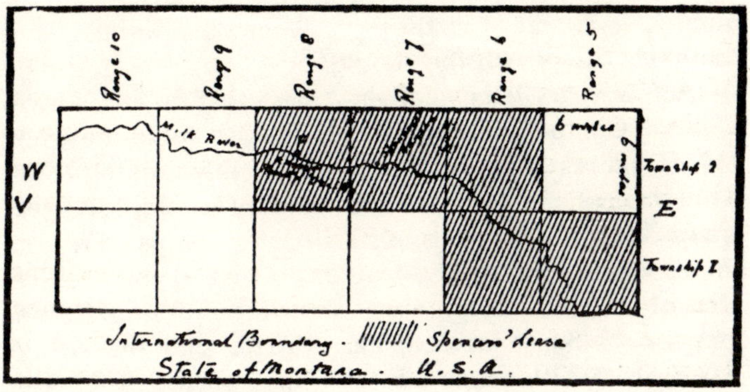

the leased land bestrides the Milk River, which flows out of Canada into Montana in Township 1, Range 5. The Spencers thus controlled at least twenty-four miles of river frontage, and, as there was no other water within striking distance, it is evident that Townships 1 of Ranges 7 and 8 would be of no use to any stock owner who might be denied access to the Milk River. The Spencers thus virtually acquired seventy-two additional square miles of grazing land, for which they paid not a cent.

Everyone will admit that this was a long-headed scheme which deserved to succeed, but it must not be imagined that such extensive privileges could be obtained for the mere asking. Not at all! The Minister of the Interior of that day, who had control of the Dominion

Lands, was Mr. Clifford Sifton, who prior to his joining Sir Wilfrid Laurier's Cabinet in 1896 had practised law in Brandon, Manitoba. When the brothers Spencer coveted the concessions which have been described they were astute enough to reason that it might be to their advantage to do their legal business through the firm of lawyers which Mr. Sifton had ostensibly left. Results proved that their line of reasoning was unimpeachable. They had to pay a large sum of money, it is true, but they got what they wanted, and the game was worth the candle.

A few years later another American firm, the Price-Conrad Company, desired similarly to milk the good old Canadian cow, and used the same milking-stool. The concessions they wanted were near Maple Creek. Their idea was to lease detached townships here and there, selected in such a way as to give them practical control of the intervening area for nothing. The emissary whom they sent eastward to pull the strings wired from Ottawa to his principal at Maple Creek: "We can get it, but it comes high," to which the immediate answer was returned, "Must have it at any price." They got it, and it was the emissary who told the story.

Following the example of the Spencers, other American cattle men had driven their herds to the Canadian frontier in order that they might fatten on Canadian grass, of which there was an abundance, while the feed to the south of the line was eaten off, and a special officer of Customs was detailed to attend to the matter. Having himself no means of watching a long boundary line, he was perforce dependent upon us for information and assistance, his own participation being confined to making out the seizure papers and reporting to Ottawa. He made some seizures during my tenure of command at Maple Creek, between July, 1902 and July, 1906, and, except in one instance, where the owner had not apparently learned the tricks of the trade, and had, in consequence, to pay a penalty, the cattle were ordered to be returned by the Department at Ottawa without payment of duty. There was no earthly reason why they should not all have been treated alike, but so it was.

To hark back to my correspondence with the Collector of U.S. Customs, I learned from him that in November, 1901, the Spencers had shipped a trainload of cattle (176 head) from their Milk River ranche to the Chicago market. This shipment was intercepted by the U.S. Custom officers, held at St. Paul while en route to Chicago, and not permitted to proceed to its destination until after the Spencers had deposited the sum of $2,355 with the Secretary of the Montana Stock-Growers' Association as Customs duty. In November, 1900, the brothers had informed the Secretary of the Northern Montana Round-up Association that they had moved all their cattle into Canada, and on that account declined to pay their pro rata share of the Montana Round-up expenses. I saw the letters of both brothers, and took copies of them.

An indictment which the United States brought against the firm in March, 1902, failed because only ten instead of twelve jurors of the Grand Jury voted for it. A special agent of the United States Treasury Department was sent from Tacoma to take charge of the case, and the authorities were very much chagrined at having been outwitted. Great influence had been brought to bear upon the jurymen. The Grand Sovereign of the Independent Order of Oddfellows was very active in the interests of the Spencers, whose success emboldened them to think that Canadian justice could be similarly tampered with. Sam Spencer had a favourite expression, "We'll law 'em!" and he was never averse to going to law.

As the United States officials pursued their investigation they came across a great deal of evidence which was most valuable to me, and they gave me without stint all the assistance which they possibly could.

For instance, on April 25, 1900, the firm imported and paid duty on 527 calves, all less than twelve months old. My American friends obtained for me an affidavit from one of Spencers' employees, who assisted to drive about a thousand head of cattle to the Canadian frontier; the 527 calves were there cut out of the bunch and were driven to a Mounted Police detachment called "Writing-on-stone," where duty was paid on them, and the mothers were driven to the Spencers' range, where the calves subsequently joined them.

The same man also gave information as to another drive of about eight hundred, which took place in October of the same year, and as to the particulars of that I was enabled to procure an affidavit from another employee of the Spencers who took part in the importation. In addition to this every stockman in Northern Montana was eager to give us information, and we had abundance of it. This ebullition of the feeling against the Spencers on the part of their fellow-countrymen was brought about as follows:

Ever since they had been established on their Milk River lease, the firm, relying on their influence at Ottawa, had assumed that they could do as they pleased. During the winter of 1901 a great many American cattle had drifted into Canada. The range in Northern Montana had been largely burnt off by prairie fires, and the only feed available for some 15,000 head of cattle was in the neighbourhood of the Sweet Grass Hills, where the grass was good, and the stockmen concerned had no choice but to range their cattle there or let them starve to death. This meant that the cattle must be pastured within a latitude of about twenty miles of the

Canadian frontier. Within that distance there was no water readily accessible except that in the Milk River, which meandered eastward at a distance of from ten to twelve miles north of the boundary line. I had always recognised the fact that it was a sheer impossibility to hold thirsty range cattle back from water, and had always impressed upon the owners of trespassing cattle that they should do their utmost to prevent their animals from crossing to the northern bank. There were at that time no Canadian settlers on the south side of the river to be inconvenienced by incursions of stray cattle. The American cattlemen recognised their obligation to protect Canadian interests on the northern bank, and were in the habit of maintaining line riders to keep the cattle back. These men used to lodge at our detachment buildings, and, in return for their board and lodging, used to keep the Mounted Police detachments supplied with fresh beef at the expense of their employers. This system had been established by me years previously, and had been then fully reported upon and explained in my annual report for the information of Parliament. The revenue suffered to the extent that no duty was charged or paid on any animal so killed for food, and the Customs officers, who were fully aware of the cir cumstances, and never disdained to partake of the beef when their business took them into those parts, never thought proper to raise the question. In the exercise of their assumed prerogative, Spencer Brothers arrogated to themselves the right to control a large stretch of prairie about seventy miles long by twenty miles wide, and on one occasion during the winter of 1901 they gathered some 2,000 head of American cattle, which had been storm-driven to the northern bank of the river, and drove them across to the south side. One of the American cowboy line riders, George Voice, was present and pointed out that the ice was rotten. He vigorously protested against the proposed movement, but the Spencers' manager said he did not care—he would drive them across no matter what might happen, and he and his men did so. Fortunately, more by good luck than good management, there were no casualties, but the indignant cowboy told the story far and wide in Northern Montana, and there was not a cattle-owner there who was not anxious to "get back" at the Spencers, their renegade countrymen. Hence it was that I was able to collect so much information, and the report which I was able to make to my department was as full and conclusive as it was possible for a report to be.

The reply of the Customs Department at Ottawa was to send a Special Service officer to co-operate with me. His instructions were to inform the firm of Spencer Brothers that they were charged with having smuggled into Canada about 500 head of cattle in April, 1900, that the duty-paid value of these would be about $15,000, and he was to demand payment of a deposit of $7,500 subject to the final decision of the Minister of Customs.

If the firm consented to pay this demand the officer was to wire to his Minister for further instructions. Accordingly on Good Friday, 1902, Mr. Bourinot and I started by train for Coutts, a station on the boundary line, and from there by road eastward about fifty-five miles to a Mounted Police detachment situate in Pendant d'Oreille Coulée, within about seven miles of the Spencers' ranche. Bourinot drove in a police buckboard, while I rode with George Voice, the American cowboy before mentioned. He had spent the winter on the Milk River, and gave me a great deal of information which I had not previously had occasion to acquire. We might have saved ourselves a disagreeable trip, for neither of the Spencers was at home and we had

THE NORTHERN BANK OF THE MILK RIVER AND VALLEY OF WRITING-ON-STONE

The out-croppings of sandstone have been worn by wind and weather into these fantastic shapes. The Cow-boys have christened this place "China Town"

to deal with the manager, William Taylor, who told us that he was also part-owner.

In reply to Bourinot's communication, he said that his firm had paid duty on every head of stock that they had imported, and that they "would not put up a dollar." He told me that the firm then owned 6,000 or 7,000 head of cattle; he could not tell within a thousand as they had not counted them for some time. It was known to me, at least, that they had paid duty on only 1,230 animals, 854 of which were calves under twelve months of age, and I was the more disposed to believe the range gossip which assessed the cattle smuggled from Montana at from 2,000 to 3,000 head.

However, there was nothing for us to do but to go home, which we did.

Shortly after this I attended a meeting of the Western Stock-Growers' Association, and there asked a prominent stockman what it would cost the Government to hire a round-up party of fifteen riders, with the necessary etceteras, for twenty-one days. George Voice had calculated that it would take that length of time to cover the range. Mr. George Lane replied, "Fifteen hundred dollars," and I then asked if he could supply the party. He said he would. I explained that the proposition was a close secret and must remain so. He finally asked what direction the round-up would probably take, and I said, "South-east." "Then I can guess what your business is," said he. "Keep your guesses to yourself, at any rate," I replied, and we parted.

In course of time the Customs Department authorised the hiring of the round-up, and everything was arranged with such secrecy that the only people in the West who knew anything about it were George Lane, George Voice, my orderly room clerk and myself.

On Wednesday, May 14, the round-up party camped a couple of miles east of Lethbridge, and Bourinot and

I joined them there. I took my clerk with me mounted, and took two saddle-horses for my own use. Bourinot was driven in a light wagon hauled by a police team.

The captain of the round-up, William Playfair, knew what our errand was, and so did an expert cattle buyer named William Henry, whom Mr. Lane had thoughtfully included in the personnel of his party, but none of the other men knew. It was supposed to be George Lane's horse round-up, whose mission ordinarily would be to scour the range for the owner's horses, and it was amusing sometimes to hear remarks as to what was Captain Deane's connection with Lane's horse round-up! Voice had been lent to me by the Montana stockman for whom he was working at the time, and brought his own string of horses with him, ten in number. The other riders were provided with six a-piece. We should have started earlier in the year, but extensive prairie fires had in the previous autumn devastated a great tract of the country over which we wanted to travel, and so we had to wait until sufficient young grass had grown to provide for our needs. Nineteen hundred and two was the year of bad floods in the West, and our journey was very much delayed by heavy rains, which had the compensating advantage of helping the grass to grow.

I should not omit to mention something that happened on our second day out. It was after midday dinner, the camp had been struck, and we were on the point of starting again. Voice had saddled and mounted the horse he had chosen for the afternoon ("the best in the string, but mean," as he described him) when the brute began to buck. He bucked so long and so hard that he finally threw Voice over his head, turned a complete somersault, and broke his neck in the doing of it. When we turned our eyes from Voice, who was shaking himself to see if there was any harm done, we saw his late mount balanced on his rump and on the horn of the saddle, with his feet in the air, and his head where his tail had been, stone dead. He remained in that position until he was pulled over to allow the saddle to be taken from under him.

Some weeks later I wrote to his owner in Montana, and asked what value he set upon the horse, as he had been killed in our service. In his reply, he said:

"We lose horses occasionally in about the same manner in which this one acted with Voice, and in all probability we would have lost this one sooner or later, or he might have caused the death of a man. I never regret the loss of a horse that will change ends in that way, and I am thankful George escaped and the horse is dead. I do not wish any pay for him.—With kindest regards, I am, yours very truly,

"JOHN HARRIS."

Voice caught another horse out of the herd and went about his business as if nothing had happened. The chances and changes of a cowboy's life must be seen to be appreciated.

At this time we were heading for a ranch on the Many Berries Creek, about one hundred miles due east of Lethbridge, and it took us four and one-half days to make the journey. On our arrival there I found some men and horses whom I had temporarily withdrawn from my Milk River detachments. There, too, I received a report from a special envoy, who had been employed for the previous six weeks in watching the Spencer cattle, and this report told me where practically every hoof was to be found. Not a single head was on the Spencers' lease—they were all feeding on the public domain.

We now told the men of our party what our errand was, and at 6.30 next morning we all pulled out, the round-up to begin business on the nearest cattle they could find, and Bourinot and I to visit the Spencers' ranch, distant about thirty miles. On our way we were held up for a day and a half at Pendant d'Oreille detachment by bad weather and impassable roads, but I saw Mr. Taylor in the interval. He told us he was very glad the inspection was to take place—it was the very thing he wanted. As the ensuing weeks wore on Mr. Taylor's gratification visibly declined to the vanishing point. On May 21 Bourinot and I found brother John at home at the ranch. He was affability itself. He told me that he "did not know a dog-goned thing" about the cattle or anything else connected with the ranch. He said Taylor kept what books there were, and he, John Spencer, had never looked at them. He held Taylor responsible. This happened to be election day, and Taylor had gone to vote. We waited at the ranch for him until about four o'clock, and then went back to our lodgings. John Spencer promised that Taylor should bring the books for our inspection, and said that we should part good friends whatever happened, but he could not pretend to say how we might find the cattle, as he knew nothing about them, and had never told a lie in his life. From that time onwards the Recording Angel had less leisure time in connection with the rancher of pious and patriarchal appearance, who was said, by those amongst whom he had lived for years, to be the crafty member of the firm.

Taylor came to see us at Pendant d'Oreille next morning. He brought one book which showed the amount of duty paid on importations from the United States, but told us nothing that I did not know.

On the following day Bourinot and I reached our round-up camp just before noon. The party had gathered about 2,500 head of cattle, out of which in the course of the day about 400 Americans were cut out and held. The others were handed over to Taylor's men to take and keep out of our way. Next day, similarly, about 140 head of Americans were cut out of a bunch of 600. I may as well here explain how our men were guided in their selection of what I call American cattle. The Spencer Brothers had in Montana used certain brands, namely,  (double rowlock) on the left ribs, and —7K (bar seven K) and J7 on the left side. They were not allowed to use in Canada the same brands that they had used in the United States; for instance, the Canadian brand for the double rowlock cattle was the double rowlock on the right side instead of the left. Sam Spencer was awarded this brand in that place at his own request. In the same way Canadian brands were awarded in the case of —7K and J7 cattle. This story is not concerned with the particularities of brands, and for the sake of illustrating generally the system in vogue I will take the case of the  cattle.

An animal bearing that brand on the left ribs was undeniably an animal born and bred in the United States, whether it bore a brand on the right side or whether it did not. It was a common thing to find an American cow with a calf at foot and a yearling heifer or steer following her; possibly the two offspring bore the Canadian brand without any other at all. This meant that the cow was a smuggled animal. The Spencers would endeavour to call her a stray—that is, a cow which had crossed the imaginary boundary line into Canada without their knowledge or consent. But this claim was defeated by the fact that the cow had been long enough on Canadian soil to have two calves —one over twelve months old and the other, it may be, only a few weeks old; and the fact that the cow's progeny had been branded with the Spencers' Canadian brand showed conclusively that the cow had been in

Canadian territory with their knowledge and consent, and that they had given her some attention, as the two calves were still following their mother at the date of our visit. We noticed many cases of that kind.

I have previously said that the Spencers had imported and paid duty on 527 head of calves on April 25, 1900. These calves were sworn to be *under* twelve months old. That meant that any number of cows from 1,000 to 1,500 in number had been despoiled of their calves for the time being, and that they had been driven into Canada at some other point, there to meet their calves. The calves were then carefully branded; the cows were not. Some of the cows were doubtless heavy in calf at the time of their importation, and their then unborn calves would be branded when the branding season should come on and opportunities would offer.

The ordinary range expectation in the matter of calf crop was one calf to three cows or thereabouts—the casualties were so great, arising from wolves, coyotes, weather accidents, indifferent motherhood, etc., that John Spencer's claim, that every one of their cows had a calf, was a sheer absurdity. Anyhow, we found a goodly number of dry cows in their herd at the close of our visit. I will recur to this question a little later on. Two notable things happened on Saturday, May 24.

The first was that George Lane drove into camp from Medicine Hat, a distance of about 150 miles, to see how his horse round-up was getting on, and told us that he had that morning seen two men, who were evidently anxious to avoid him, riding hard in a north-easterly direction.

The second was that in the course of the afternoon I met Art Strong, Sam Spencer's very capable foreman. I had left word in various quarters that I should like to talk to him, and as a result of some such communication he now came to visit our camp. He had formerly been a line rider on the Milk River in the employ of some Montana stock-owners, and I knew a good deal of him and about him. I knew, for instance, that, although he would serve his employer's interests to the utmost, he would not swear to a lie. I feared from the first that by moving Sam Spencer's cattle he might hinder our inquiry, and I had taken the precaution, before I left Lethbridge, of laying an information and obtaining a warrant for his arrest in connection with the importation of calves in April, 1900. I intended to have no scruples in putting him out of harm's way if I should have any reason to suspect him of playing tricks with us. It was this I wanted to tell him.

After the usual greetings I said that I wanted to point out to him that if he took upon himself the task of carrying out the unlawful commands of his employers, he might find a difficulty in devoiding himself of responsibility for the execution of orders which he of necessity knew to be unlawful. I told him I had a warrant in my pocket, but I did not want to execute it unless he obliged me to do so, and I also pointed out that all the Spencer cattle were now under seizure by the Customs Department, and it would be a serious matter for any person to interfere with the due process of law. He said, "They accuse me, don't they, of smuggling 1,000 head of cattle at the Bone Pile in April, 1900?" I replied, "Yes, that's what they say of you." "Well," he retorted, "I didn't do it. There were only 900 in the bunch anyhow; and after I had cut out the calves for Customs entry at Writing-on-Stone, my orders were to leave the mothers at the line, and I left them there." The "Bone Pile," I should say, was a pile of bones which marked the boundary line. Having got such an admission as this from a hostile witness, I thought myself so fortunate that I said, "Oh! well, I'll keep the warrant in my pocket for the present, and I hope you won't give me any occasion to use it." He promised he would not, and we went our respective ways.

Strong's statement about the 900 cattle, if accepted, and I accepted it unreservedly, emphasised the fraudulent nature of the sworn Customs entry as to the 527 calves being all under twelve months of age. There must have been among them a considerable number of yearlings which had reached the age of puberty, and were, doubtlessly, in some cases, in process of becoming mothers themselves. It was no uncommon thing to find on the range a two-year-old heifer with a calf.

On May 25 our herd of American cattle numbered about 750 head. Taylor came to our camp for dinner that day, and after looking through the seized stock, told Bourinot that there was not a four-year-old steer in their herd. This was an indication of what his line of argument was likely to be, and, in the course of a thirty-mile ride with George Lane that morning, I asked him how a dispute as to age between our experts and the Spencers' representatives could be conclusively settled. He said the only way would be to have a veterinary surgeon on the spot. As a last resource an animal in dispute could always be thrown and its mouth could be examined, and a disinterested veterinary surgeon would be the best person to examine the teeth. He would be able to tell to a certainty. When Lane left us, as he did that afternoon for home, he carried with him from me a letter to the Commanding Officer at Calgary asking him to send his veterinary officer to join our camp, and he did so.

The significance of the two riders reported by George Lane appeared about this time. It was proposed to move the camp in a north-easterly direction for about eight miles, and Voice was sent to look over the ground. The north-east corner of the range was black with cattle when we first began our work, but Voice came back and reported now that they had been driven off. He found a trail leading south-west (showing tracks of a large band of cattle and of galloping horses), which had been used in herding them off the hills into the coulées. By the sign of the tracks this had been done within about thirty-six hours. We also found deep-cut wheel marks of a wagon going in the same direction. This was no more than we had expected, and we were in no way disconcerted. At the worst it could only mean that we might have to prolong our stay and go over the range again. There was no hope of the cattle being able to get away from us, as if they went into Montana the Customs officers there would seize them, so we did not worry.

Our routine from day to day was pretty much the same. Breakfast at about 4.15 A.M. or 4.30 A.M. Ride all the forenoon, dinner at noon; ride all the afternoon, supper at 6 P.M. or thereabouts. Sometimes we had to move camp every day, sometimes it would be a fixture for two or three days, according to how we found the cattle. We had to drive with us our seized herd, wherein were innumerable calves. They had to be moved slowly, and the number of cattle, of course, increased from day to day.

Matters by this time reached such a stage that some definite pronouncement had to be made as to the plan upon which the seizure was to be conducted. My colleague and I had never been able to agree upon this point. He had spent most of his life in the Maritime Provinces seizing bottles of illicit rum from fishing smacks and the like, and knew as much about cattle as a cow knew about side-pockets. He was not even willing to learn. He argued that the Spencers had paid duty on 1,230 head of stock, and that we should seize all over that number of American brands that we could find. This proposition was too childish to waste time in discussing, and I told him so. For want of something better to say, he finally observed that his "Depurtment" (sic) was in charge of the operations and that what he, as representative of the Customs, said was final. Considering that he was as useless as a fifth wheel to a coach, this was calculated to make a plain man mad, and I am free to confess that it made me "as mad as a wet hen." I stumped out of the tent, leaving behind me as a Parthian shot, "You'll find that I shall settle this question, irrespective of your Department's representative."

I called to my clerk to bring writing pad and pencil, and together we retired to a convenient spot, where he sat on the prairie and wrote, and I walked about and dictated.

The following is a verbatim copy of what he wrote:

"MEMORANDUM

of details for settlement with Spencer Bros. and Co., by Supt. Deane.

"On April 25, 1900, they imported 527 calves.

"Of these, 224 were entered at Coutts as being 'under six months old.'

"The remaining 303 were entered on the same date at the same place as being 'over six and *under* twelve months.'

"As a yearling is not properly so-called until he has become twelve months old; as a two-year-old is not properly so-called until he is twenty-four months old; and as a three-year-old is not properly so-called until he has completed thirty-six months of age, it will be seen that none of the 527 calves was thirty-six months old on April 25, 1902.

"By May 25, 1902, one month later, it might be plausibly claimed that some of them had become three-year-olds.

"A liberal method, therefore, of estimating the possible

number may be arrived at in the case of the 303 calves which were entered as being over six and under twelve months on April 25, 1900.

"In the first place, it may be fairly presumed that the 303 calves were half steers and half heifers. We may thus consider them to have been 152 heifers and 151 steers. *Place aux dames!*

"As the ages of the calves were spread over a period of six months, it is reasonable to divide the number of heifers and steers by six, and thus to assume that twenty-seven heifers and twenty-six steers had, on May 25, 1902, entered the category of three-year-old animals.

"The entry at Coutts giving the ages of these animals, as shown by the Customs records, will, I presume, be held to mean exactly what it expresses, neither more nor less. It is important that this should be definitely understood, as, in conversation with Mr. Bourinot the other day, Mr. Taylor prepared the way for a change of front by saying that a mistake had been made in the entry at Coutts. He appeared to claim that a mistake had been made in the number of calves entered, but he also mentioned quite incidentally that some of the calves were fourteen months old. I called Mr. Bourinot's attention to this remark afterwards. Upon this premise, namely, that the entry at Coutts was correct, and was made in good faith, I am, in the opinion of competent stockmen, making a liberal computation when I allow one-sixth part of the 303 calves to be classed as three-year-old steers and heifers on May 25, 1902.

"This pre-supposes no casualties to have happened to any of them.

"These animals are said to have been all branded  and J7 on the left side.

"I desire to draw particular attention to these twenty-six steers qualifying as three-year-old animals, *because it will account for the only three-year-old steers of American brands lawfully in possession of Spencer Bros. and Co. in Canada.*

"On December 7, 1900, the firm imported and paid duty on 189 cows and 80 heifers. The calves (268) imported on that occasion are too young to require attention.

"The brands on these animals were entered as , J7, and  (quarter-circle F).

"On April 20, 1901, the firm paid duty on eighty-two cows and twenty heifers, described as being then about two years old. The brand on this importation was entered as  on the left side.

"The total number then of cows and heifers three years old and upwards which Spencer Bros. and Co. have lawfully in their possession on May 25, 1902, equals 189, plus 80, plus 82, plus 20, plus 27, all of which amount to 398.

"A certain proportion of female stock is always unprolific, being called 'dry stock.' Competent stockmen tell me that, estimating the proportion of 'dry stock' at 30 per cent. is in reality an under-estimate, so that, if it be conceded that Spencer and Co. should receive a calf with each of the 398 cows to which they are entitled, they cannot complain of illiberality. This very number, 398, should be subject to deduction from losses, etc., but the fact that none is claimed by the Government again bespeaks liberality.

"In the number of cattle which have been rounded up there are a number of steers of three, four, five years old and upwards.

"These animals all bear American brands, have not been entered at Customs, and are thus valuable and seizable property.

"I may here again say the allowance of the twenty-six just turned three-year-old steers, as previously mentioned, is a liberal concession to the firm of Spencers.

"Following the same rule as is suggested for the steers, all cows bearing American brands of three years old and upwards, whether with calves or not, are liable to seizure and confiscation, and these and the steers will constitute the most valuable part of the seizure.

"There is no difficulty whatever in conducting the seizure upon these lines. Competent cattlemen are as well able to tell the age of a two, three or four-year-old animal, etc., as they are to read the lines of a book. Mr. Lane had provided in the personnel of his round-up an expert in this matter, and, in the event of any dispute arising as to an animal's age, we have, upon Mr. Lane's advice, fortified ourselves with professional veterinary opinion in the person of Staff-Sergeant Hobbs. The dictum, therefore, of Mr. Henry, the expert, of Mr. Playfair, captain of the round-up, and of Staff-Sergeant Hobbs may be held as to be unassailable wherever they are agreed upon a point of age, and such opinion need not fear to be controverted in a court of law.

"Spencer Bros. and Co. may plausibly plead that the American-branded steers, etc., now on their range here have strayed across the boundary line and joined their cattle here without their knowledge. Against that there are two circumstances to be considered. First, Arthur Strong told me on May 24 last, in connection with the entry of 527 calves at Writing-on-Stone on April 25, 1900, when I told him that I held a warrant for his arrest for aiding and abetting in smuggling cattle into Canada (as per affidavit of John Rice), that he had not smuggled any cattle as charged; that on the occasion in question he had, in accordance with his orders, driven 400 head of cattle over and above the calves aforesaid as far as the boundary line and left them there. He protested that he did not know whether they came into Canada or not.

"Secondly, we know from Mr. Stock Inspector Bray's report that, on May 2 last, Spencer Bros. shipped four beef cattle branded  on the left side, viz., the American brand. It remains for the firm to show whether these animals were ever duly entered at Customs. The two circumstances are at least suspicious.

"I have thought it advisable to record for the information of the Department at Ottawa, and possibly for future reference, in the event of the matter ever finding its way into a Court of Law, exactly what my views and line of reasoning are while we are on the spot.

"To pursue this matter to its logical conclusion, there is, in my opinion, but one course open to us. We have now over 1,400 head of cattle. After the claims of Spencer Bros. and Co. have been satisfied as aforesaid, it will be found that in the balance remaining there will still be a considerable number of steers and cows of three years of age and upwards, and these should be seized, as Spencer Bros. and Co. cannot have them lawfully in their possession, and the onus of proving that they are so rests with them.

"Badwater Lake, Alberta.

"*May* 31, 1902."

As soon as a fair copy had been made I took it to Bourinot and said, "That is an outline of the basis of settlement; if you agree with it you should sign it; if you do not agree with it you would do well to detail your objections in writing." He studied it for a while, and then said, "It's all right," so we had no further dispute.

Bourinot left on June 3 for Coutts, from whence he sent to his Department at Ottawa a long telegram which we had concocted. The reply read as follows:

"Commissioner instructs you to demand deposit of duty paid value for stock seized, such deposit not exceeding $10,000. Forfeited stock may be sold by private sale, if you deem this advisable, in case deposit not paid."

The $10,000 limit was absurdly inadequate, and rendered it useless for us to waste time and money by going again over the range in pursuit of the cattle that had been driven out of our way, so we turned over to Mr. Taylor and his men:

(1) 398 cows, three years old and upwards, with a calf to each cow.

(2) 26 steers which had just attained the age of three years.

Taylor, as was expected, kicked like a steer about everything. I explained to him our method of settling the dispute, and quoted from my record the maximum number of cows which he was entitled to receive, according to his own sworn Customs entries. He retorted that he had never heard of such a thing as holding a man to months in the ages of cattle. Bourinot chipped in then, "I told you in March, Mr. Taylor, that we would hold you to your entries, and that is what we are doing." We were quite firm, so finally he said he was satisfied with the cows and steers, and took them over as being three years and upwards.

Next we handed over to him some 348 head of less than three-year-old animals which we did not want.

This brought us down to the herd that we intended to seize—all three-year-olds and upwards. We asked Taylor if he had any objection to offer in respect to these, and he and his men started in and recklessly cut out about 150 head which he claimed were two-year-old animals.

We sat round and looked on, and, in some cases, laughed. Several of the cows were followed by two calves —a yearling and a calf, and he thought it good business to take the yearlings away from their mothers, as if we were such fools as not to see through this absurdity.

One amusing incident happened. Taylor and our man, Playfair, disagreed about a steer. Playfair said, "Look here, Taylor, I've just got fifty dollars here. You say that steer is not three years old and I say it is. I will bet you fifty dollars on it, and if you will bet I will take the money over to the Captain there, and he shall hold it while we throw the animal and let the vet. examine its mouth." Taylor was not such a fool as to give away his money in that fashion, and declined the offer. Playfair then refused to take his objections seriously.

After Taylor and his men had finished their afternoon's fun, we instructed our experts to cut back into the seized herd all of the 150 animals that they would positively swear to as being three years old. They cut back all but nineteen head. They said there might be doubt as to these nineteen, and they would not be prepared to swear without a mouth examination. This Taylor was particularly anxious to avoid; he was too good a cattleman not to know that he was wrong, and a mouth examination not only would have discredited him in the eyes of his own men, but would have subjected him to derision all over the range and in the stockmen's world. It was no part of our business to compel an examination. In the first place, the Customs Act throws upon the importer the onus of proof. Taylor was the importer, and the proof lay with him. In the second place, we were dealing with Spencers' cattle. If there was any throwing to be done, it had to be done by the Spencers' men. We should never have heard the last of it if an animal had been thrown by our men and a leg had been accidentally broken perhaps, as was always possible. It was better policy for us to concede the nineteen head, which we did.

We then asked Taylor if he was satisfied that the herd under seizure consisted of cattle three years old and upwards. He replied, "To the best of my judgment."

We then proceeded to count the seized herd, and found 587 head. Taylor was nervous and lost the count. Voice gave it to him once, but he lost it again, and was content to accept our figures, the more so as we had spent ten hours in the saddle "chewing the rag" over this very simple proposition.

Next morning the round-up left us, as its work was done, and well done, too. They had worked with us and for us loyally and well, and our personal relations were all that could be desired. Bourinot and his teamster left at the same time, heading for the railway. He had an engagement to meet Taylor at Medicine Hat, there to receive the required deposit, and it was my duty to stay with the herd, with Voice and the few men that I had as herders, until I should hear from Bourinot. The nights of the 14th, 15th, and 16th June were bitterly cold, with driving rainstorms at frequent intervals during the day. The cattle were restless and hard to hold, and I was mighty glad when word came about 3 P.M. on the 17th that the deposit was made and that the cattle might be released. I sent for Taylor to come and take them over, and we counted them out to him:

198 steers, worth $42.50 each.
164 cows, with calves, worth $35 each.
225 dry cows, worth $28 each.

The total value was over 20,000 dollars. The prices quoted were the market prices of the day, and we knew of a man who was prepared to buy the cattle at those prices if there had been any hitch with the deposit.

On June 18 we broke up our camp and started for the Mounted Police detachment at Writing-on-Stone, about forty miles distant, and it was about time, for our grub had run out, the rains had spoilt most of the little flour we had left, and we had but a scanty breakfast that morning. Having to make a detour on business, I had a ride of fifty-three miles before I got my next meal, and that was not till half-past three in the afternoon. We had all become a little tired of the job—the work had been very tiresome and monotonous during the last few days. We had driven an ever-increasing number of cattle, which finally amounted to about 1,400 head, for about seventy miles, and had not lost even one calf. My two horses had carried me for over 900 miles between May 14 and June 19, which was as much as I dared take out of them, considering that one was twenty-two years of age ("Dandy" by name, dandy by nature), and the other turned out to have a poor constitution. Old "Dandy" delighted in cutting a refractory steer out of a bunch. He would cock his ears and watch the brute, and turn like a flash at the slightest touch of a rein laid flat on his neck. That is the cowboy fashion, and I never insulted the old chap's mouth by pretending to know that he had a bit in it.

He and I, on one of the closing days of the round-up, had finally cut out a steer that had given us a lot of trouble. Willard Humphries, an American cowboy, one of Spencers' men, had been looking on from the outside of the circle, and when I pulled up alongside of him, said, "The old horse did that well, Cap'n, but I don't like to see him do it." "Why not?" I queried. "Oh! because he's too old; he shouldn't have that to do in his old age." "I believe you're right," said I. "I'll never do it again," and I never did.

For my share in this seizure I was peremptorily ordered to be transferred from Lethbridge to Maple Creek. I had been in Lethbridge for fourteen years, so there was, as the Western expression goes, "no kick coming to me." I simply packed up and went, and, by the irony of fate, stumbled upon the other instances of graft which I have previously mentioned. I carried with me the grim satisfaction of knowing that I had worked up a case in which there was not a single flaw, and which could not fail to be upheld by every tribunal in the Dominion.

In spite of all the information at their disposal, the Customs Department became weak-kneed (how this malady was induced may be better imagined than described), and returned to the Spencers or their representatives 4,000 of the 10,000 dollar deposit, thus defrauding the revenue of the round sum of $14,000, besides the further unknown quantity represented by the hundreds of smuggled cattle which we had not been permitted to round-up.

The Spencers then had the audacity to bring a suit against the Government for the $6,000 which the Customs held. This action was tried in the Exchequer Court at Medicine Hat on December 2, 1904.

They had filed in the Court a perfect avalanche of affidavits, in which they denied pretty nearly everything that had been reported against them. One instance will serve to show the class of impotent falsehood that they generated, for the falsity of every document was exposed at the hearing. One of the affidavits purported to have been made by Art. Strong, wherein he flatly contradicted the story that I had told about meeting him near the camp, and said that such a conversation never took place. In the witness-box, under cross-examination, Strong freely and unequivocally admitted that he had met me and had told me about his connection with the 900 cattle in April, 1900. So open and ingenuous was his admission that the judge remarked, "Ah! these affidavits have been prepared."

One of our witnesses, Peter Ennis, who had helped Sam Spencer to smuggle some 800 cattle into Canada at Pendant d'Oreille in October, 1900, and was coming from Montana to tell his story under oath, swore in the witness-box that while he was on his way the then Mayor of Great Falls (a bosom friend of the Spencers) had offered him $250 not to come to Court. When that inducement failed he was plied with liquor and made so helplessly drunk that it was quite a job to sober him up in time to give evidence. However, we managed it, and he gave good evidence, too.

The result of the trial was a foregone conclusion, and

Mr. Justice Burbridge said he could give the suppliants no relief. He remarked that the amount sued for represented only a small proportion of the value of the cattle seized, and this was an indication of the trend of his thoughts.

The disappointed suppliants appealed from the decision of the Exchequer Court to the Supreme Court of Canada, which affirmed the judgment of the Court below, and that settled the matter.

Some years ago I cut out a fragment of some newspaper, the name of which I do not know, the following poem, with which, with apologies to the author, it seems to me I may fitly close my narrative of this episode. It was a unique experience for a police officer, and I would not have missed it for the world:

THE COWBOY'S PRAYER

The following poem, written under the above caption, signed Charles B. Clark, Jr., contains a whole sermon whose broadness might be commended to some clerical teachers:

O Lord, I've never lived where churches grow;
  I love creation better as it stood
That day You finished it so long ago,
  And looked upon Your work and called it good.
I know that others find You in the light
  That's sifted down thro' tinted window panes,
And yet I seem to feel You near to-night
  In this dim, quiet starlight on the plains.

I thank you, Lord, that I am placed so well;
  That You have made my freedom so complete;
That I'm no slave of whistle, clock and bell,
  Or weak-eyed prisoner of wall and street.
Just let me live my life as I've begun,
  And give me work that's open to the sky;
Make me a partner of the wind and sun,
  And I won't ask a life that's soft or high.

Wholesale Cattle Smuggling

Let me be easy on the man that's down,
  And make me square and generous with all;
I'm careless, sometimes, Lord, when I'm in town,
  But never let them say I'm mean or small.
Make me as big and open as the plains,
  As honest as the horse between my knees,
Clean as the wind that blows behind the rains,
  Free as the hawk that circles down the breeze.

Forgive me, Lord, when sometimes I forget;
  You understand the reasons that are hid;
You know the many things that gall and fret,
  You know me better than my Mother did.
Just keep an eye on all that's done and said,.
  Just right me sometimes when I turn aside,
And guide me on the long, dim trail ahead
  That stretches upward to the Great Divide.

CHAPTER XVI

LOUIS RIEL: EXECUTED FOR TREASON

I HAVE often wondered whether, if there had been no rebellion in 1885, real estate in the business centre of Calgary would have been selling for $4,000 per foot frontage* in the year 1912. I trow not. The subject-matter of my sketch, prior to July, 1884, had been living in the United States, where he had become naturalised, and where he was earning a living as a school teacher. He was induced to return to Canada by a deputation of prominent men among the French half-breeds of the North Country, with a view to assisting them in obtaining sundry rights from the Dominion Government, and the redress of certain grievances which they had, or claimed to have.

At that time the country had rather fallen short of the expectations which had been raised about it, and settlers generally were far from being in a prosperous condition. The winter of 1882 had been a very hard one—witness the loss of some 8,000 or 9,000 head of Senator Cochrane's ranch cattle. This was due in part to bad management, it is true, but the historical fact is indisputable. New-comers felt that the conditions of life in the country were cruel. The winter of 1883 was also hard, and a good many people in the western country began to regret having come. Money was

* The Royal Bank of Canada paid that figure for the Hudson's Bay property in Eighth Avenue.

scarce, and, to use a popular expression, "The bottom was falling out of the whole thing." I knew a man who had a place about eight miles out of Regina, who used to make periodical trips to the Pile of Bones Creek with three barrels in a wagon to take home water for domestic and stock purposes.

With the outbreak of the Rebellion in 1885 every farmer who owned, or could provide himself with a team of horses and a wagon, could hire himself out to the Government at ten dollars per day. Money poured into the country to feed and supply the troops and police. Militia officers and men visited the country on service when otherwise they would never have thought of coming so far west, and the North-West Territories and their possibilities thus became widely known. In short, the Rebellion saved the country which, as an eastern correspondent wrote to me in 1884, "was not what it had been cracked up to be."

The climate alone was a factor that compelled very serious consideration. On New Year's Eve, 1884, the thermometer registered 58° below zero. On the following day it stood at 48° below zero, with a wind blowing at the rate of fifty-five miles an hour.

We had a set of instruments at Regina, and used to keep records for the Meteorological Department.

It was the custom on New Year's Day for the gentlemen to call upon the ladies, who remained at home on purpose to receive them, and offered to their visitors whatever refreshment they happened to have in the house, from tea to liqueurs. In this way one had to drink warily, because one was bound to take something in every house one entered, and it sometimes became a problem how to regulate oneself without doing violence to one's own feelings or of offending the susceptibilities of the hostesses, whose hospitality was always profuse.

On this occasion, however, my visits were very short. I could not keep my horses standing in the bitter wind, and a handshake, with a "Happy New Year" wish, was as much as could be compressed into each ceremonial.

Nor was the weather inclement only in the winter. I find from my diary that on the night of June 20, 1885, a hard frost cut off potatoes and tomatoes, so that the climate was as uncertain as it was unsparing.

All this helped to make the ordinary settler view the half-breed agitation with indifference. He had so many troubles of his own that he did not care whether the half-breeds were given scrip or not. In the north, at Prince Albert, Carlton and Battleford, it was different. The public there viewed with growing apprehension the agitation of the half-breed element, which largely predominated in the population. The prelates and priesthood of the Roman Catholic Church sent warning after warning to the members of the Dominion Cabinet, and the Mounted Police reports, which passed through my hands, sounded an ever-increasing note of alarm as the later months of 1884 and the early months of 1885 rolled on.

In the autumn of 1884 Mr. Fred White, Comptroller of the Mounted Police, and Sir John Macdonald's chief political agent, came westward and travelled through the Battleford-Prince Albert country, in company with the Premier's son, Hugh John Macdonald.

When he returned from that trip to Regina, he handed me a long telegraphic dispatch, to be converted into cipher and sent to the Minister, Sir David Macpherson, who was then taking Sir John Macdonald's part of the Administration, the latter having gone to England. As Mr. White was a special emissary, one would have supposed that his communication would have received some attention; but nothing was done. No steps were taken to check the conflagration which was evidently brewing, and on March 26, 1885, the first shot was fired at Duck Lake.

Riel was brought to Regina by train and handed over to me on May 23 by Captain George Young, of the Winnipeg Field Batteries.

In reporting his arrival to the Police Department at Ottawa, I said that I intended to allow no visitor to have speech of the prisoner without a permit from the Prime Minister. I religiously held to this regulation of my own making, and it saved me a great deal of trouble. There was a stock answer ready for everyone who applied at the guard-room, and all applicants were informed that they might take it as a final reply without pestering me to death. Riel had quite a number of sympathisers in Quebec, and from that province came the funds which provided him with legal assistance at his subsequent trial. Not long after his arrival at the guard-room, I was accosted one day in town by a gentleman, who said that he was the editor of a Quebec newspaper, and had come to Regina on purpose to see the prisoner. I replied that if he had taken the precaution of providing himself with Sir John Macdonald's permit there would be no difficulty in arranging an interview with Riel, and I asked if he had made any arrangements to that end at the Police Department in Ottawa. He said he had not done so, he had not supposed any such course to be necessary. I had to regret, then, that I was not at liberty to allow him to see Riel. He looked at me with a sort of pitying smile and said, "My dear sir, I think you hardly realise that I have come all this long way from Quebec on purpose to see this man." I assured him that I fully appreciated the length of the journey which he had taken, but Louis Riel, who had led two rebellions in Western Canada, was a very important prisoner, who would unquestionably be tried for his life, and that, until the policy of the Government was made known with regard to allowing him to receive visitors, I was not at liberty to relax the rule which existed. There was nothing more to be said or done, and the unfortunate editor returned to Quebec. It was not until June 21 that the Lieutenant-Governor showed me a telegram from Ottawa to the effect that "Government do not wish prisoners to be interviewed before arrival of Crown counsel at Regina."

The matter was placed in the discretion of Mr. Christopher Robinson, Q.C., the senior counsel for the Crown, and his were the only "permits" that I recognised.

Riel himself was given to understand from the first that visitors would have no access to him. He then wanted to be given newspapers, but these, too, were denied to him. He was told that he might have books or magazines or literature of that nature, but nothing respecting the topics of the day.

He, of course, wanted to have a spectacular trial, preferably in the East, before the eyes of the whole world, and little dreamt that his case would be disposed of by a stipendiary magistrate, a justice of the peace, and six jurors, in a little embryo town like Regina.

A letter which he addressed to the Premier summed up his views in its opening sentence. When he had any particular clerical work that he wanted to do, I used to let him use the Commissioner's office. This was a small office opening off mine, which was not otherwise used, as the Commissioner was in the north, and Riel and his escort could sit there without inconveniencing anyone.

The following is a copy of a letter he wrote; he made three copies of it—one for the Premier, one for the Lieutenant-Governor, and one for me:

Louis Riel: Executed for Treason

JESUS:	*MARIE:*	*JOSEPH:*
Sauvez nous :	*Intercedez pour nous :*	*Priez pour nous :*
Prison de Regina.	16 *Juillet*, 1885.	(*Confidential.*)

Au Très Honorable
Sir John A. Macdonald,
Premier Ministre,
de la Puissance,
du Canada.

Monsieur le Premier Minïstre,

J'implore un proces complet, et à la Cour Supreme. Je desire me d'esculper, depuis quinze ans. Si vous cèdez a mes instances, si vous m'accordez toute la latitude dont j'ai besoin pour me défendre Dieu me secourant, non seulement je me clairerai. Mais la grande responsibilité des troubles du Nord Ouest en 69—70 *et en* 85 *tombera courdement sur les Honorable Messieurs Blake et McKenzie et sur les journaux leurs principaux organes. Votrę politique au sujet du Nord Ouest se trouvera comme débarrassée des obstacles que ces deux hommes puissants se sont efforcés de vous susciter depuis* 69.

Mon intéret n'est pas seulement de me d'esculper. Je desire me réhabiliter. Si par le soutien de Dieu et la faveur des bonnes gens, il n'est permis de viser aux avantages d'une vraie réhabilitation et d'une indemnité équitable, ce serait pour rentrer dans la politique Manitobaine.

Je m'en coute d'abandonner ma patrie, ma mère, mes frères, mes sœurs, mes parents, mes amis.

De plus j'ai à cœur de continuer mon œuvre j'apprécie le grand talent des hommes qui ont gouverné et qui gouvernent, encore à l'heure qu'il est Manitoba. Mais il me semble qu'ils ne comprennent pas sa fondation. C'est pour cela que cette province n'est pas à l'aise et que la confédération s'en sent. La Manitoba profite, mais il ne fait penser. à ces personnes qui engraissent sans avoir de santé. Il ne lui serait peut-être pas inutile que j'arrivasse un jour à son ministre. Et il me serait particulièrement avantageux à moi, d'y arriver pour continuer avec vôtre Gouvernement ce que a été commencé, il y a quinze ans par l'acte de Manitoba.

J'avais l'honneur de vous dire dans ma communication du 6 courant que l'Irlande, c'est que je pense, pouvait devenir heureuse, et en même temps les Seigneurs Anglais continuer a avoir leur revenue comme l'ordinaire.

Le principe que j'aurais à proposer pour arriver à ce résultat me parait clair et simple. Si mon pays natal m'honnorait un jour au point de me faire asservir au premier siège de son ministre je vous soumettrais mes vues.

Dans le cas où il vous serait possible de les approuver je vous les présenterais pour mettre fin aux "Better terms" qui fatiguent la Conféderation sans apporter d'amélioration definitive au Manitoba. Vous me procuriez sans doute l'avantage de modifier en mieux ce que je n'aurais pas encore assez mûre dans mes manières de voir. Apres les avoir inaugurées dans la jeune province, vous seriez à même d'examiner comment mes idées fonctionneraient. Si elles réussissaient, vous pouvriez les generalizer a tout la Puissance. De là Mère Patrie en jugerait elle-même. Et avant trop long temps peut-être auriez-vous vous la gloire, et moi, le plaisir de les voir appliquer à la situation de l'Irlande par la Haute Autorité de Parlement Anglais même.

Le principe et les vues dont j'ai l'honneur de vous dire un mot sont en germe dans la constitution, l'acte du Manitoba.

Monsieur le Premier Ministre les meilleurs idées ont besoin d'être comprises pour-être mises en vogue. Et lors même la main de Dieu et celle des mes amis me feraient sortir de ma prison pour me porter à la tête du Ministère Provincial du Manitoba, il me serait encore bien difficule de fair mon chemin, s'il n'y avait pas là un gouverneur qui me compris.

Depuis que je suis à Regina tous mes écrits ont passé par les mains de Monsieur le Capitaine Deane. Ce noble officier connait mes facons de penser. Et pour ne pas le gêner, en lui faisant auprès de vous, des louanges qui ont a passer par son office, je vous disais tout court que ce serait, à mon avis, un honneur pour le Manitoba d'avoir un Lieutenant-Gouverneur tel que lui, pour l'Honorable Monsieur Aikens un successeur d'aussi grand merits et pour moi un guide dont les conseils me seraient si utiles.

Mes bien-veillants avocats sont arrivés d'avant hier. J'ai en la joie d'une entrevue avex eux. Ils vont insister pour que mon proces ait lieu en Bas Canada et par devant la cour Suprême. Veuillez m'accorder cela à moi: Veuillez cèder aux bonnes réprésentations de mes savants avocats.

Lorsqu'on me conduira dans l'est, si vous consentez bien que j'y sois conduis, arrangement pouvrait être pris pour qu' a mon arrivé trois avocats conservateurs, un Canadien Français, un Irlandais, et un Anglais Protestant m'offrent leurs bons services. Grande serait ma reconnaissance pour un tel honneur.

Ma cause serait plaidée au point de vue des interêts du parti opposé.

Monsieur le Capitaine pourrait me conduire. Il suiverait tout le procès. Il vous verrait souvent. Ce serait comme naturellement que vous pouvriez le nommé Lieutenant-Gouverneur du Manitoba.

Moi, j'aurais le bonheur de m'en retourner à St. Vital, goûter le paix qui m'y attend depuis quinze ans.

Et vous (que mes vœux ne vous soient pass suspects) vous aurez augmente de beaucoup le thème de vos re-

compenses. Si mes bons souhaits peuvent sortir au travers des barreux de ma petite et sombre cellude, si ma stricte captivité n'empèche pas ma voix de se faire entendre, puissiez vous un jour occuper le trône Vice-Royal de la Puissance, pour le plus grand bien de cette conféderation Canadienne, dont vous êtes l'un des Glorieux fondations.

J'ai l'honneur d'être,
avec beaucoup de respect,
Votre très humble serviteur,
(*Sd.*) LOUIS RIEL.

A perusal of this letter must, to my mind, irresistibly convey the idea that the writer was "cracked." I do not know of any word in the English language which so aptly fits the occasion.

Here was a man on the point of being tried for his life, for crimes committed in the North-West Territories in the year of grace 1885, blandly making suggestions as to the Government of Manitoba—and of Ireland, of all places. It has been said that Riel's grandfather was of Irish descent, and that his name was Reilley, but I have heard the statement contradicted just as positively as it was made. Be that as it may, it can excite no wonder that Louis Riel was a heavy burden for his legal advisers to carry.

These gentlemen had been retained by Riel's sympathisers in the Province of Quebec, and sent westward to give the unhappy man as good a run for his life as possible.

Appeals had been made on behalf of the French-Canadian race in the Province of Quebec, and this dispatch of counsel to defend Riel was one of the results. The names of the gentlemen in question were Mr. Charles Fitzpatrick (now Sir Charles, Chief Justice of Canada), Mr. F. X. Lemieux, and Mr. I. N. Greenshields, all of Quebec Province; with them was associated Mr. (now Hon. Mr. Justice) T. C. Johnstone, of the North-West Territorial Bar.

The Quebec gentlemen arrived at Regina on July 15, and Riel was arraigned on the 20th.

There and then began the most momentous trial that had ever taken place in Western Canada. Mr. Osler in his opening address to the jury called it "The most serious trial that has ever probably taken place in Canada." At the opening of the court Mr. Justice Richardson announced that Mr. Henry Le Jeune would be the associate justice of the peace. The clerk opened the court and the prisoner was placed in the dock.

In reply to a question by the presiding magistrate, Riel admitted that he had been furnished with a copy of the charge, of the panel of the jurors, and of the list of the witnesses for the prosecution.

He was then arraigned.

There were, based upon an old statute of Edward III., six charges, almost identical, and the wording of them was so quaint that it is perhaps permissible to quote the first charge at length, and to point out wherein the other five differed from it.

The first charge read:

"That Louis Riel, being a subject of Our Lady the Queen, not regarding the duty of his allegiance nor having the fear of God in his heart, but being moved and seduced by the instigation of the devil as a false traitor against Our said Lady the Queen, and wholly withdrawing the allegiance, fidelity and obedience which every true and faithful subject of Our said Lady the Queen should, and by right ought to bear towards Our said Lady the Queen, in the year aforesaid, together with, on the 26th day of March, divers other traitors, to the said Alexander David Stewart, unknown.* Armed and arrayed in a warlike manner, that

* The information was laid by Mr. Alexander David Stewart, who was at that time Chief of Police of the City of Hamilton, in Ontario, and who had come westward with the Crown counsel to assist in these cases.

is to say, with guns, rifles, pistols, bayonets, and other weapons, being then unlawfully, maliciously and traitorously assembled and gathered together against Our said Lady the Queen, at the locality known as Duck Lake, in the said North-West Territories of Canada and within this realm, and did then maliciously and traitorously attempt and endeavour by force and arms to subvert and destroy the Constitution and Government of this realm as by law established, and deprive and depose Our said Lady the Queen of and from the style, honour and kingly name of the Imperial Crown of this realm, in contempt of Our said Lady the Queen and her laws, to the evil example of all others in the like case offending, contrary to the duty of the allegiance of him, the said Louis Riel, against the form of the Statute in such case made and provided and against the peace of Our said Lady the Queen, her Crown and dignity."

Charge No. 2 read exactly like No. 1, except that it charged the offence to have been committed "At the locality known as Fish Creek," and the third charge quoted "The locality known as Batoche."

The first three charges averred that Louis Riel was "A subject of our Lady the Queen."

Charges four, five and six were exact reproductions of one, two and three, except that they averred that Louis Riel was "Then living within the Dominion of Canada and under the protection of our Sovereign Lady the Queen."

The alternative charges were necessitated by the fact that Louis Riel had, between 1870 and 1885, become a naturalised citizen of the United States.

Mr. Fitzpatrick then submitted a plea to the jurisdiction of the court which, briefly, set forth that "The said Hugh Richardson, in open Court with a Justice of the Peace and a jury of six, has no jurisdiction to try the offences charged in the information."

Counsel for the Crown entered a demurrer against this plea, and the prisoner's counsel joined issue upon the demurrer.

It was a very pretty quarrel as it stood, but Providence was on the side of the big battalions. The Government had provided some legal giants to uphold their end of the stick, to wit: Mr. Christopher Robinson, Q.C., and Mr. B. B. Osler, Q.C., of the Ontario Bar; the then Deputy-Minister of Justice, Mr. Burbridge, together with a French advocate from Quebec named Mr. T. C. Casgrain. With these gentlemen was associated a member of the local Bar, Mr. D. L. (now Hon. Mr. Justice) Scott. I should perhaps note here that Mr. B. B. Osler was a Liberal in politics, and Mr. Robinson a Conservative.

The two main questions before the Court at this stage were these: (1) Had the Court, constituted as it then was, authority under the statute of 1880 to try the case? (2) Did not that statute interfere with and entirely override the provisions of Magna Charta?

Mr. Fitzpatrick opened the ball.

He dived manfully into the recesses of Magna Charta, and stirred up the dry bones of King John's unruly barons, to show that the statute of 1880, passed by the Dominion, under which Louis Riel's court was constituted, was repugnant to the provisions of the Great Charter, which provided that "no man shall be arrested, nor imprisoned, nor banished, nor deprived of life, etc., but by the judgment of his peers and the laws of the land." He quoted authorities to show that "a trial by jury is understood to mean ex vi termini, a trial by a jury of twelve men, impartially selected, who must unanimously concur in the guilt of the accused before a legal conviction can be had."

He spoke very ably and at great length, and was followed by Mr. Greenshields, who, in another speech of considerable length, contended that the statute of 1880 was entirely ultra vires of the Dominion Parliament.

It was a great treat to hear Mr. Christopher Robinson's reply. He spoke easily and unaffectedly, with an absence of effort that to me was quite remarkable, and in a quiet conversational tone. He took an interest in all the odd little incidents that occurred in court. If there were a window to be opened or shut he followed with his eyes the entire operation. A man on the opposite side of the table was sketching a head on his blotter, and Mr. Robinson seemed to take the greatest interest in this head, which promised at first to be that of a girl, but afterwards developed some hair on the face, and was possibly intended for a sketch of the prisoner. Be that as it may, Mr. Robinson watched the progress of the drawing, and any other little incident that attracted his attention, all the while dropping some such commonplace platitudes as these:

". . . As regards the larger portion of my learned friend's arguments, which was addressed to the reasonableness or unreasonableness of those different enactments, we decline to follow them into that argument at all. . . . Those laws are Acts of Parliament, passed by British subjects for British subjects; they have existed for years, and until the past few months their validity has never been questioned. As regards their reasonableness or unreasonableness, I would say this also—that we must have regard always to the circumstances and conditions of the country for which the laws are enacted, and it is impossible that everything which my learned friend calls the fundamental principle of the British Constitution can be extended to all parts of the Empire; but if they rely upon that argument, it is a further answer to say that there is no greater fundamental principle of the British Constitution than the Supremacy of Parliament. Neither the right of Grand Jury, nor the petit jury, nor the right of a jury of any kind, is so much a fundamental principle of the British Constitution as the Supremacy of Parliament. . . . So that we have this course of legislation. First we have the Imperial legislature saying to the Parliament of the Dominion: You can make such laws as you think proper for the Government of Rupert's Land. Next we have the Parliament of the Dominion under that power making laws, and then we have the Imperial Parliament again, in view of the enactments which they have passed, making this enactment valid. . . . For these reasons it has been thought on the part of the Crown that nothing could be plainer than the course of legislation under which this Court is constituted, and from which it derives its jurisdiction. . . ."

After all the arguments were concluded, Mr. Justice Richardson delivered himself as follows: "Now if I understand the contention of Mr. Fitzpatrick, it is that this Act of 1880, so far as it relates to the trial of criminal offences such as this, is ultra vires."

Mr. Fitzpatrick: "My contention is that the Act of 1880, in so far as it relates to the trial of capital cases, is ultra vires."

Mr. Justice Richardson: "Well, as I cannot hold that, I must sustain the demurrer."

The discomfited counsel's face was a study. It was certainly the face of the most disgusted man in British North America at that time. It looked around the court-room with an expression of wonderment, which seemed to ask, "Is this all the expression of opinion that is due to me? After all my research, after all my eloquence, are my arguments to be turned down by a ruling of less than a dozen words?" I followed his gaze around the court-room and failed to see any expression of sympathy on any face there. The prevalent feeling in the North-West Territories was this: We have taken our lives in our hands to open up a new country, and in working out our own salvation we do not want to be let and hindered by old-time provincial prejudices.

To such an extent did this sentiment prevail that the North-West Council, which was then partly appointed and partly elective, had passed an Ordinance practically prohibiting the collection from a North-West settler of a debt incurred by him in the older provinces. This was, of course, disallowed by the Governor-General in Council, but the feeling was very much alive all the same.

The plea to the jurisdiction of the Court having been disposed of, Mr. Johnstone was put up to demur to the information on the ground that the first three charges were laid against the prisoner as a British subject, and that the other three were silent as to his nationality—that is to say, that charges four, five and six did not allege that the prisoner was the subject of a foreign state at peace with Her Majesty.

Mr. Burbridge replied: "In three counts we have charged him as a British subject and with having violated his natural allegiance, and in three counts we have charged him with having acted contrary to his local allegiance. It is quite sufficient that a man may live in a country to be guilty of treason."

The magistrate overruled this demurrer, and the prisoner was called upon to plead, which he did: "I am not guilty."

One whole day had been taken up, and the end was not yet so far as preliminaries were concerned.

At the opening of the court on the following morning the prisoner's counsel applied for an adjournment of the trial. They said that three witnesses named Dumont, Dumas and Nault, who were in Montana, were material to the defence. Mr. Greenshields represented that they would come to court to give evidence on the assurance of counsel that they would be protected.

He also said: "It is an undoubted fact, competent of proof, that the accused was confined in the Beaufort Asylum for a period of three years, from 1872 to 1875." The defence required certain medical witnesses from Quebec and Toronto to testify to the condition of the prisoner's mind at that time.

Mr. Greenshields said:

"The court can see the necessity in a trial of this kind, where life is involved, that we should be given the fullest opportunity to make a proper defence. What we want is a fair trial. That is what we are here for, and we should obtain the fullest and fairest trial; and if after a full and fair trial the court and jury find that the prisoner is guilty of the offence charged, we will have done our duty before the court and the people. The people of this country will be satisfied that no injustice has been done. If, after the production of such affidavits as these, the prisoner is forced on to trial on the charge of high treason, public feeling will not be satisfied. A trial of this kind, in which the public are all interested, must be a fair and impartial trial."

This was simply playing to the gallery of the Quebec party, which was "agin the Government," and Mr. Robinson, when his time came to reply, metaphorically boxed Mr. Greenshields' ears for his insinuations. He said:

"I regret extremely that my learned friend Mr. Greenshields should have departed so far from what I regard as professional courtesy and professional etiquette as to make the remarks which he thought it right to make in the discharge of his duty. . . . As to part of his remarks, I understood, and I think everyone else must have understood, that if they meant anything they certainly meant to imply a threat against those acting for the Crown; that if they declined to accede to the contention, public opinion would be brought to bear upon them, and public opinion would not support them. We are answerable to public opinion, and we are perfectly content to be answerable to public opinion, but I repeat again my surprise that that tone of spirit and sort of address should have been thought necessary in a case of this description."

The defence at this time were asking for an adjournment of about a month to enable them to produce necessary witnesses, and had represented that the prisoner was a man of little or no means, and that the necessary witnesses could not be produced without the assistance of the Crown.

In replying to the defence, with regard to a proposed safe conduct for Dumont, Dumas and Nault, Mr. Robinson said:

"It is a matter of history that a rebellion has broken out in this country. It is a matter of notoriety that those three men were not only participators in that rebellion, but were active and leading spirits concerned in it. It is a matter of notoriety that the result of their connection with that rebellion has led them to flee from justice. . . .

"We have no authority, at all events, and we have no power whatever to give to any of those persons who have fled from justice anything approaching protection or safe conduct if they choose to enter this province. If they enter it in innocence they can prove their innocence. If they enter it guilty, they must take the chances of all others who are guilty."

As to the production of witnesses for the defence from a distance, Mr. Robinson said:

"What those representing the Crown have thought is that it would be right for them to accede to an adjournment or postponement of this case for one week. All those witnesses who are in this country can be got in a week as well as in a month or a year. The Crown will do more. The Crown will join with my learned friends in telegraphing to those three gentlemen who are at Quebec, or those three gentlemen who are at Prince Albert. I desire that to come from the Crown as well as from them, and the Crown will pay their expenses."

The court then adjourned until July 28, and on that morning the trial began in earnest. Six jurors were sworn and empanelled, and Mr. Osler opened the case for the Crown.

The various speeches by the Crown counsel were so cogent that it was a privilege to hear them, and it is almost an act of desecration to mutilate them as I am doing. I have them all before me *in extenso,* together with full stenographic reports of the evidence, and all manner of literature connected with the rebellion.

The addresses of counsel are too long to reproduce, and therefore I can but make extracts here and there to suit the purpose of this brief sketch.

Mr. Osler outlined to the jury the story which he proposed to prove by the evidence, and I need do no more than record his closing remarks:

"I believe the facts as I have opened them to you will be fully and thoroughly sustained by the evidence, and there will be this further matter appear in evidence—that the prisoner was not there for the purpose so much of aiding the half-breeds as he was there for the purpose of utilising the half-breeds for his own selfish ends. You will find throughout the evidence in this case that it was not so much the rights of the half-breeds he was making as the power and benefit of Louis Riel, and money that Louis Riel wanted to extort from the Government. It will appear that this so-called patriot, leader of an oppressed people, was willing to leave the country and go wherever the Government wanted him, if he got a sum of money from the Government.

"Gentlemen, when he found that the Church to which he belonged, to which his principal supporters belonged, was against him in the movement, he had more ground to play upon his material, and (to feed his own vanity and ambition) he had himself named as the leader and prophet of his new religion. The 'Prophet of the Saskatchewan' was the cry under which his poor dupes, and many of them should have known better, were supposed to rally, intending by combining religious power to follow on the North Saskatchewan the methods of Eastern leaders. . . . I think you will find the evidence shows that he was utterly careless of his methods, and had but one object—his own power or money—and he did not care whose lives he sacrificed. . . ."

These statements were, in every instance, fully justified by the evidence which followed.

It was shown beyond doubt that Riel himself was the head and shoulders of the whole movement.

In the camp of Poundmaker, an Indian Chief, was found a letter in Riel's writing, signed by himself, dispatched after the Duck Lake skirmish, wherein nine men were killed, in which he said:

"Praise God for the success he has given us. Capture all the police you possibly can. Preserve their arms. Take Fort Battle, but save the provisions, munitions and arms. Send a detachment to us of at least one hundred men."

In another letter, proved at the trial to be in his handwriting, addressed to the French and English "mètis" (mixed breeds) from Battle River to Fort Pitt, he said:

"We will help you to take Fort Battle and Fort Pitt. Try and have the news which we send to you conveyed as soon as possible to the mètis and Indians of Fort Pitt. Tell them to be on their guard, to prepare themselves for anything. . . . Take with you the Indians; gather them together everywhere. Take all the ammunition you can, in whatever stores they may be. Murmur, growl and threaten. Rouse up the Indians."

A good many of the Indians whom he talked so lightly of rousing were refugee Sioux, who had come into Canada after the Custer massacre, and had not gone back with Sitting Bull when he returned to the United States. Very undesirable persons to rouse up.

Dr. John H. Willoughby deposed that he went from Saskatoon, where he was practising medicine, to Batoche, a distance of about fifty miles, on March 16, and there saw Riel with about sixty or seventy armed half-breeds. Riel told him that his plans were now mature, and that, as soon as he struck the first blow he would be joined by half-breeds and Indians, and that the United States were at his back.

He intended to divide the country into seven portions, and they were to be given to the Bavarians, Poles, Italians, German and Irish. There was to be a new Ireland in the North-West, and the Irish of the United States were to be given a chance, as well as the inhabitants of the "disthressful counthry."

He pointed to his men, and said to Dr. Willoughby, "You see now I have my police. In one week that little Government police will be wiped out of existence." He added that the rebellion of fifteen years ago "would not be a patch upon this one."

Mr. Charles Nolin had the time of his life. He was a very prominent half-breed, who had strongly sympathised with Riel and his aspirations, so long as he kept them within bounds. When Riel told him that he had decided to induce the people to take up arms, Nolin decided that it was time to drop the connection. He did so and gave evidence for the Crown.

He said, in part: "In the beginning of December, 1884, he (Riel) began to show a desire to have money; he spoke to me about it first, I think. I think he said he wanted $10,000 or $15,000."

Q. From whom would he get the money?

A. He said that the Canadian Government owed him

about $100,000, and then the question arose who the persons were whom he would have to talk to the Government about the indemnity. Some time after that the prisoner told me that he had an interview with Father André, and that he had made peace with the Church. He said that he went to the church with Father André, and in the presence of another priest and the Blessed Sacrament he had made peace, and that he would never again do anything against the clergy. Father André told him he would use his influence with the Government to obtain for him $35,000."

Counsel for the prisoner exploited, for all that it was worth, the argument that Riel came to Canada at the request of others, which was true; and that, having come here, he desired to return to the United States, and would have done so but for the pressure put upon him by his friends. This was not true, witness the evidence of a man who was more in Riel's confidence than anybody else.

CHARLES NOLIN: There was a meeting on February 24, when the prisoner was present.

Q. What took place at that meeting? Did the prisoner say anything about his departing for the United States?

A. Yes.

Q. What did the prisoner tell you about that?

A. He told me that it would be well to try and make it appear as if they wanted to stop him going to the States. Five or six persons were appointed to go among the people, and, when Riel's going away was spoken about, the people were to say "No, no." Riel never had any intention of leaving the country.

Q. Who instructed the people to do that?

A. Riel suggested that himself.

Q. Was that put in practice?

A. Yes.

Q. When did you finally differ from the prisoner in opinion?

A. About twenty days before they took up arms. I broke with the prisoner and made open war upon him.

Q. What happened on the 19th?

A. On March 19 I and the prisoner were to meet to explain the situation. I was taken prisoner by four armed men.

Q. Did you have occasion to go to the Council after that?

A. During that night I was brought before the Council.

Q. Was the prisoner there?

A. Yes.

Q. What did he say?

A. I was brought before the Council about 10 o'clock at night. The prisoner made the accusation against me.

Q. What did you do?

A. I defended myself.

Q. What did you say—in a few words?

A. I proved to the Council that the prisoner had made use of the movement to claim the indemnity for his own pocket.

Q. You were acquitted?

A. Yes.

Q. You were in the church after that?

A. The prisoner protested against the decision of the Council.

Q. Why did you join the movement?

A. To save my life.

Q. You were condemned to death?

A. Yes.

Q. When were you condemned to death?

A. When I was made prisoner I had been condemned to death, when I was brought to the church.

It was during the cross-examination of this witness by Mr. Lemieux that the "little rift" between the prisoner and his counsel became apparent.

The witness was about to leave the box when the prisoner spoke:

Your Honour, would you permit me a little while——

Mr. JUSTICE R.: In the proper time. I will tell you when you may speak to me. Not just now, though.

PRISONER: If there was any way, by legal procedure, that I should be allowed to say a word, I wish you would allow me before this witness leaves the box.

Mr. JUSTICE R.: I think you should suggest any question you have to your own counsel.

PRISONER: Do you allow me to say? I have some observation to make before the Court.

Mr. FITZPATRICK: I don't think this is the proper time, your Honour, that the prisoner should be allowed to say anything on the matter.

Mr. JUSTICE R.: I should ask him at the close of the case, before it goes to the jury.

Mr. FITZPATRICK: That is the time to do it.

Mr. JUSTICE R.: I think you should mention it quietly to your counsel, and if they think it proper for your defence they will put it.

Mr. FITZPATRICK: I think that the time has now arrived when it is necessary to state to the Court that we require that the prisoner at the bar should thoroughly understand that anything that is done in this case must be done through us, and if he wishes anything to be done he must necessarily give us instructions. He should be given to understand that he should give any instructions to us, and he must not be allowed to interfere. He is now endeavouring to withhold instructions.

Mr. JUSTICE R.: Is there not this difficulty under the statute, saying that he shall do so?

Mr. FITZPATRICK: I think the statute provides that he may make statements to the jury.

Mr. JUSTICE R.: The prisoner may defend himself under the statute, personally or by counsel.

Mr. FITZPATRICK: Once he has counsel he has no right to interfere.

Mr. ROBINSON: He has the right to address the jury.

Mr. FITZPATRICK: I am not aware of any right then.

Louis Riel: Executed for Treason

PRISONER: If you will allow me, your Honour, this case comes to be extraordinary, and while the Crown, with the great talents they have at its service, are trying to show I am guilty—of course, it is their duty—my counsellors are trying—my good friends and lawyers, who have been sent here by friends whom I respect—are trying to show that I am insane——

Mr. JUSTICE R.: Now you must stop.

PRISONER: I will stop and obey your Court.

Mr. JUSTICE R.: I will tell you once more, if you have any questions which you think ought to be put to this witness, and which your advisers have not put, just tell them quietly and they will put it, if they think it proper to do so.

Mr. FITZPATRICK: I don't think he ought to be allowed to say any more. For the last two days we have felt ourselves in this position—that this man is actually obstructing the proper management of this case for the express purpose of having a chance to interfere in this case, and he must be given to understand immediately that he won't be allowed to interfere in it, or else it will be absolutely useless for us to endeavour to continue any further in it.

Mr. JUSTICE R.: Is that a matter that I ought to interfere in? Isn't that a matter entirely between yourself and your client? Suppose you cannot go on, and my ruling was called in question, and the question was raised and the Court allowed such and such a thing to be done?

Mr. FITZPATRICK: I don't pretend to argue with the Court. It is not my practice, it is not my custom. I have stated to the Court what I think of this case. I think the Court here is bound by the ordinary rules of law, and so long as the prisoner is represented by counsel, it is his duty to give such instructions to his counsel as to enable him to do his duty to his case.

Mr. JUSTICE R.: I admit he ought to do so. But suppose he does not; and suppose counsel think fit to throw up their brief?

Mr. FITZPATRICK: We are entirely free to do that, and that is matter for our consideration at the present moment, if the prisoner is allowed to interfere. Of course, I have to take the ruling of the Court.

Mr. JUSTICE R.: I don't like to dictate to you, but it strikes me that now an opportunity should be taken of ascertaining whether there is really anything that has not been put to this witness that ought to have been put.

Mr. FITZPATRICK: We have very little desire to have questions put which we, in our discretion, do not desire to put. What has this Court to do with theories about inspiration and the division of lands, further than we have gone into it? However, I, of course, have to accept the ruling of the Court as it is given, and then it will be for the counsel for the defence to consider the position.

Mr. ROBINSON: It must be quite understood that no rulings of the Court are given with the desire or at the request or with the concurrence of the Crown. We have nothing to do in the shape of interference. We must not be drawn into the position that there is a ruling of the Court on a question of that kind. I think it would probably be right for the Court to ask the prisoner whether the case is or is not fully in the hands of the counsel. It is for the prisoner to say.

Mr. FITZPATRICK: We accept that suggestion.

Mr. JUSTICE R.: Are you defended by counsel? Answer my question, please. Is your case in the hands of counsel?

PRISONER: Partly; my cause is partly in their hands.

Mr. JUSTICE R.: Now stop. Are you defended by counsel or not? Have you advisers?

PRISONER: I don't wish to leave them aside. I want them, I want their services; but I want my cause, your Honour, to be defended to the best which circumstances allow.

Mr. JUSTICE R.: Then you must leave it in their hands.

PRISONER: I will, if you please, say this reason: My counsel come from Quebec, from a far province. They have to put questions to men with whom they are not acquainted, on circumstances which they don't know, and although I am willing to give them all the information that I can, they cannot follow the thread of all the questions that could be put to the witnesses. They lose more than three-quarters of the good opportunities of making good answers; not because they are not able; they are learned, they are talented, but the circumstances are such that they cannot put all the questions. If I would be allowed, as it was suggested. This case is extraordinary.

Mr. JUSTICE R.: You have told me your case is in the hands of advisers.

PRISONER: Partly.

Mr. JUSTICE R.: Now you must leave it there until you get through. I will give you an opportunity of speaking to the Court at the proper time.

PRISONER: The witnesses are passing and the opportunities.

Mr. JUSTICE R.: Tell your counsel.

PRISONER: I cannot—all. I have too much to say.

Mr. JUSTICE R.: If there is any question not put to this witness which you think ought to be put, tell it to your counsel, and they will say whether it should be put.

PRISONER: I have on cross-examination 200 questions.

Mr. ROBINSON: We had better understand this. Counsel for the Crown are taking no part. Our inclination is, if counsel for the prisoner agree to it, to let the prisoner put any questions he pleases to the witness. We don't wish to interfere in any way between the prisoner and his counsel.

Mr. FITZPATRICK: Would your Honour allow us, say, five minutes of a consultation?

Mr. JUSTICE R.: I was just going to suggest that you should take a little time, and that the prisoner should go with you.

An adjournment here took place, and on the Court re-assembling, the conversation was resumed along the original lines. The conference had produced no practical result.

Mr. Lemieux explained that although he and his confrères had done their very best to help the prisoner, "It appears that he is not very well pleased, or it appears he thinks we did not put all the questions to the witnesses that we should have put."

Mr. Robinson interjected: "If the prisoner under the special circumstances of this case desires to join his counsel in conducting the examination or cross-examination of witness, the Crown do not object to it."

But the prisoner's counsel were obdurate. As Mr. Lemieux put it: "If the prisoner insists upon putting questions to the witnesses, we object to it, and we, moreover, say that we will not continue to act in the case as counsel. We think, however, it is too late for him to now disavow or refuse."

It was a hopeless *impasse,* the prisoner would not discharge his counsel, he would not confide to them the questions that he desired to ask; they would not concede to him the right to ask them himself, and at one time he said: "Here I have to defend myself against the accusation of high treason, or I have to consent to the animal life of an asylum. I don't much care about animal life if I am not allowed to carry with it the moral existence of an intellectual being."

Mr. JUSTICE R.: Now stop.

PRISONER: Yes, your Honour, I will.

Mr. JUSTICE R.: I think I shall have to tell you that you are in your counsel's hands, and if you and they cannot agree, then will come another question—whether the Court will not further interfere and say counsel must go on.

The examination of Charles Nolin was then continued, and the witness said that the Council that condemned him to death was one that was called "Exovede.' He said that the prisoner had separated entirely from the clergy: that the half-breeds were people who need religion, which had a great influence on their mind.

Asked, if without religion, the prisoner would have succeeded in bringing the half-breeds with him, the witness answered: "No, it would never have succeeded. If the prisoner had not made himself appear as a prophet he would never have succeeded in bringing the half-breeds with him."

Mr. Lemieux re-cross-examined the witness after this.

The witness was asked, if the prisoner did not lose a great deal of his influence by the fact that he lost the influence of the clergy, and he replied that at the time the prisoner gained influence by working against the clergy and by making himself as a priest.

Asked if he meant the people did not have confidence in their clergy, he said, "No," but they were ignorant, and advantage was being taken of their ignorance and simplicity.

PRISONER: I wish to put a question myself to the witness in the box, your Honour.

Mr. JUSTICE R.: If your counsel see fit to put it they will put it, and if not the witness is discharged.

Mr. LEMIEUX: I asked the prisoner if he had any questions to put to the witness through me, and he said he had none, that he would only put questions by himself.

Some little further conversation continued along the same lines, and another witness was called.

Several papers were produced in Court at different times bearing the signature, "Louis David Riel, Exovede."

One was a demand addressed, "To Major Crozier,

Commander of the Police Forts, Carlton and Battleford," calling upon him to surrender his forts to the Provisional Government of the Saskatchewan.

Another was addressed to Messrs. Charles Nolin and Maxime Lépine, who were instructed to deliver the first mentioned document.

A third was addressed to Major-General Middleton, and dated May 15.

In order to explain the meaning of the word "Exovede" I have to refer to the testimony of Captain George Young, of the Winnipeg Field Battery, who received Riel from General Middleton on the evening of May 15, and remained in charge of him until he delivered him to me at Regina on May 23.

This witness said, inter alia:

"During the term of eight or nine days that I was living with him (Riel) entirely, there was an immense amount of conversation. We conversed almost constantly and very freely. He conversed on almost every subject connected with the rebellion. When we found the books and papers in the Council room we found the word 'Exovede.' This bothered us a great deal, and one of the first things I asked the prisoner was what it meant. He wrote the meaning of the word in my note-book. It is lengthy."

Mr. GREENSHIELDS: No matter, let us have it.

It is as follows:

"From two Latin words *ex*, which means from, and *ovede*, flock. That word I made use of to convey that I was assuming no authority at all. And the advisers of the movement took also that title instead of councillors or representatives, and their purpose for doing so was exactly the same as mine, no assumption of authority. . . . Several times, it is true, we made use of the words 'Representative Members of the Council,' but we had to do it until the word *Exovede* was understood and until it would begin to become usual amongst even the men of the movement. So the council itself is not a council, and being composed of *Exovedes,* we have called the *Exovedate.*"

In examination-in-chief this witness was asked by Mr. Robinson:

Q. From first to last of these conversations with you, did you observe anything to arouse a suspicion or indicate that he was of unsound mind?

A. Not at all—certainly not. I found that I had a mind against my own, and fully equal to it; better educated and much more clever than I was myself. He would stop and evade answering questions with the best possible advantage.

In the hands of Mr. Greenshields the witness acknowledged that he had had no experience in dealing with people of unsound mind, nor had he received a medical education.

Q. You do not consider yourself in a position to give an opinion as to the sanity?

A. I could not give a medical opinion, but I consider that during the nine days I was living with him I would know if I was living with a lunatic.

The next witness whom I call into the witness-box of this court of reminiscences is Dr. James M. Wallace, who told Mr. Osler that for about nine years he had been in charge of the asylum for the insane at Hamilton, Ontario, but had studied insanity for more years than that. He had been present during the sitting of the Court, had heard the evidence, had interviewed the prisoner alone for about half an hour, and had discovered no indication of insanity. He thought the prisoner was of sound mind and capable of distinguishing right from wrong.

In answer to Mr. Fitzpatrick, the doctor said he had heard of the particular form of mental disease known as megalomania, a term which was scarcely ever used, and that by only one writer.*

Q. You are aware that this particular form of insanity is characterised, among other things, by extreme irritability on the part of the patient?

A. Not megalomania. Megalomania simply applies to grandiose ideas. It can have no other definition than that, and these ideas, allow me to explain, are delusions; they are delusions such as a person holding or believing himself to be a king, or possessed of immense wealth, and that the world is at his feet.

Q. But are you quite sure that the character of irritability is not one of the characteristics of this malady?

A. It is not a malady. It is merely a symptom, commonly found in paralytic insanity.

Q. Where the disease exists, is the idea, the result of disease, fixed and constant?

A. It is the result of the disease.

Q. But is it fixed or intermittent?

A. In those cases it is fixed.

Q. So that when a "queen" has taken herself to be a queen, she remains a queen?

A. She usually dies a queen.

Q. In her own idea?

A. Yes.

Q. Not sometimes a queen and sometimes otherwise?

A. No.

The next witness to be called upon to tell his recollections was Father Alexis André, Oblate, who had lived with the half-breeds of the Saskatchewan for about twenty-five years.

He was one of the witnesses who were brought from Prince Albert, at the expense of the Crown, to give evidence in Riel's favour, and Mr. Lemieux tried to extract from him an opinion adverse to the sanity of the prisoner.

* The reader must remember that this was thirty years ago.

Q. You have had a good deal of experience with people, and you have known persons who were afflicted with mania?

A. Before answering that I want to state a fact to the Court regarding the prisoner. You know the life of that man affected us during a certain time.

Q. In what way?

A. He was a fervent Catholic, attending the church and attending to his religious duties frequently, and his state of mind was the cause of great anxiety. In conversation on politics and on the rebellion and on religion he stated things which frightened the priests. I am obliged to visit every month the fathers (priests) of the district. Once all of the priests met together, and they put the question: "Is it possible to allow that man to continue in his religious duties?" And they unanimously decided that on this question he was not responsible, that he was completely a fool on this question, and that he could not suffer any contradiction. On the question of religion and politics we considered that he was completely a fool.

Mr. Lemieux rather incontinently dropped this witness, who was taken in hand by Mr. Casgrain for the Crown.

Q. I believe in the month of December, 1884, you had an interview with Riel and Nolin with regard to a certain sum of money which the prisoner claimed from the Federal Government?

A. Not with Nolin. He was not present.

Q. The prisoner was there?

A. Yes.

Q. Will you please state what the prisoner asked from the Federal Government?

A. I had two interviews with the prisoner on that subject. When he made his claim I was there with another gentleman, and he asked from the Government $100,000. We thought that was exorbitant, and the prisoner said: "Wait a little; I will take at once $35,000 cash.

Q. And on that condition the prisoner was allowed to leave the country if the Government gave him the $35,000?

A. Yes, that was the condition he put.*

Q. When was this?

A. On December 23, 1884.

Q. There was also another interview between you and the prisoner?

A. There have been about twenty interviews between us.

Q. He was always after you to ask you to use your influence with the Federal Government to obtain this indemnity?

A. The first time he spoke of it was on December 12; he had never spoken a word about it before, and on December 23 he spoke about it again.

Q. Is it not true that the prisoner told you he himself was the half-breed question?

A. He did not say so in express terms, but he conveyed that idea. He said, "If I am satisfied the half-breeds will be." I must explain this: this objection was made to him that even if the Government granted him the $35,000 the

* As we now learn from the late Lord Strathcona's-biographer that that nobleman himself, when he was plain Donald A. Smith, at the request of Governor Archibald, paid Riel $3,000 to leave the country for the time being, after the Rebellion of 1870, and after he had perpetrated the cold-blooded murder of Thomas Scott, and as we learn from the same authority that Archbishop Taché declared that the Government authorised him to promise Riel an amnesty, it is quite evident that there was more method in poor Louis' madness than any of us at the time had any idea of.

The same biographer tells us that when the Liberal Party came into power after the *exposé* of the "Pacific Scandal" in 1873. Louis Riel was elected for Provencher, and "actually travelled to Ottawa for the purpose of being sworn in a member of the House of Commons. At this time he was a fugitive from justice. . . . He succeeded in taking the oath and in writing his name in the book. . . . In the hurry and confusion of the moment he was allowed to slip away from the House undetected." No one seemed to bother about him greatly, and he "was accordingly permitted to escape."

It would be interesting to know if the warrant then issued was in existence, and if so, who had the custody of it, during the traitorous agitation among the half-breeds of the North-West.

It would have meant the saving of a little blood and a good deal of treasure, but the development of the Great Lone Land would have been delayed for at least a generation.

half-breed question would remain the same, and he said in answer to that, "If I am satisfied the half-breeds will be."

Q. Is it not a fact he told you he would even accept a less sum than the $35,000?

A. Yes. He said, "Use all the influence you can, you may get all that, but get all you can, and if you get less we will see."

Mr. Osler's cross-examination of the next witness was of absorbing interest.

Dr. François Roy was one of the prisoner's witnesses from Quebec, whose expenses were paid by the Government. He told Mr. Fitzpatrick that for more than fifteen or sixteen years he had been medical superintendent of the lunatic asylum at Beauport, in Quebec, and it had been his duty to visit the principal asylums in the United States and see how the patients were treated there. He had made a special study of diseases of the brain. He said that the prisoner was an inmate of the asylum for about nineteen months prior to January, 1878, suffering from megalomania, and passing under the name of La Rochelle. He was placed therein by the Provincial Government of Quebec.

In reply to Mr. Fitzpatrick, the doctor said: "I am perfectly certain that when the prisoner was under our care he was not of sound mind, but he became cured before he left, more or less; but from what I heard here to-day I am ready to say that I believe on these occasions his mind was unsound, and that he was labouring under the disease so well described by Dagonot."

In cross-examination, Mr. Osler elicited from the witness that he was one of two proprietors of a private asylum, having an average of from 800 to 900 inmates. He said they had a medical superintendent and a treasurer.

Q. The proprietors only have a general supervision?

A. More than that, I, myself, am a specialist. The

doctor admitted that he had brought no books or papers. Before starting he had looked into the register to refresh his memory as to the date of La Rochelle's discharge, and for the rest said, "I thought they would ask me my opinion of the case."

Having satisfied his legitimate curiosity on matters in general connected with the conduct of the institution, Mr. Osler came at length to the disease and its characteristics in this wise :

Q. You say the main feature of this disease is what? What is the leading feature of this disease, do you say? Do you say that it is a fixed idea incapable of change?

A. That is one thing I may say.

Q. Will you answer the question? Do you say that the leading feature of the disease is a fixed idea incapable of a change by reason?

A. I did not succeed in changing.

Q. I ask you is that the leading feature of the disease?

A. That is one of the features.

Q. Is it the leading feature?

A. It is one of them. It is one of the characteristic features.

Q. A fixed idea with a special ambition incapable of change by reasoning?

A. Yes, we did not succeed in changing the idea of the patient.

Q. Well, that fixed idea is beyond his control?

A. I would not be prepared to say entirely.

Q. If it is beyond his control he is an insane man?

A. Yes.

Q. Is not this fixed idea beyond his control?

A. Yes.

Q. If within his control, it is an indication of sanity?

A. That he was trying to get better, he may have had intermissions in which he understood his condition.

Q. It is subject to control, it is not a fixed idea; that

is what we have agreed upon as the leading characteristic, do you understand?

A. I do not know what you are after.

Q. If this idea is subject to control, then this man is sane?

A. There may be intermissions when he can control himself, because then the insanity disappears.

Q. And then there is a lucid interval?

A. Yes.

Q. During the period of the insanity the idea possesses the man and it is not controllable?

A. No.

Q. Is that the leading feature of the disease?

A. Partly.

Q. Do you know of any other?

A. I am not an expert in insanity.

Q. Can you give me any other leading feature of the disease?

A. I have no other feature to give.

Q. That is the only one you can describe?

A. I gave you the features and characteristics of the disease well enough.

Q. I am going to keep you to that unless you want to enlarge upon it. I am going to build my theory upon that. You can enlarge it as much as you like now, but do not go back upon me afterwards. Is there any other leading feature of the disease?

A. I have given you the principal characteristics of his disease.

Q. I want to get the peculiar characteristic of this form of mania.

A. They have intermissions sometimes for months and sometimes for days. The least contradiction excites them.

Q. There is a class of healthy intermissions. Sometimes a man likes beer and sometimes whisky. I want to get the characteristics that distinguish him from a healthy man, not those that we have in common with the insane.

A. We always answer reasonably, but when a man

comes and pretends to know everything, and talks nonsense, we suspect that, to a certain extent, he has lost his reason.

Q. We want to get at the leading characteristic. You have given us one feature. Is there only the one feature? If there are any other features say so.

A. I won't give you any.

Q. Will you stick to it?

A. Yes.

Q. Then what leading idea not subject to change by reason is it that you have fixed upon in the evidence yesterday and to-day bringing you to the conclusion that he is of unsound mind?

A. It is because of some symptoms.

Q. Tell me the symptoms that bring you to the conclusion that this man is within the rule you have laid down. Tell me the facts that bring him within that rule?

A. The facts are that he has always kept that characteristic.

Q. Answer that question.

Mr. FITZPATRICK: This witness has been speaking in English for some time past. If the witness does not understand the questions properly he should answer the questions in French.

Mr. OSLER: If the man wants to hide himself under the French he can do so.

Q. You understand what I mean?

A. Parle-moi François?

Mr. OSLER: It will be for the jury to say whether he is making the change at his own suggestion or at that of the counsel on the other side.

Q. Having given a rule to test this insanity, what fact is there disclosed in the evidence which leads you to say that the prisoner comes within the rule?

A. That part of the evidence given by the clergy to-day shows in a positive manner that the prisoner has manifested symptoms that we meet with in megalomania.

Q. That is no answer to my question. I want the fact

on which you bring the prisoner within the rule that you have laid down.

A. I want to take the fact proved by the evidence.

Q. Tell me the fact on which you rely.

A. The prisoner gets his theory from the idea that he has a mission.

Q. Do you understand that to be the fixed idea not controllable by reason?

A. I believe so because reason has never so far succeeded in changing the idea that he has.

Q. Is that the only reason you have for saying that the prisoner is insane?

A. It is, and I believe it to be sufficient.

Q. Is it consistent with labouring under an idea not controllable by reason that he would abandon that idea for $35,000?

Mr. FITZPATRICK: I object to that. That has not been proved.

HIS HONOUR: What is the question?

Mr. OSLER: Is it consistent with a man having an idea not controllable by reason that he will abandon that idea for $35,000? Let that be a hypothetical question.

Mr. FITZPATRICK: I object to the question.

HIS HONOUR: He can put hypothetical questions.

Mr. OSLER: My learned friend must know that the question is regular, and should not interfere at a critical part of the examination so as to give the witness a cue.

Mr. FITZPATRICK: I did not have any such intention. We have the right to object, and intend to exercise that right.

Mr. OSLER: You should not exercise it in such a way as to give the witness a cue. That is the second cue that you have given the witness. You gave him a cue in regard to speaking French.

It would be unprofitable to follow Dr. Roy's evidence any further. He was hopelessly out of his depth, and his counsel had to do something desperate to save his face.

When, in order to evade answering a question, he told Mr. Osler that he was "not an expert in insanity," a good many people who heard him wondered what he was doing there at all.

Mr. Osler finally dismissed him with a gesture of great contempt and in these words: "Well, doctor, if you will not answer the question in French or in English, I may as well let you go. You can go."

He then turned his broad back upon him, and the doctor stepped blithely out of the box as if he were a hero.

Father Vital Fourmond was another of the prisoner's witnesses brought from Prince Albert at the expense of the Crown. It was he who consulted the other Reverend Fathers as to whether Riel should be allowed to continue in his religious duties. He told Mr. Lemieux that Riel

"had extraordinary ideas on the subject of the Trinity. The only God was God the Father, and God the Son was not God; the Holy Ghost was not God either; the second person of the Trinity was not God, and as a consequence of this the Virgin Mary was not the Mother of God, but the Mother of the Son of God. Instead of saying 'Hail, Mary, Mother of God,' he said, 'Hail, Mary, Mother of the Son of God.' He did not admit the doctrines of the Church, of the Divine Presence. As to his political ideas, he wanted first to go to Winnipeg and Lower Canada and the United States and even France. He said he will take your country even, and then he was to go to Italy and overthrow the Pope, and then he would choose another Pope of his own making."

Mr. LEMIEUX: Have you made up your mind about the prisoner being insane as far as religious matters are concerned?

FATHER F.: We were much embarrassed at first, because sometimes he looked reasonable and sometimes he looked as a man who did not know what he was saying.

Mr. LEMIEUX: Finally?

Louis Riel: Executed for Treason

FATHER F.: We made up our minds there was no way to explain his conduct but that he was insane, otherwise he would have to be too big a criminal.

Father Fourmond gave this evidence on July 30 as a witness for the defence. He was somewhat less guarded on August 7 following, when he made an affidavit appealing for mercy on behalf of Philip Carnot, Maxime Lafime, Moise Ouilette, Pierre Parenteau, Emmanuel Champagne, and Philip Carnot, "All of whom I firmly believe (so the affidavit runs) were kept in the rebel camp through terror of their own lives and for fear of their families being punished should they attempt to escape."

The following are extracts from the same affidavit:

"To impress the people and keep them within his power this man, Riel, reverted to all kinds of trickery. Often have I seen him praying aloud, prostrating himself in prayer, and ordering all the others to do so. Then he made a deep impression on his poor, ignorant dupes, and so convinced them of his Divine mission that it was impossible to convince them that he was a trickster and would lead them to destruction. Riel so played on their ignorance that he made them believe in his power to work miracles; they firmly believed this. I heard them say that Riel could make it thunder and could cure disease without medicines. Riel himself declared that he was once the victim of an incurable disease of the heart, but that on May 24 he had cured the disease by his Divine power. He also declared that if he should be killed it did not matter, he would be with them again alive, and that would prove to them his Divine mission. He cried: 'It is the Holy Ghost that speaks, who shall dare disbelieve me? . . . Oh! my poor people!' I could not restrain them, they were under the infatuation of this arch traitor and trickster till he got them committed by the effusion of blood. I heard him say and proclaim, 'Death, death, death to anyone who tries to desert,' and many of the poor people had guns pointed at their hearts by Riel's orders, because he suspected them of wishing to get away; and to complete his terrorism over the poor people he declared it to be his determination to put me (this deponent) in the front of the battle."

This affidavit, of which I have quoted a very small part, is interesting as showing that a week's further reflection was sufficient to bring the Reverend Father to the conclusion that, after all, criminality, and not insanity, was the preponderating weight in the scale.

The insanity plea was ridiculous from the first. What did a couple of partizan doctors, hurriedly imported from the East, after one or two brief interviews, know about the prisoner and the state of his mind compared with us who were in daily communication with him? It was no uncommon thing for us to have lunatics in our charge, and very skilful and sympathetic treatment they used to receive at the hands of Dr. Jukes, the Senior Surgeon of the Force. He was in daily communicatibn with Louis Riel in the discharge of his duties, and never had any reason to suspect him of insanity. Nor had I, nor had Sergeant Piggott (the provost in charge of the prison), and we had had the prisoner in custody for over two months. I was asked at the trial if I had ever seen anything to indicate that the prisoner was not of sound mind, and I replied, "Nothing whatever."

Q. Anything to indicate the contrary?

A. Yes, I think so, he always gave me the impression of being very shrewd.

As I left the witness-box to return to my place in court, I had to pass the dock, and as I did so Riel said to me, "Thank you, Captain," and he meant it.

He particularly resented the imputation of insanity, and did not seem to realise that it was the one hope of saving his life. I have no doubt in my own mind that if Father Fourmond had laid an information before a Justice of the Peace that Louis Riel was insane and dangerous to be at large, and had adduced in corroboration of his complaint some of the evidence which he embodied in his affidavit before mentioned, the accused man would have been committed to one of our guardrooms for temporary detention pending inquiry and observation. This was not done, and as Father Fourmond and his confrères held their peace, the outside world knew nothing of the prisoner's eccentricities as alleged. If the matter had ever been brought to the notice of the Mounted Police they would have been glad of an opportunity to remove this firebrand, and would have attended to it, but, in truth, insanity was never mentioned in connection with Riel's name until his counsel originated the idea at the trial.

Mr. Fitzpatrick made a very long and very able address on behalf of his client, and at the close thereof the prisoner was informed by the Court that if he had any remarks to make to the jury then was the time to speak.

This is a special privilege accorded by statute to a person charged with high treason, and before Riel opened his mouth, Mr. Lemieux told the Court that his counsel must not be considered responsible for any declaration he might make.

Riel made a long, rambling speech, from which it is not an easy matter to make extracts.

The following is, however, material to the question of sanity or otherwise:

"To-day when I saw the glorious General Middleton bearing testimony that he thought I was not insane, and when Captain Deane proved that I am not insane, I felt that God was blessing me and blotting away from my name the blot resting upon my reputation on account of having been in the lunatic asylum of my good friend Dr. Roy. I have been in an asylum, but I thank the lawyers for the Crown, who destroyed the testimony of my good friend Dr. Roy, because I have always believed that I was put in the asylum without reason.

"Even if I was going to be sentenced by you, Gentlemen of the Jury, I have this satisfaction if I die—that if I die I will not be reputed by all men as insane, as a lunatic. A good deal has been said by the two Reverend Fathers, André and Fourmond. I cannot call them my friends, but they made no false testimony. I know that a long time ago they believed me more or less insane. . . .

"As to religion, what is my belief? What is my insanity about that? My insanity, your Honour, Gentlemen of the Jury, is, that I wish to leave Rome aside, inasmuch as it is the cause of division between Catholics and Protestants. . . . The nineteenth century is to be treated in certain ways, and it is probably for that reason I have found the word *Exovede.* I prefer to be called 'one of the flock.' I am no more than you are, I am simply one of the flock, equal to the rest. If it is any satisfaction to the doctors to know what kind of insanity I have, if they are going to call my pretensions insanity, I say humbly, through the grace of God, I believe I am the prophet of the New World."

Mr. Robinson closed the case for the Crown in a magnificent speech, and freely castigated the counsel of the other side who preceded him. I should explain here that we had in the barracks at that time some fifty half-breed and Indian prisoners, including Poundmaker, the Indian Chief, and these men were all awaiting trial for treason felony.

Mr. Robinson said among other things:

"It will not be necessary to go over the evidence in detail, for a reason we seldom find in cases of this kind. There is no contradiction, there is no dispute, there is not a single witness whose word has been doubted, there is not a single fact proved on the part of the Crown which anybody has been called to contradict; and it stands, therefore, as an admission, and an admission made by counsel for the defence, that the case as presented has been made out beyond all question. . . .

"What my learned friends' addresses amounted to was practically this. They told you, in fact, that this rebellion was justifiable. My learned friend, Mr. Greenshields, told you that the men responsible for the blood that was shed were the people who had refused the petitions which the half-breeds made under the direction and guidance of the prisoner at the bar. In the next breath he told you that this rebellion was directed and carried on by an irresponsible lunatic. . . .

"My learned friends must make their choice between their defences. They cannot claim for their client what is called a niche in the Temple of Fame and at the same time assert that he is entitled to a place in a lunatic asylum. . . .

"What in reality is the defence which you, as sensible men, are asked to find by your verdict? You are asked to find that six or seven hundred men may get up an armed rebellion, with its consequent loss of life, its loss of property; that murder and arson and pillage may be committed by that band of armed men, and we are to be told that they are all irresponsible lunatics. It is my duty to put these facts to you plainly and strongly, because it is our duty to protect society, and all that I can say is that, if such folly as finding this man insane is possible in this country, you say in effect to men who desire to come here to live that there is no sufficient protection by law for either life, property or liberty.

"Are you prepared to say that? Because that is the single issue placed before you by counsel for the Crown; disguise it as you like, speak of it as you like, that is the simple result and the plain consequence. . . .

"My learned friend, Mr. Fitzpatrick, must have forgotten what is due to a prisoner when he charged those who were acting for the Crown with some warmth for not having called

Poundmaker to prove the receipt of that document. [*N.B.*—That is the letter signed by Riel, found in Poundmaker's camp.]

"He was good enough at the same time to say that those who were conducting the case for the Crown were persons who understood fair play. It was because we did understand fair play, because it would have been improper to have called Poundmaker to swear to that that we did not call him. If we had attempted to put Poundmaker in the box to prove the receipt of this document we would have been asking Poundmaker to declare on his oath his own complicity in this rebellion, and Poundmaker would have said to us:

"'I decline to answer your questions,' and any judge would have said to those who acted for the Crown, 'Gentlemen, you had no business to put a man in that position.' Now that is our answer on the part of the Crown to the charge that we did not call the prisoners to prove their own guilt out of their own mouths. . . . Those who are guilty of this rebellion, and those who have not a proper excuse, have taken the step upon their own heads, and they must suffer the punishment which the law from all time, and which the law for the last five centuries, has declared to be the punishment of the crime of treason."

The case was left to the jury in a very full charge, and the law, as regards the defence of insanity, clearly stated in a manner to which no exception was taken either at the trial or in the Court of Queen's Bench of Manitoba or before the Privy Council.

The jury brought in a verdict of guilty, with a recommendation to mercy, and were discharged.

The prisoner was asked if he had anything to say why sentence should not be pronounced upon him, and made a very long, rambling speech, after which he was sentenced to be executed at Regina on September 18.

An appeal was taken to the Court of Appeal in Manitoba and also to the Privy Council, but the judgment was affirmed by both courts.

Louis Riel: Executed for Treason

Riel, after his sentence, was not long in attending to his spiritual affairs, and was then received once more into the bosom of the Church. Before this could be done, however, he had to recant his errors, which he did in a long manuscript document, dated the 4th day of August, and of which a translation is as follows:

"Renunciation made by Mr. Louis Riel, whose name is also 'David' Riel, of all his errors in the presence of the Reverend Father Fourmond, Oblate of Mary Immaculate, his Father Confessor, the 4th day of August, 1885.

"I, the undersigned Louis Riel, being in full possession of my faculties and of my free will, without any other motive than to ensure my eternal salvation, in reconciling myself with the God whom I have offended, and to amend the scandals which I have been so unhappy as to cause, do solemnly abjure all the errors which I have believed, professed and taught contrary to the doctrine of the Holy Apostolic and Roman Church, beseeching her in the person of her charitable ministers to bestow upon me her holy absolution for all my crimes and iniquities, as I renounce my false mission of prophet, the prime cause of my errors and of all other backslidings.

"I particularly abjure my sins against the most Holy and Adorable Trinity, against the Divine Motherhood of the August and Immaculate Mother of God, against the Most Holy and Adorable Eucharist, against the Eternal punishment of Hell, against the infallibility of the Holy Catholic and Apostolic Church of Rome and of her visible Head, the Holy Father the Pope, against the authority and integrity of Divine Inspiration of the Holy Scriptures and of the Catholic tradition; against the Apostolic institution of the Sabbath Day.

"I believe with all my heart, and with my mouth freely and fervently confess that there is one God in three Persons. Consubstantial and perfectly equal in all things, that is to say, that the Father is God, the Son is God like unto the Father, begotten by Him from all Eternity, Consubstantial with His Almighty Father, Eternal, Infinitely perfect like unto Himself, who, when He, the Divine Son of God, abased Himself so as to make Himself like unto us, except as to sin, took our likeness upon Him in the womb of the Blessed and Immaculate Virgin Mary—ever a Virgin by the Operation of the Holy Spirit, and consequently Mother of the Person Who is God : Mother of God according to the Catholic Faith, solemnly confirmed at the Œcumenical Council of Ephesus. I believe, therefore, that there are two natures in Jesus Christ our Lord, the Divine nature and the human nature, although He can only be one Person, the Person of the Son of God. He is perfect God and perfect Man, so that when He says that His Father is greater than Himself it is not the teaching of the Holy Catholic Church that He is not wholly Man and wholly God. I further believe that the Holy Ghost, the third Person of the Most Holy and Adorable Trinity, is God, like unto God the Father and the Son, proceeding from the Father and the Son, being One God with the Father and the Son. I believe in the Seven Sacraments of the Holy Church, and more particularly that an ordained priest only can hear the confession of Christians and give them Holy absolution; that the Blessed Eucharist is a Sacrament instituted by Our Lord Jesus Christ in His abundant love for us, and that it contains in verity and truth His Body, Blood, Soul and Divinity, under the Holy species of bread and wine, living in that adorable Sacrament not only for this mortal and temporal life, but more for the glorious and eternal life, enjoying in His Body and in His Holy Spirit all the priceless treasures of His triumphant resurrection.

"I believe in the infallibility of the Church and of Our Holy Father the Pope, speaking ex Cathedra and as the lawful successor of Saint Peter, in his supremacy over all other bishops of whom he is the One Visible Head on earth, as well as in his authority and jurisdiction over all priests and the faithful, believing that to him, as to Peter, it was said, 'Feed my sheep: feed my lambs.' I believe in the eternity of the pains of Hell, that they will forever endure and never cease, Purgatory alone having temporal punishment proportioned to trespasses against Divine Justice. I believe that the Holy Sabbath Day is at least an apostolic institution designed to replace the Sabbath of the ancient law, and that consequently the divine obligation to keep it holy is as binding upon us as was the obligation with regards to the ancient Jewish Sabbath, abolished by the new dispensation.

"Most humbly I solicit pardon from the public at large, particularly from the venerable representatives of the Holy Catholic Church, from the representatives of the Civil Power and all my Christian brethren, for the scandalous offences which I have committed against God and His Ordinances, commending myself to the pity of all men, and particularly so to that of the Almighty God Whom I have set at naught.

"(Signed) LOUIS RIEL or LOUIS 'DAVID' RIEL."

"(Witness) V. FOURMOND, O.M.I."

,, L. COCHIN, O.M.I."

Riel asked to see me one day, and handed me the document of which the foregoing purports to be a translation. So far as I recollect now, a recantation in the foregoing form had been presented to him by the priests for acceptance and signature, and he stipulated that he should be allowed to make a copy of it. This copy he then entrusted to me, asking me to keep it. Why, I do not know. He did not ask me to publish it, or I would not have received it, for it was not a time in the country's history when it would have been advisable to add fuel to the fire.

Having explained what the foregoing document was, he then handed me another paper, which was to be signed in my presence by the two priests, Fathers Fourmond and Cochin, and was to be witnessed by myself.

This document also was to remain in my custody. A translation of it reads as follows:

"We, the undersigned, certify as witnesses the authenticity of the answers made by Louis David Riel and of his recantation, and of the authenticity of the document of his renunciation; and we declare ourselves responsible before God and man for the legitimacy of the questions which we have put to him and for the legitimacy of the recantation which we have required from him as ordained priests.

"Regina Prison, 7 August, 1885.

"(Sd.) V. Fourmond, O.M.I.
"(Sd.) L. Cochin, O.M.I.

"(Witness) R. Burton Deane,
"Superintendent, N.W.M.P."

He made a great point of my witnessing this document, and I did so, although I did not want to be involved in any matter which might give possible offence to the priests. Similarly, I did not want to give offence to a moribund man, and accepted both papers from him accordingly. After a lapse of thirty years I presume there is no harm in publishing historical documents.

I never discussed religious subjects with Riel. The only occasion on which he ventured to obtrude his pretensions on me was on November 14, 1885, two days before his execution, and long after the recantation of his errors, when he sent me a note by the orderly officer, written by himself, which purports to be:

"The Narration of a Vision as seen this evening, 14th November, 1885, by Louis 'David' Riel, 'Prophet of the New World.'

"Care of Mr. the Inspector Dowling."

On the other side of a half-page of foolscap was written:

"Capitaine R. B. Deane,

"A little before half past eight o'clock this evening, as I had knelt down to make the way of the Cross, my eyes being shut, while I was beginning to pray, and being turned toward the West, I saw before me at a distance of about twenty or twenty-five yards a man, dark complexion, black moustache. It struck me that it was the Honourable Hector Langevin. While I was considering his face his features changed and reminded me (sic) the decomposed features of late Sir George E. Cartier, and he disappeared. An instant after my mind was in doubt whether those features were not those of the Hon. Minister of Militia."

The before-mentioned appeals to the Manitoba Court and the Privy Council had necessitated the postponement of the execution, and it was not until November 15 that the Commissioner of Dominion Police brought the death warrant from Ottawa. We had known, of course, that it was on the way, and arrangements had been made for the morning of November 16, at eight o'clock. Riel was informed by Sheriff Chapleau of the arrival of the warrant at about 9 P.M. on the 15th, and said in reply, "I am glad that at last I am to be released from suffering." The strain upon him during the previous three months had been tremendous, and he had become constitutionally weaker, although his mental condition was unchanged. He was attended at the last by Fathers André and McWilliams, and died with the courage of a man and a Christian, and it was not possible to doubt his sanity.

He had asked that his body should be given to his friends, to be laid at rest in St. Boniface, the French cemetery across the Red River from Winnipeg, and we handed it over to a Mr. Bonneau, upon an order from the Lieutenant-Governor, for conveyance thither.

While the coffin was thus awaiting transfer to Mr. Bonneau, it was kept in a corner of the prison yard, and, while there, report was made to me that a rumour was in circulation that after the dead man had been cut down from the scaffold, a brutal Mounted Policeman had, to the accompaniment of a blasphemous oath, stamped his booted foot into the dead man's face as it lay on the ground.

It seems now, as I write these words after the lapse of more than a quarter of a century, that it is almost incredible that such an improbable, senseless story should have obtained currency; but it is to be borne in mind that race prejudices and passions were running high, that the neighbourhood was seething with excitement, and that it was impossible to allow the body to pass out of our possession until the falsity of this report had been demonstrated beyond all question. Colonels Irvine and Macleod were both in barracks, as were Superintendent Gagnon and Dr. Jukes, and I took them all across to the prison yard and had the coffin opened.

Gagnon was a native of Quebec, so it was very fortunate that he was able to be there.

As was expected, there was no trace of any disfigurement of any kind. A few locks of hair had been taken from the brow, but this had not been done by any unsympathetic hand, and the lie that had found its way into circulation was killed in its infancy.

If this had not been done we should never have heard the end of it.

I will close the story of Louis Riel, so far as his life came into conjunction with mine, by reproducing a poem which he handed to me on July 13, 1885, and which I believe was his own composition :

JESUS :	MARIE :	JOSEPH :
Sauvez-nous.	Intercedez pour nous.	Priez pour nous.

Beni soit Dieu qui glorifie
Le Règne de Victoria:
C'est un Dieu que je me confie
Puisque c'est lui qui me créa.

Louis Riel: Executed for Treason

Dieu venielle que la Règne voie
L'eclat des plus beaux cheveux blancs;
Et qu'elle avance dans la joie
Du plus gracieux de ses ans.

Fasse Jésus-Christ qu'elle atteigne
Ce grand age qui n'est pas vieux,
On la grâce des années règne
Plus, en remontrant vers les cieux.

Plaise a Jésus-Christ qu'elle vive
Pour le moins encore vigt-ans:
Que Sa Majeste soit active
En bonne sante, tout le temps.

Qu'elle aime, mais sans préfèrence,
Le peuple Canadian Français:
Que toute la Nouvelle France
Trouve auprès d'elle un libre accés.

Sous son admirable couronne
Sous son règne majestueux
Puissant race Anglo-Saxonne
Rendez les Irlandais heureux.

Que Jesus le Fils de Dieu même
Fasse etinceler sur les mers
Et les terres, le disdème.
De la Reine, dans l'Univers.

Au bureau du Commissionaire à Regina,
12 Juillet, 1885.

Dédié à Monsieur Le Capitaine R. B. Deane.

Complimentary for my being allowed to write in the Commissioner's Office.

CHAPTER XVII

THREE TRIALS FOR MURDER

THE TUCKER PEACH MURDER (1910). THE BENSON MURDER AND ARSON (1913). THE WILSON MURDER AND ROBBERY (1914)

The Tucker Peach Murder

ON June 29, 1910, a dead body was reported to have been found in the Bow River, not far from the Roman Catholic Industrial School at Durbow. A coroner was notified, and in company with a Mounted Police constable from Okotoks, visited the spot on the following day. The body had been washed against the trunk of a fallen tree in the river; part of it, which was out of the water, was very much discoloured, and the whole of it was considerably decomposed. When brought to land there was found to be no head on the body; a shirt and undershirt were all the clothing, and these gave no clue to the identity of the man who had come to so untimely an end. No one was known to be missing, and after a somewhat perfunctory examination the coroner issued his order for burial, and the remains were buried on the river bank by a couple of near-by settlers who volunteered to do the work. It happened that my wife and I were at this time on a month's holiday in British Columbia, and it was not until the month of November following that I first heard of the occurrence. In the course of that month a long-distance telephone message informed me that a skull had been found in the bed of the river, just under the tree where the body had been discovered, and that a hole in the forehead indicated foul play. Detective Sergeant Murison was sent to the spot; he found the skull as stated, and close to it, half buried in the sand, a blanket, cowhide and two pieces of rope. These were matted together and frozen solid, and it took a long time to thaw them out. The skull had a small, clean hole in the centre of the forehead, such a hole as could only have been made by a bullet, a piece of cotton batting in one of the ears, and a slight dent, apparently the mark of an old injury received during lifetime some years previously, which extended both ways across the forehead from the centre.

Obviously the first thing to do was to find a name for the dead man, and to take that as a starting point for further inquiries. Gradually it transpired that one of the earliest settlers in that sparsely settled district, a man who had been settled there for upwards of a quarter of a century had, earlier in the year, disappeared in a mysterious sort of way, that is to say, he had gone away without saying "good-bye" to sundry neighbours, who were surprised at his omission to go and see them before he left. It was common talk that he had sold his place and his horses to a young fellow who had taken possession, but this unceremonious departure, without a word, rankled in the minds of the neighbours, because there was no reason for it, and they could not understand it. The absentee's name was A. C. Tucker Peach, but he was popularly known as "Old Tucker." A few neighbours, those who knew him, said from the first that that skull, with its few iron-grey hairs, its missing teeth and general contour "looked like old Tucker." One witness subsequently deposed how the deceased man came by the wound on the forehead when a horse had kicked him in his own stable many years previously, and how he had helped dress the wound. The same witness said, speaking of the iron-grey hair, "Many a time I've cut it!" with the suspicion of a tear glimmering in his eye.

The skull was sent to the Provincial bacteriologist at Edmonton for examination, and very masterly treatment it received at the hands of Dr. Revell. The body, which had been buried on the Bow River bank in June, was exhumed, but the cleansing and thawing of it for the examination took several days, and nothing was said about it at the inquest, which was opened on November 29, at Okotoks. Dr. Revell showed the coroner's jury how a bullet had entered the skull at the forehead, and after a somewhat eccentric course had emerged at the inside corner of the left eye. He told the same story to two other juries later on, and they all believed him.

The inquest was called for November 29, 1911, and on November 28 our position was this—we believed that we had evidence enough to convince the jury that the body was Tucker Peach's, and that he had been murdered by a bullet wound in the head, but as to how or by whom the fatal shot had been fired we were in complete ignorance.

We had not, however, been idle since the finding of the skull on November 12. We had been searching high and low for Tucker Peach and making inquiries as to his business relations with T. M. Robertson, the young man to whom he was alleged to have sold out. Robertson at that time was working as a brakesman on the Canadian Pacific Railway, between Calgary and Medicine Hat, and we found ourselves depending exclusively on him for any intelligence whatever respecting his deal.

Robertson had left word with the postmaster at Gladys to forward to his care, at his Calgary address, any mail that might arrive for Tucker Peach, and a report had in some manner become circulated that

Tucker Peach had written to him from England, where is was known that he had a sister living.

On being served with a summons to attend the inquest, Robertson told us that he had bought the Peach ranch of 160 acres for $26 per acre, half down, half payable in twelve months. That after the deal was made Peach went to Carstairs, and from there to England, and that, in the month of September, Peach had written to him asking how he would be able to meet the remainder of the payment.

Immediately on receipt of this report I sent a non-commissioned officer to Carstairs, but no trace of the missing man could be found there.

Robertson was interviewed as soon as he returned to Calgary from Medicine Hat, and told a slightly different story; he said now that he had paid $1,000 down by a cheque on the Bank of Montreal, Calgary, and that the transfer had been drawn up by Peach's lawyer. He said that he had received his money by means of a draft from P. Coats & Co., and that Tucker Peach had written to him from Lancashire where his sister was living. The transfer he said he had left at Medicine Hat, and he did not know the name of the lawyer who had drawn it. We ascertained without difficulty that his account of his monetary transactions was fictitious; but beyond that we had nothing to warrant our depriving him of his liberty, and my men had positive instructions to say nothing which might alarm him at all. Another report as to Peach's whereabouts, namely, that he was in Stettler, was investigated and found to be untrue. There was nothing for it but to wait and see what the inquest might bring forth.

On the day before the inquest was due to be held, Robertson duly started by train for Okotoks (about thirty miles from Calgary), but instead of stopping there went on to Macleod, some eighty miles farther south.

Arriving at Macleod in the afternoon he went to a "sporting house," where he gradually became maudlin under the influence of liquor, and eventually said that he was escaping from the police, that he had stolen about $75,000 in Alaska, that the police were after him, and that he wanted to catch "the Spokane Flyer" that night. The woman of the house wrote a note to the officer commanding the Mounted Police at Macleod, and Robertson was gathered into the fold. At the guard-room, where he was searched, the summons to the inquest was found on his person, a coroner's warrant was applied for and issued, and Robertson was presented in custody at Okotoks next day. He was feeling very much the results of his potations of the previous day, and was in no condition to withstand the gruelling examination which he was called upon to undergo. In the witness-box he told a story different from any of his previous stories. He said now that he had bought two quarter sections from Tucker Peach, being 320 acres at $26 an acre, which price included the twenty horses on the place. This purchase money, to the extent of $5,000, had come to him by bank draft from Scotland to the Bank of Montreal at Calgary, where he cashed it for notes and gold. He did not remember the respective amounts of each, and so the silly story went on, until at last he was informed that the Bank of Montreal officials could, and would, be called to contradict his statements in detail, and he was asked if he had any explanations to offer as to the conflict of evidence between himself and them. His answer to that was, "Well! I guess this is not the place to say it. I do not wish to say anything further."

Inspector Duffus, the officer who was watching the case for the police, saw that the psychological moment had arrived—he obtained the coroner's permission to speak to the witness, asked the latter if he had anything he would like to say to him privately, and, on an affirmative gesture, took him to another part of the house. There, having given the prisoner the full caution enjoined by the Criminal Code in presence of witnesses, he wrote down Robertson's confession and asked him to sign it, which he did. The confession briefly set forth that on the morning of King Edward's funeral Robertson and one John Fisk had murdered Tucker Peach in his own shack, that they had wrapped the body in the dead man's blanket and cowhide, and, with his own wagon and horses had carried it into the middle of the stream. The jury, of course, brought in a verdict accordingly, and the question was how to arrest John Fisk before he could be warned by his sympathisers.

It happened that he had recently bought a livery stable business in a new place called Carbon, about seventy-five miles from Calgary, in a north-easterly direction.

It was after 10 o'clock before I had heard and digested the reports made by the returning inquest party, and there was no time to lose. We had a detachment at Carbon, but the wires were down, and we could not communicate with them—in addition to which there was the possibility that both men might be away from home on patrol, so there was only one thing to be done.

Soon after midnight of November 29 the most powerful motor that I could hire in Calgary, containing two non-commissioned officers, crept quietly out of the city on its seventy-five miles run to Carbon. The men had positive orders to wait for the opening up of the stable in the morning and to take Fisk while he was engaged in his work, for he was well known to be a desperate man, who would not scruple to use firearms if he had a chance. The arrest was effected without difficulty, and the motor discharged its passengers into barracks in Calgary by 1 P.M. of November 30. Thirteen hours at $5 per hour paid the motor-man's account.

Now that the two perpetrators of the murder were secured there was obviously only one course to pursue in order to convict both men, namely, to use Robertson's evidence against Fisk and Robertson's confession against himself.

Robertson never weakened in the stand that he had taken. On the contrary, he seemed to be anxious to tell all he knew. A great load seemed to have been lifted off his mind, and he never was dull or dispirited from first to last. He told the cross-examining counsel at Fisk's preliminary hearing that he was not afraid to meet his God, and even later, ten days before his execution was due to take place, before the news of his reprieve had been received, a fellow-prisoner remarked of him that he was cracking jokes and laughing, and did not seem to realise at all the terrible position in which he was standing. But I am anticipating.

Only one person was allowed to talk to him, and that was the officer to whom he confessed at the time of the inquest. To him, after he had been a day or two in the guard-room, he, Robertson, made an amplified statement, and this revealed such an extraordinary state of affairs that I reproduce it as it was given. This was not used in Court, of course, and was intended for our guidance in hunting up corroborations of the story of an accomplice.

As to the law on that very important point I had, many years ago, to wit, in the month of November, 1889, clipped from the *Weekly Times* and pasted in one of my textbooks a little nugget of wisdom enunciated by the President of the Parnell Commission on Wednesday, November 13, 1889. There had been a conversation between the President and Sir Henry

James as to the principle of law governing the admission of an accomplice's evidence, and the President disposed of it in these words:

"I rather regard it as a doctrine of expediency and prudence than a principle of law. Juries are strongly recommended not to act upon the uncorroborated evidence of an accomplice, but it has never been a rule of law. I may add that the corroboration required is only of the surrounding circumstances so as to lead up to a general presumption as to the truth of the evidence. *It would be an absurdity to say* [the italics are mine] that no evidence of an accomplice can be received unless corroborated by other independent testimony, because then there would be no need of an accomplice's evidence."

Robertson's confession was as follows:

"The latter end of January, 1910, I was working at Bob Begg's, at the corner of the Bow and High Rivers. One day in February Jack Fisk drove down with a team and bob sleigh to Begg's place. Mrs. Begg, the two children and I were the only ones there; he sold her a washing machine and a couple of patent fasteners for horse-collars. This was the first time I met Jack Fisk. Two or three weeks after this old man Tucker came down to the river at Begg's for water. He said Jack Fisk's pigs disturbed the water at the top of the hill and he couldn't drink it. He took a barrel of water with him in his wagon. I rode the range for Begg for about a month looking after the cattle, and one day I rode over to Begg's gate at the N.E. corner of his place, where I met Jack Fisk chasing his milk cows into Begg's place. I had some conversation with him about some horses, and he told me that old man Tucker was getting after him about some horses, which he, Tucker, had lost. He said, 'I'm scared the old man will get me into trouble,' and as Tucker had no friends and no relations and no one to take care of him, he thought it would be a good thing to get him out of the way. I said, 'If you have his horses the old man is right and you should get into trouble.' He then said to me, 'If you will help me to get Peach out of the way, you can have his land and I will take his horses as I want them.' I didn't say anything about this as I was scared; he then threatened me and said, 'If you say anything about this I will put a shot into you.' I said nothing to anybody, and rode home to Begg's, and he went on rolling his fall wheat. I used to meet him nearly every morning after this when I was riding, and he would ask me what I thought about it, and if I had said anything to anyone. We discussed the thing on and off for about two months until the last Saturday in April; I think it was Saturday when I came into town to see about my job on the Canadian Pacific Railway and stayed at the 'King Edward' while in Calgary. Begg was in town and stopped at the 'Dominion.' The two of us went home on Monday—this would be the beginning of May. That afternoon the team I was working got up in a bunch and got away from me. Mrs. Begg sent me up to the top to look for them. While I was up on the hill I met Fisk, and he began talking about getting rid of old Peach, and said that if I helped I could have the land and he would take the horses. He was to take them at any time he wanted them.

"I then agreed to help him.

"Two weeks after this I went into Calgary and started working on the Canadian Pacific Railway as brakesman. I made a couple of trips and went out to Fisk's place the following Wednesday. Before going out to Fisk's I hired a rig from Frank Pashak, who runs a store at De Winton, and told him that I was going to drive to Tucker Peach's.

"When I got to Fisk's place he sent me to Tucker's shack, about 300 or 400 yards away. This was Thursday afternoon. I helped Peach to clean his grain that afternoon, and talked to him about selling his place and horses. He made a memorandum on a sheet of paper which is now in Medicine Hat in my box. The memorandum showed what he wanted for the horses, land, etc. I went back to Fisk's that night and slept there. Fisk and I agreed that night we would kill Tucker Peach the next morning. He was to fire the first shot and I was to fire the second. He wanted me to fire the first, but I wouldn't.

"The next morning, Friday, the day of King Edward's funeral, about 6 o'clock, Fisk and I went to Peach's shack and tried to look into the window. We couldn't see anything as it was covered over with a tent."

[*Note.*—The old man had an instinctive dread of Fisk, and on that account always fastened his door and covered his window. He would not have opened his door to Fisk.]

"I knocked at his door, and the old man called, 'Who is there?' I said I was there, telling him my name. He opened the door. He had his drawers and shirt on. He sat down on his bed, which was on the floor, and started to put on his trousers. Fisk then fired a shot at Peach with a revolver. Blood started to trickle down his face and he fell back. Fisk handed the revolver to me and told me to do the same. I took the revolver, pointed it at Peach, and fired. I don't know whether I hit him or not, I was so excited—but I guess I did. Peach never spoke. He was dead after the shot. We both came out of the shack and looked round to see if anyone was there, but there was no one in sight. We then hitched up Tucker's team and drove up to the door, rolled the body in some blankets, and drove it down to the Bow River at Tucker's lower place. We drove into the river along the west fence, on the west side of his property, and dumped the body into it. The blankets and cow-skin which we rolled him in were tied round him. The river at this point runs east. From what I heard the body was found about a quarter of a mile from where we dumped it. After this I came into town, having stayed at the Durbow School on Saturday night. I told some of them there that I had bought the place. The team I took in were Peach's. I sold them to the Alberta barn for $200, and put the money in the savings bank of the Bank of Montreal. I was to give Fisk any money he needed. I gave him two payments—one was $50 and one $30. The amounts show in my pass book. I went back to the ranch in about two weeks. I saw Ernest Adams then, and he told me that Fisk had been looking after the horses and that four two-year-old horses were missing. Adams said he thought Fisk had stolen them. I didn't say anything. Shortly after this the body was found. Fisk, I think, was living on his place at the time, but shortly after this left for Carbon. Shortly before the body was found I brought one of Peach's horses into town and traded it for one belonging to Mr. Gilmour, the plumber of 827 5th Ave., West Calgary. I sold the horses I got from him to a grocer, who has a store east of the Post Office, for $18. I gave him a bill of sale. I sold a stud about two weeks ago. My cousin sold it for me. My cousin is E. Davis and is looking after the place for me. He knows nothing about this affair. Fisk threw the revolver we shot Peach with into the middle of the river.

"*Sd.* THOMAS M. ROBERTSON."

With these details to guide us, our next task was, of course, to verify the story. We tried, first, to find the revolver in the river. I sent Robertson with Inspector Duffus and others in a motor to the spot. The days were short, the distance from Calgary was about twenty-five miles, and nothing but a motor could cover the ground in the hours of daylight. Slush ice was found to be running down the river. The water was very cold and up to a man's middle. It transpired that Robertson could not tell within a hundred yards where the pistol had been thrown in, and the party returned without having accomplished anything in the way of corroboration.

The headless trunk was at this time lying at an undertaker's place in Okotoks, and was in process of being cleaned and thawed out. When it was ready Dr. Revell's services were again called in. He spent several hours with the evil-smelling corpse, and the thoroughness of his examination was manifested when he found the bullet which Robertson had fired tucked away under the skin just over the eighth rib on the left side. In the shirts that were on the body when found there were holes corresponding to the situation of the bullet. Adhering to the 32-calibre bullet were some minute particles of the underclothing through which it had passed, together with a single red fibre from the blanket, where it had passed through a stripe. The indications were that the bullet had struck the floor and glanced upwards. Robertson had said that his hand was very shaky. In the floor of the shack, close under the bed, which consisted of nothing more than a few gunny sacks filled with hay, we found an indentation made by the bullet in its course. The corroboration of Robertson's story, therefore, in that particular was complete. We had once before examined this shack in a search for the dead man's money. He was known to have a sum variously estimated at from $1,200 to $1,500, but nobody knew where he kept it.

He would not entrust it to a bank, and we were able to place in the witness-box only one man who had ever seen him with a large sum of money in his hand. When we first entered the shack we found that it had been thoroughly ransacked and the money evidently found and carried off. We were utterly unable to place before Fisk's jury any evidence to connect him with the missing currency, but in April, 1911, after Fisk's conviction, the one man who could have supplied the missing link permitted himself to talk to a neighbour, and I soon heard of it. It happened that he met Fisk at a little place called De Winton, and had supper with him at the "Minto House" hotel. He saw Fisk pay for a twenty-five-cent supper with a ten-dollar bill, drawn from a large roll of bills which he had in his hand. He was surprised to see so much money as Fisk was notoriously impecunious.

This incident is a fair sample of the difficulty we experienced in collecting evidence. John Fisk seemed to have terrorised the entire neighbourhood. It was no uncommon thing to hear a witness say, "If Fisk gets off I shall have to quit the country."

It was some weeks before I could obtain corroboration of Robertson's story as to the conveying of the body to the river, but it presently transpired that a settler named Robert Jones, who lived between Tucker Peach and the river, was working at a fence on his quarter section with an Indian boy when the funeral cortège passed down the trail. Both he and the boy recognised the Tucker Peach team and wagon, saw John Fisk in a khaki-coloured shirt sitting on the front seat with the reins in his hand, and a person, whom they took to be Robertson, at the rear end of the wagon-box.

A bitter controversy raged over this testimony when, at length, it was given, and desperate attempts were made to discredit it. One witness went the length of swearing that on a particular Sunday after church service he had had a conversation with Robert Jones, who had told him that he had not seen the team and wagon on the road to the river.

This evidence was offset by a constable of the Mounted Police, who deposed that on the Sunday in question he spent the forenoon with Robert Jones and that Jones did not go to church at all that day.

It came out later, after Fisk had been hanged, that another settler and his daughter had also seen the team and wagon as described by Jones and the Indian boy, but refrained from saying a word about it for fear of Fisk's vengeance in case of his acquittal. Both father and daughter had given valuable testimony but suppressed this important item. After sentence of death had been carried out, as I have said, the father met a juryman at High River, and said: "Your conscience may be quite clear about the verdict you gave: John Fisk was guilty all right." He then intimated, in a round-about way, affected by the denizens of the Western States, that he and his daughter had seen the outfit and that what Jones and the boy had said was true.

Robertson was mistaken in telling us that the murder was committed on the day of the late King's funeral. It doubtless would have taken place on that day but for the circumstance that, when Fisk looked round in the morning, he saw Ernest Adams, Tucker Peach's nearest neighbour, moving about on a hill between their two houses, which commanded a view of Peach's shack, and his attention would possibly have been attracted by any shots fired then.

Robertson went to visit Tucker Peach that afternoon, at Fisk's suggestion, and found him fanning some barley which he had contracted to sell for seed, and to fan which the old man had borrowed Adams's fanning mill.

Robertson's evidence was to the effect that, after the barley had been cleaned, he helped Peach to load the mill on to his wagon, and he, Peach, returned the mill to its owner at about supper-time. Adams, on the other hand, deposed that his mill was returned to him by Peach at dinner-time, midday. He said he couldn't be mistaken because he asked Tucker to stay to dinner on that occasion, but the old man declined.

Fisk was being defended by the most eminent criminal lawyer and K.C. in the Province of Alberta, and he was not slow to make the most of this conflict of evidence. Robertson was in the witness-box for two whole days, and the learned counsel in effect said to him: "You have admitted spending with Tucker Peach his last afternoon on earth—you killed the old man then and now try to lay the blame on John Fisk."

Herein, to my mind, lay the one chance that Fisk ever had of provoking a disagreement of the jury, and if his counsel had stopped there a "reasonable doubt" might have been raised, particularly as we were unable to show the money motive on Fisk's part. But the difficulty settled itself. Lord Brampton in his memoirs gives an interesting instance of a counsel who did not know when to stop cross-examining, and in consequence lost his case. There was something of the same sort here. Cross-examination, prolonged *usque ad nauseam,* presently elicited the fact that, in the course of the fanning operations, a man with a team and wagon arrived to fetch the seed barley for the purchaser, and took it away. He had to wait until the work was finished, and his evidence was conclusive proof that Robertson was right, and that Adams was wrong in saying that the mill had been returned to him by midday. This, too, disposed of the suggestion that the murder was committed by Robertson that afternoon.

This evidence was all news to me. Nobody knew the name of the purchaser of the barley, and we were only able to secure his attendance at the last minute before the trial closed. From him we learnt the name of the hired man who had fetched the barley, and after extensive search, found him near Montreal. He arrived just in time to give his evidence against Robertson, and deposed that the dead man had told him that he was in process of selling out to Robertson.

The trial of John Fisk began on February 21, 1911, and lasted ten days, forty-one witnesses being examined for the prosecution.

The jury brought in a verdict of "Guilty," with a recommendation to mercy. This was to salve the susceptibilities of one of their number who was not in favour of capital punishment, and who required that concession.

It had no effect whatever at Ottawa so far as mitigation of the penalty was concerned, and John Fisk was executed in the guard-room yard at Calgary on June 27, 1911.

A Western politician once remarked in my hearing that he admired the Mounted Police, not so much for what they did, but for what they prevented. I wonder under which category such cases as this would come!

Robertson's trial began on May 16, and continued four days. Forty-three witnesses were examined for the Crown and six for the defence.

The jury appended a "strong recommendation to mercy" to their verdict of guilty, and the death sentence was in due course commuted to life imprisonment.

There is no ground for any such supposition, but one might very readily believe that Robertson was acting under hypnotic suggestion.

Sir Allan Aylesworth, the Minister of Justice, remarked to the Comptroller of the Mounted Police that these murder trials were the best worked up cases that had ever come under his notice.

The Benson Murder and Arson

The following extract from a newspaper published in the State of Missouri, U.S.A., tells so concisely and accurately the story of a brutal murder committed on the confines of my district in May, 1913, that I reproduce the item intact.

The Alberta coroner's explanation, as given to us afterwards, of his reason for not having had a post-mortem examination made, was that there was no doctor within fifty miles, that an adjournment of the inquest for the necessary three or four days would have caused great inconvenience to everyone concerned, including the widow, and that, so far as he and his jury were able to judge, there was no necessity for incurring the expense of the professional services and of the delay.

From the Kansas *City Star,* Sunday, December 21, 1913.

"JUSTICE AT QUICK STEP.

"The Story of the Swift Moving Court of Canada and a Missourian Who Will be Hanged.

"A man from Missouri was sentenced last week to be hanged in Canada.

"The manner in which the Canadian Government prosecuted the case, the sure-fire way in which the murderer was brought to justice without technicalities to befog the issue, the directness and speed of it, are lessons the court of this country might take with profit.

"The ten witnesses who were taken by the Canadian

Government from Missouri to Calgary, Canada, to testify against the murderer, at a total cost of $3,000 to that Government, have returned. They are loud in their praise of the sureness and swiftness with which the sword of justice is swung up there, compared with the leisurely manner in which it is wielded here.

"One of those witnesses was M. E. Feltis, Sheriff of Caldwell County, Missouri.

"'The courts of Canada waste no time in technicalities, dilatory tactics, nor meaningless legal phrases,' he said. 'It would be a good thing if our courts would copy them in some things.'

"THE CRIME

"Last April, John P. Benson, a lawyer, of Braymer, Mo., and William Jaspar Collins, a young ne'er-do-well, of the same town, went to Canada to take up land claims. Benson had $3,500. Collins had no money, and Benson paid all of his expenses for the trip to Canada and for filing on the homestead.

"Benson built a small frame house and barn on his claim, which was in the country, 150 miles from Calgary, and Collins lived with him. Benson sent for his wife and young son to come, but before they reached Calgary she got word from Collins that her husband had been burned to death in a fire which started from an exploding oil stove. She went on to the claim, where the body of her husband, the face disfigured with burns, awaited her.

"The coroner in that district held an inquest, and as the indications were that Benson had been burned to death, the verdict was to that effect. Mrs. Benson, her son, and Collins returned to Braymer, Mo., with the body, Mrs. Benson loaning Collins the money to pay his fare. None of the money which Benson had when he died was recovered, and the supposition was that it had been destroyed in the fire, which burned the greater part of his clothing.

"With $1,800 in His Pocket

"Soon after the funeral in Braymer, Collins began spending money freely, and this excited suspicion. The Masonic Lodge in Braymer, of which Benson was a member, engaged a detective from the Pinkerton agency in Kansas City, and he went to Braymer last August and exhumed the body of Benson. The Pinkerton detective made it appear that he was working in the interest of an insurance company that wished to make sure that it was Benson's body before it would pay the policy it had on his life. This was to quiet any suspicion Collins might have.

"The body was identified by J. A. Neville, a dentist, who had put some bridgework in Benson's mouth. An examination disclosed that one side of the skull was crushed in as if with the blow of a club, and a revolver bullet had entered the breast and pierced the heart.

"Collins was arrested, and in his pocket was found $1,800, consisting of ninety $20 bills, all new, and all of consecutive numbers, issued by the First National Bank of Braymer. The bank officials said they had paid those bills to Benson just before he departed for Canada. In the pockets of Collins were also found a bunch of keys and a knife that had been owned by Benson.

"Collins made a full written confession, telling how he first stunned Benson with a blow on the head and then shot him, robbed him, and poured oil on his body and set it on fire.

"The Canadian authorities were notified, and within a few days the Canadian Government in Ottawa sent to President Wilson in Washington a request for the extradition of Collins.

The Benson Murder and Arson

"A Document Without 'To-wits'

"If this had been an official request from this Government to Canada for the extradition of a person charged with murder it would have been a formal and lengthy document, full of antiquated verbiage and numerous 'whereases' and 'to-wits' and 'as aforesaid.' But the request of the Canadian Government was couched in fewer than fifty words. It stated simply that on May 1, 1913, William Jaspar Collins had murdered John T. Benson in the Province of Alberta, Canada, and that Collins had taken refuge in the United States, and was in jail in Caldwell County, Missouri, and the Canadian Government requested this Government to deliver him to the Canadian authorities at Portal, on the national boundary in Manitoba.

"President Wilson put his 'O.K.' on the brief document, and gave it to W. J. Bryan, Secretary of State. He O.K.'s it and sent it to Governor Major, who sent it to the Sheriff of Caldwell County.

"Then began delays. A hearing must be had to determine if Collins should go. That was held in Chillicothe, Collins fighting against extradition and repudiating the confession he had made. But in due time, having exhausted every legal cudgel for the prevention of his extradition, the court said Collins must go to Canada for trial.

"Meanwhile the authorities in Alberta had their plans all set for a speedy trial once they should get Collins in custody. They sent enough money to Sheriff Feltis for him to bring to the Canadian border Collins, Neville, the dentist; E. H. Michaels, the undertaker; James Burnett, a constable; William H. Pye, a merchant; Dr. H. A. Schroeder, Dr. Gus S. Dowell, Louis W. Reed, prosecuting attorney of Caldwell County; the widow of Benson, and the Pinkerton detective, all to be used as witnesses against Collins. They promised to pay all their expenses from the time they left home until they returned and, to see that Collins had fair play, they paid all the expenses of his brother from Caldwell County to Calgary and back home again. The total cost was $3,500.

"The party was met at the international boundary by the Canadian officials, and went straight to Calgary, where it was met by a party of witnesses from the scene of the crime, who had come 150 miles.

"A Preliminary 'Next Day.'

"The day after arrival in Calgary, a preliminary hearing was given Collins in the barracks of the Mounted Police. The Government appointed an able lawyer to defend him, but how different from the American method; there were no motions for continuances, nor changes of venue, nor any other dilatory tactics whatever. Within twenty-four hours after his arrival in Calgary, Collins was given a hearing and held for trial.

"Only one day intervened between the preliminary hearing and the beginning of the trial, which was held in the supreme court room in Calgary, before Chief Justice Harvey, with James Short as prosecutor for the Crown.

"In any American Court a day or two, at least, would have been consumed in getting a jury, and in many cases, in murder trials in Missouri, weeks and even months have been spent at this. It took just twenty minutes to select a jury to try Collins. In America a jury of twelve men try a man for murder. In Canada a jury of six does it.

"A Jury in a Hurry

"There was no quibbling; no man was asked if he had 'conscientious scruples against concurring in a verdict of guilty if that verdict might mean the infliction of the death penalty.' All the long and complicated questions asked jurors in this country were omitted. Twelve men were called from the venire and were sworn, the State struck off three names, the defence struck off three, the remaining six were sworn to try the case fairly and return a verdict according to the law and evidence; all done in twenty minutes, and the trial began at once. It lasted two days. There was not a quibble nor a trick nor a subterfuge in the whole of it. Only one objection was made by the defence throughout the trial, and that was to the introduction of the confession made by Collins. His lawyer rose to object to it and was stopped by the Judge, who raised his hand in warning, and said:

"'There is no use wasting time in arguing that point. The Court decides that the confession was given voluntarily by the defendant, without the use of threats or promise or hope of reward or clemency. It will be introduced in evidence.'

"And He Will be Hanged 'That Day'

"The different witnesses told their stories. Collins declined to testify in his own defence. There was no witness nor evidence for the defence. The arguments were made very briefly. The jury retired, and within ten minutes returned with a verdict of guilty, and the judge, without leaving the bench, sentenced Collins to be hanged on February 17.

"And he will be hanged that day. His lawyer will appeal and it will be passed on at once. No delay of two or three years, as in this country, and no hope of reversal.

"February 17 Collins will be hanged in an enclosure in the barracks of the Mounted Police, and his body will be buried there in an unmarked grave, for it is a rule there that the body of a person hanged for murder cannot be claimed by relatives nor others.

"The party of Missourians who assisted the Canadian authorities in the enforcement of Canadian law was given a banquet before they returned, and Sheriff Feltis, of Caldwell County, was told that if he would come back to Calgary to see Collins hanged all his expenses would be paid by Canada."

The fifty-word communication alluded to in the foregoing was a night lettergram, sent at my instigation by the Attorney-General's Department to the Secretary of State at Ottawa, asking him to expedite proceedings, and the result as described followed.

The Wilson Murder and Robbery

John Wilson was chief clerk of the Canada Cement Company, which had its works at Exshaw, on the line of the Canadian Pacific, about forty miles west of Calgary. The Company used, in the month of May, 1914, to pay their men every fortnight, and the money for this purpose was transmitted by the Bank of Montreal in Calgary, by means of the Dominion Express Company, to the Cement Company at Exshaw.

It was part of the duty of the chief clerk in question, on receiving notification from the Express Company that the necessary currency for paying the wages had arrived at their office, to go to that office and receive the package of money.

On May 22, 1914, the package consisted of a small sack, at the bottom of which was the silver, while the bills were on top.

It had been the custom for about twelve months preceding this date for one of the other officials of the company to go with the chief clerk to fetch the money, and on this occasion a young man named James Gordon went with Wilson.

The Company had provided an automatic pistol for the use of the chief clerk on these occasions, and he was in the habit of letting his assistant carry the money and of walking a pace or so behind as an armed escort.

This little procession was within about twenty yards of the railway gate giving egress from that Company's premises when it was met by three men, who had just come in from the outside. These were Russians, whose names were Max Manelek, Afancy Sokoloff and Serkey Konuch, alias "Joe Smith."

Without a word being said, "Joe Smith" walked up to young Gordon, presented a revolver at his head with his right hand, and with his left grabbed the bag of money which the boy was carrying in his right hand, and ran off. In his surprise and dismay, Gordon called out to Wilson to the effect that the money was gone, and almost simultaneously heard two shots fired behind him. Wilson fell dead. Someone, probably Sokoloff, came up behind Gordon and felt his pockets, and then Sokoloff and Manelek followed "Joe Smith" into the bushes fringing the Bow River. Sokoloff, before going, took Wilson's pistol out of his pocket and carried it off.

Wilson was killed by a bullet which entered his body at the fleshy part of his left arm, passed through both lungs, and was found between the under and outer shirts on his right arm. The pistols carried by Sokoloff and "Joe Smith" were automatic Lugers—wicked-looking weapons, sighted up to 2,000 yards.

It happened that there was no Mounted Police detachment at Exshaw, and so pursuit of these ruffians devolved on the men on the spot. Within fifteen to twenty minutes of the occurrence a force of six men started after the murderers, crossing the river on a raft as their quarry had done. On the other side this party split up, and Ingram Dobson, carrying a shot gun, and William Murby, carrying a rifle, came upon fresh footmarks, which they followed. Dobson saw one of the fugitives hiding behind a stump, and promptly emptied his gun into his stomach, while Murby covered him with his rifle and ordered him to throw up his hands, which he did without loss of time. This man turned out to be Max Manelek, the only one of the three who was not armed. His captors took him into custody and handed him over to the police. They had certainly earned the reward of $200 offered for the capture of each of the three murderers.

Within half an hour of the receipt of the telegram reporting the murder some constables were dispatched in a motor to Exshaw, upon which point the three neighbouring detachments at Canmore, Morley and Banff were also ordered to converge. "Joe Smith" and Sokoloff managed to get away from their pursuers, and the next we heard of the former was shortly after midnight on May 23. A freight train had pulled into a place called Cochrane, where a Mounted Police constable was stationed, and he, with the assistance of the railway police, organised a thorough search thereof. "Joe Smith" was found in a car loaded with timber, and after a desperate struggle, was arrested by Constable Watts and two of the railway police. It was a fortunate thing that the safety catch of his Luger revolver had become jammed in some way, so that he was unable to use it, or somebody would have been hurt.

On his person was found the stolen money, $2,340.20—the silver in one of his pockets and the bills, together with the Bank of Montreal pay slip, in the bag inside his shirt. This aroused queries as to what had become of his companion, for it seemed incredible that he should have allowed "Joe Smith" to carry off all the plunder. I was so much of opinion that the third man had been disposed of that I circulated the offer of a reward of $200 for Sokoloff's body, dead or alive, but nothing came of it.

The Calgary City Police Force had on its staff at that time a detective named Ernest Schoeppe, who, in addition to fluent English, could speak German, Polish, Slavish, Bohemian, Russian, Ruthenian and another Slavonic language. He was thus a most desirable accessory to a police force having to do business in such a cosmopolitan city as Calgary had become. He managed to obtain, from a Russian, information that Sokoloff was hiding in a northern suburb of Calgary, and on June 2 the Chief Constable went thither with a strong squad of his men. The hiding-place turned out to be an empty grocery store, which had a small cellar, and in this the fugitive proved to be. As he would not respond to polite invitations to come out, the Chief sent for the fire brigade, and shortly had two streams of water pouring into it. After a while a knocking was heard, and a voice in Russian said, "I come out; I give up." Sokoloff passed up his pistol and cartridges first and then came up himself.

Schoeppe's next move was to obtain from his informant John Wilson's pistol, which Sokoloff had taken from the dead man's pocket. He had been trying to sell this to the man who gave information of his whereabouts to the detective.

The three prisoners were tried together on June 16 and 17, and the jury, after forty-five minutes' consultation, found them all guilty, with a recommendation to mercy in the case of Manelek.

They were sentenced to be hanged in the Mounted Police guard-room at Macleod on August 26 following, and were sent thither next day.

After sentence was pronounced, Sokoloff asked Schoeppe to go and see him, as he had something of interest to tell him, and in order to explain what followed, it is necessary to go back a little.

The man who gave the information as to Sokoloff's whereabouts was a Russian named Fred Erenenko. He was a witness at the trial of the murderers, and told how Sokoloff had admitted to him that he had shot Wilson, and that he had tried to raise money on Wilson's pistol. He admitted having been intimate with Sokoloff and "Joe Smith," and the trend of his cross-examination went to show that he had been more or less the prime mover of a gang of ruffians, of whom Sokoloff and Smith were the principal tools. Erenenko was asked by the prisoners' counsel, "Why did you give Sokoloff away?" and he replied, after a moment's reflection, "I had to." At all events, as I have said, Sokoloff sent for Schoeppe and told him that Erenenko had tried to persuade him to kill Schoeppe on the ground that he was the only man in the country that he had to fear. He made several suggestions as to how this should be done, but Sokoloff either thought that the proposed methods were too risky or did not want to hurt Schoeppe.

One plan that Erenenko proposed was that they should visit Schoeppe at his home and kill him with some blunt instrument. They should visit the house a few times so as to become thoroughly acquainted with the plan of it, and Schoeppe then remembered that Erenenko had gone to him on two or three occasions in the previous winter with some papers which he professed himself unable to understand. Schoeppe refused to receive the reward payable for Sokoloff's arrest, and said he had promised to have it paid to Erenenko.

In connection with this matter I received from the Attorney-General's Department the following letter:

The Wilson Murder and Robbery

Copy of letter received 27/5/14.

Department of Attorney-General,
Edmonton, May 26, 1914.

Superintendent DEANE,
Royal North-West Mounted Police,
Calgary, Alberta.

SIR,—I beg to convey to you the appreciation of this Department for the very efficient manner in which you have conducted the Wilson murder case. The Attorney-General is home, and is much pleased with the result of your work. I trust that you will be able to capture the third man. I am writing Mr. Short, the Attorney-General's agent at Calgary, to arrange for trial of prisoners as soon as possible, as I deem this is a case in which justice should be meted out speedily.

I have the honour to be, Sir,
Your obedient servant,
(Signed) JOHN D. HUNT,
Acting Deputy Attorney-General.

I replied that we could not have done what we had done but for the valuable assistance received from the Canadian Pacific Railway Police and the City Police of Calgary, both of whom helped us to watch all avenues of escape. Mr. Deputy Attorney said he would write a letter of thanks to each of the Departments in question. The Judge in summing up gave due credit to everybody concerned.

CHAPTER XVIII

INCIDENTS OF MOUNTED POLICE LIFE

A DROWNING FATALITY

A VERY sad accident occurred in June, 1889, whereby a promising young constable named Albert Perry lost his life. He was one of a small detachment of a corporal and three mounted men who were camped on the right bank of the Little Bow River where it runs into the Belly River on the west side thereof.

This detachment had been placed there in the spring of 1889, and was intended to furnish protection to a large number of cattle, which ranged over a great tract of land, much of it affording excellent feed, in a locality where settlers were very few and far between.

The few settlers that were in that neighbourhood were much afraid of the Indians, whose main fault was their insatiable curiosity. Men, women and children were all curious to see the inside of a white man's house, and to that end would prowl about the premises, peer in at the windows and eventually try the doors. If the doors would open the entire outfit would probably walk in, sit on the floor, and wait to be asked if they had an appetite. We had already had an hysterical complaint from the C.Y. Ranche, where there were men enough to stand off a few inquisitive Indians, but it devolved upon us to send a patrol, which tore down the visitors' tents and ordered them back to their Reserve.

There was always the possible making of trouble in

a proposition of that kind, for the Indians were under no obligation to confine themselves to their Reserves—their treaties with the Government made no provision of that kind, and it is a certainty that they would not have signed them if they had.

As it happened, our "bluff" was never "called" by the Indians, who invariably did as we wanted them to do.

The owners of the large number of cattle that ranged in the Little Bow country were naturally apprehensive that a body of Indians travelling at large would not hesitate to kill cattle if they happened to run out of grub.

This was the *raison d'être* of the Mounted Police camp on the Little Bow, which was situated at a distance of about twenty miles from Lethbridge in a direct line. But Lethbridge is on the east side of the Belly River, which it was thus necessary to cross. All mountain streams are very dangerous to cross during the spring freshets, and strong teams of horses or oxen with wagons have been known to be carried off their feet and swept away by the rush of water. There was a ferry across the river at Lethbridge at the time of which I speak, and by that route the distance to the Little Bow Camp was about thirty-five miles. This increase in the distance was caused by a large coulée which struck westward from the river, and round which it was necessary to make a detour.

Opposite the mouth of the Little Bow there was a ford across the Belly River. The ford was freely available in low water, but not in the month of June when, owing to the melting of the mountain snows, the river was running like a torrent.

It was the custom of all detachments to render weekly reports to Divisional Head-quarters, and Constable Perry had been sent to Lethbridge with his detachment's returns, etc., and had been instructed that the Belly River could not be forded, and that he must travel by the long route. He delivered his reports, etc., at Lethbridge and, in the ordinary course of routine, left barracks one morning to rejoin his detachment. Three or four days later a man rode in to ask what had become of Perry, as he had not returned to camp. We began to make inquiries. The ferryman told us that he had taken him across in the morning, but had recrossed him in the evening, as the boy had come back and had said that he had lost his way. He announced his intention of taking the shorter cut in the morning, but the ferryman warned him against trying to ford or swim the river, and advised him to go to barracks and tell his troubles. Poor Perry was afraid of the inevitable "chaff" as to being a "tenderfoot," which would make his life a burden in the barrack room, and disregarded the ferryman's advice.

He took the trail instead to a small settlement known as the "Eight Mile Lake," about eight miles east of Lethbridge, and there asked a rancher to put him up for the night. No rancher in those days ever refused such a request as that, but when he heard of the young man's predicament, he earnestly remonstrated with him as to attempting to cross the Belly River in flood. Remonstrances had no effect, and Perry started out in the morning after breakfast on his foolhardy errand, and that was the last we could hear of him.

As soon as the report of his being missing reached me I organised a large patrol to scour the country within a radius of twenty miles or so, and started with Staff-Sergeant Charles Ross at four o'clock next morning. We went first to the Eight Mile Lake, where the aforesaid rancher, whom we knew well, told us all that he could tell, and we then headed for the mouth of the Little Bow. Ross was a very highly trained and experienced plainsman. Perry's horse was shod in front but plain behind, and we had not long left the Lake when Ross said, "Here's his trail." Now and again we had to stop and cast about when crossing a hard piece of clay prairie, but for the most part we followed that trail at a hand gallop for from ten to twelve miles, eventually arriving at the river and seeing Perry's horse, saddled and bridled, standing under a cut bank on the opposite side of the river. There was nothing for the poor beast to eat, and he must have felt pretty sorry for himself.

Fortunately, Ross knew of a punt that was in the neighbourhood, and having borrowed that, we made the horse re-swim the river to our side. Perry's body was recovered, about a fortnight later, some twenty miles farther down the river. There was nothing to show how he had come by his death. He was said to be a first-rate swimmer, and had apparently fallen a victim to over-confidence.

Singularly, some light was thrown upon the subject a few years later, when the same horse (reg. No. 1,570; I have never forgotten the brute's number) was on detachment duty on the St. Mary's River. At this detachment we used to run our herd of spare horses, and as the river bounded the Blood Indian Reserve, it happened occasionally that some of the herd would cross the river and graze on the other side. One afternoon, when it was nearly time to give the horses their oats, before locking them up for the night, the corporal in charge ordered one of his men to cross the river and bring back some of the herd that were there.

No. 1,570 happened to be the horse whose turn it was to perform such duty for the day, and, on his back, the constable rode into the river, which was, fortunately, not at high water mark. The corporal stood on the bank watching the proceedings, and saw the horse, as soon as he found himself out of his depth and obliged to swim, deliberately roll the rider off his back.

In the circumstances, no harm resulted on that occasion, but there is no doubt that that is how Perry lost his life, and no man was ever after asked to ride that particular brute into swimming water.

Lynch Law

On the evening of February 13, 1895, it was reported to me at Lethbridge that a man named Willis had blown his brains out. I went to his house and found that the report was in no way exaggerated, as brains were scattered all over one of the walls of his bedroom. He had put the muzzle of a Winchester rifle into his mouth and pressed the trigger with his great toe. The deceased, whom I had known for some years, had had good situations, but had lost them through drink, and he had been steadily going down the hill for some time, his earnings being very precarious. At this time he was out of work and the wolf was at his door. The household, in fact, was kept going by a lodger named James Ronald. "But for him," Mrs. Willis had said on one occasion, "we should have had nothing to eat." Willis had, however, frequently complained to various people of the undue intimacy between his lodger and his wife—an intimacy extending over a period of years—and not a little indignation had been aroused by the treatment which the husband complained of having received.

It was said that on one occasion when Willis arrived at home somewhat the worse for liquor he found his wife sitting in her lodger's lap, and when he remonstrated with them, the lodger put him quietly but firmly out of the house, shut the door and turned the key in the lock. Ronald had been away from Lethbridge for a time, but had now returned, and it is no disregard of the obligation "De mortuis" to say that, when Willis readmitted Ronald to his household he knew what his past experience had been.

Ronald attended the funeral as chief mourner, and it was said that this helped to precipitate matters.

Be that as it may, soon after midnight on the second day after the tragedy a band of masked and armed men broke into the house on the outskirts of the town occupied by James Ronald and his brother Maxwell, who were in bed together at the time. Maxwell was covered by a rifle and ordered not to move. His brother James was pulled out of bed, tarred, feathered, dressed and led with a rope round his neck by a half-mile route to the front door of the Lethbridge House which was the principal hotel in the town. He was pushed into the hall, the door was temporarily fastened from without, and the masked gang rapidly and quietly dispersed. James Ronald was then at liberty to make his way home without molestation. It was rather a stormy night, with drifting snow; a night on which few people would be about the streets, and no noise was made.

Maxwell was detained in bed under the guard of two men, and was forbidden to stir for twenty minutes. At the end of that time his guards departed, and he was allowed to dress and to find his way to my house, where he arrived at a quarter past one. I rang up the town police station and asked the sergeant in charge what had become of James Ronald, and he replied that Ronald had gone home. There was nothing to be done that night. Maxwell had told me that the masked gang were very sparing with their words. Any orders that were given were given by a stranger, who acted as captain, in a quiet, incisive voice with a drawl. Neither of the brothers was able to identify any of their assailants, nor could they give us any information which would help us to trace them, so they decided to let the matter drop, and James left town at once for the East, declining either to make or support a complaint.

The incident, however, found its way into the papers, and in a few weeks' time I received from Mr. Ronald, Senior, the father of the brothers, a letter urging me very strongly to bring the masked gang to justice. He said he made a great point of this, because a new association had come into being, calling themselves the "Patrons of Industry," and one of the planks in their platform was the abolition of the Mounted Police. I felt there was a covert threat in the letter, but as I had no intention of letting the matter drop, I could not understand why the old man should write to me in such a strain. The reason, which I heard some months later, will appear in its proper place.

In my reply to the old man I said that the matter would unquestionably receive my very serious attention, provided he would guarantee that his son James would return to the West to give evidence when called upon to do so. Ronald, Senior, readily gave the required guarantee, and as soon as it came into my hands I issued for execution a warrant which had been locked up in my drawer for some little time. Just here I must go back for a little space to recount some circumstances that had taken place in the interval.

I had not actually imputed blame to the sergeant in charge of the town detachment for (1) having permitted this outrage to take place, and (2) for having no trace of the perpetrators, but I allowed him to see what was in my mind, and it was no surprise to me when, a few days later, he asked to be relieved of his charge and to be returned to duty in the barracks. He was subsequently, in the course of that duty, exercising a horse when the brute bucked, threw him against the stable wall and broke his arm. Thereupon he went into hospital. We had our own hospital within the barrack grounds.

A few days after this accident it came to my knowledge that Sergeant Phair was one of the members of the tar-and-feather gang, and that he had been seen on that eventful evening with a black mask in his possession and tar and feathers on his Winchester carbine.

About the same time, while I was corresponding with Mr. Ronald, Senior, his son Max came to me one day and said that he had found the captain of the gang. He said that, in an idle moment, he was smoking a pipe and basking in the afternoon sunshine in front of the Lethbridge House when he heard a voice, the incisive drawl of which he can never forget. He abandoned all other business that afternoon and devoted it to studying this man and finding out all about him and where he was living. The man's name was Charles Warren; he was an American citizen, had been in town for a few months, doing no work, and having no visible means of support, but quiet and inoffensive withal. He habitually carried a six-shooter in his breast pocket, and had been asked to lead the gang because he was supposed to have had previous experiences in like exploits, and there was less chance of his voice being recognised. Entreating Max to keep his secret rigidly to himself, I took his information and issued a warrant for Warren's arrest. It was then that I began to look rather anxiously for a reply from Mr. Ronald, Senior, as to his son James's intentions.

I should explain here that the entire community—ministers of religion, men, women and children of all sorts and conditions—were of opinion that poetic justice had been done. The Presbyterian minister voiced the sentiments of the local public when he said to me one day that James Ronald had committed a moral offence for which the law was powerless to punish him, and it was not well that he should go unpunished altogether. He admitted that he was in no way in favour of mob law, but he could not regret what had happened.

"Of course, Captain," he queried, "you have to do your duty, and I suppose this matter will have to come up some day?"

"Oh, yes," I replied, "it will go into Court some time before Christmas, and in the meanwhile I am not losing any sleep over it."

With such a feeling of sympathy with the law-breakers in the minds of the public, it can be readily understood that any punitive proceedings had to be very warily undertaken.

I took but one person into my confidence, and he was a man whom I could trust out and out—Staff-Sergeant P. H. Belcher, who was then Quartermaster-Sergeant of the Division. He had a little room, wherein he lived, behind the store-rooms, and to him I betook myself. I could not myself have visited Sergeant Phair in the hospital and held lengthy conversations with him without attracting a certain amount of attention, and I therefore deputed Staff-Sergeant Belcher to tell him that I was in possession of evidence which would enable me to convict him of "disgraceful conduct" under the Police Act, and to give him twelve months' imprisonment, in addition to any other sentence that might follow a conviction for burglary in the Supreme Court. I desired that he would take time to think it over because, if he should choose to turn Queen's Evidence, I would undertake to lay no charge against him at all. He took time to consider whether he would tell what he knew or take his medicine, and finally decided that he would tell. I asked in the first instance for the names of the gang. There were eight of them altogether, and two had left the country by the time I wanted them, so that I had only four to locate, and that was soon done. On June 7 Warren was arrested by Sergeant Brymer, and summonses to witness were at once served on three members of the gang. I issued a warrant for the fourth upon information sworn that he would probably leave the country rather than obey a summons.

I held the preliminary examination myself, the Crown being represented by Mr. Conybeare, the private prosecutor by a Mr. Wrigley, a young barrister of repute, and the accused by an ex-partner of Mr. Conybeare's, who thought he could make more money by defending than by prosecuting criminals. In accordance with the authority conferred upon me by the Criminal Code, I informed the legal gentlemen, at the opening of the Court, that I intended the inquiry to be private, and that I proposed in the first instance to examine the witnesses myself.

This rule I designed to apply more particularly to the four witnesses who had been participators in the outrage, and I took them very minutely over the whole of the evening of February 13, and pinned them down to a sworn statement as to where they were and how they spent that particular evening from about seven or eight o'clock until well after midnight. They told their respective stories with an amplification and lucidity of detail, which not only branded them as most prolific liars with a wonderful fertility of imagination, but showed also that they had no knowledge of the tar-and-feather proceedings, the making of the masks, etc., and effectually headed off any question of an alibi for the accused. There was no need for counsel to examine further or cross-examine these witnesses, and after their perjured testimony had been duly recorded and signed by themselves they were allowed to depart. Max Ronald was examined and cross-examined in the usual way, and on his evidence the accused was committed for trial, as he reserved his defence.

The next step was to obtain a change of venue, and this was granted by the judge upon the affidavit of Messrs. Conybeare, Wrigley and myself that we believed ourselves to be the only residents of Lethbridge who were of opinion that the accused would not receive an impartial trial in that town.

The trial was set for July 6, at Macleod, a place about thirty-two miles westward, and thither the accused was sent by a four-horse team in good time. Thither, too, was dispatched James Ronald on his arrival from the East. As he, like his brother, would be able to identify Warren by his voice alone, I asked Superintendent Steele, who was in command of the Macleod Post, to arrange to have some conversation with the accused within the hearing of James, the witness. This was easily brought about, and Superintendent Steele told me that, on hearing Warren's voice, James became so nervous that he trembled and could hardly stand.

It became a grave question whether or not we could put him in the witness-box at all. He had permitted himself at the inquest to say that he had had no improper relations with the woman, and the defence made no secret of their intention to produce the woman to contradict him if he should repeat such a statement.

During my journey to Macleod on the day before the trial, while my team was crossing the Old Man's River, the first rain fell during that year. The country was in a terrible state of drought, and the grass would hardly grow on the prairie. The seasons had been growing gradually drier ever since 1888, and the climax was reached in the year of which I am speaking, 1895. During those dry years we invariably had hard winters, with some snow, which furnished the only moisture that the soil received until the autumn, when heavy rains set in, generally when our hay crop was being harvested. At Lethbridge the only hay that we could get at that time was grass cut round the edges of sloughs or swamps in the Milk River Ridge district, forty miles distant, and often it happened that contractors after hauling their racks into our barracks, had to unload and dry their hay before stacking it.

In the following year, 1896, when the Liberals were returned to power, the wet cycle began, and there was a plentiful growth of green grass; and Sir Wilfrid Laurier was held accountable for the era of prosperity which then set in and has continued ever since!

So far as the trial went, we did not fare much better at Macleod than we should have done at Lethbridge. There had just been at Macleod a pigeon-shooting match between the gun clubs of the two places, and the visiting team had imbued the residents with their own ideas, as we very soon found from their conversation.

On July 6 Charles Warren was placed in the dock to answer two counts of burglary and two of riot.

Some members of the Lethbridge Gun Club had told their friends in Macleod that Sergeant Phair had been a member of the gang, and this reached Mr. Conybeare's ears, with the result that he insisted on his being called as a witness. I explained to him that my word was pledged to the non-commissioned officer that he should not be prosecuted, and that he must take the responsibility of calling Phair as a witness.

I sent a telegram to Lethbridge ordering Sergeant Phair to be sent to Macleod next morning in time for the opening of the Court, and met him at the door of the court-house on his arrival. It was rather fortunate that I did, for I had an inkling that he might deny all knowledge of the affair, and I think that is what he would have done. That would have attracted to himself all the sympathy of the two towns, by whose residents he would have been hailed as a hero and a martyr, and I should have been placed in an awkward position by reason of the promise I had given him. I pointed out to Sergeant Phair that in the event of his taking such a stand as that it might be my duty to convict him of perjury. This would not conflict with my promise, and I should assuredly be able to do it. I said this because evidence had already been given by the proprietor of the Lethbridge Hotel that he had seen the masked gang conducting their victim down the street and, indeed, he seemed to think it an excellent joke. He had made the audience in Court laugh once or twice, and did so again when he described James Ronald as looking not unlike a Red Indian, when the judge looked up from his note-book and asked the Crown Prosecutor, "Why has this man not been indicted?" "Well, my lord," began the counsel, cudgelling his brains for a suitable answer. "Have it done at once," said his lordship, and down went the witness's jaw as far as it could go—there was no more jocularity left in him. As a matter of fact, neither counsel nor I knew what the witness would tell until he found himself in the box.

The evidence of this witness, in conjunction with that of my original informant, would have sufficed to convict Sergeant Phair of perjury, and, on my advice, he finally consented to tell the truth. He went into the witness-box and confirmed Maxwell Ronald's story as to Warren being the man who had stood at the end of his bed with a revolver in his hand and had superintended the proceedings of the lawless gang. James Ronald was in such a state of nervous prostration that he was unable to give evidence at all, but the case was proved to the hilt, and his absence did not seem to matter. Counsel for the prisoner called no witnesses and made no defence. Counsel for the Crown waived their address to the jury, and the prisoner's counsel thus secured the last word. The judge summed up against the prisoner, and the jury disagreed.

The law required only six jurors, and of these, as we learned later, two were determined to convict, two were determined not to convict in any circumstances whatsoever, and two were in a state of indecision.

There was no prospect of their coming to an agreement, so they were discharged and a new trial ordered.

It was unmistakably established afterwards that this impotent conclusion was brought about by a juror who was playing to the gallery of Lethbridge, where he had one or two bosom friends who sympathised with the prisoner. He had so little sense of truth and honour as to falsify his oath of office, which bound him to render a true verdict according to the evidence. Towards the close of the afternoon on which the jury were discharged I was in a room in the Macleod hotel, changing from uniform into plain clothes, when I was drawn to the window by the sound of a heavy shower of rain and the patter of footsteps on the sidewalk across the street. I looked out and saw two men taking shelter under the overhanging eave of a doorway in a house opposite—they were the juryman of whom I have made mention and the learned counsel for the prisoner. They were both well "loaded," and it was enough to make a cat laugh to see them fall on one another's necks. The juryman was obviously taking credit for holding out against a conviction, and the other was only too willing to give him all the credit he wanted. I stood at the window and watched them until the shower ceased, as suddenly as it had begun, and they staggered off arm-in-arm.

A new trial was ordered for July 10, and on the

night of the 9th Sergeant Phair deserted. The new trial was not unlikely to make some trouble for sundry prominent people in Lethbridge, in that the charge was to be altered so as to dispense with the intervention of a jury. A subscription of $100 was hastily raised by the persons most interested in Sergeant Phair's absence, and he was persuaded to leave the country. Sergeant Phair's arm was at the time in a plaster splint, and he could move about freely. The hospital wherein he was housed stood in the south-east corner of the barrack enclosure, within a few feet of a road, with nothing but a wire fence intervening, and Sergeant Phair was persuaded to climb into a waiting buggy and was driven across the international boundary line into Montana. He only received $40 of the $100 which had been subscribed, as the driver thought that $60 was due to himself.

Warren was released on bail until the winter assizes, and took advantage of his freedom to cross the boundary; one of his sureties followed him. The case was called at Macleod in the following November, but the accused did not appear, and his bail was ordered to be estreated. The prosecution, however, had its effect, and was such as to discourage further experiments with Lynch Law.

A little later in the summer, when I was inspecting my Milk River detachments, I met a well known rancher, who chatted about the tar-and-feather episode. He told me that the men who were mainly instrumental in carrying out the project had written full accounts of it to their friends in Ontario, and in one of the letters occurred the expression, "And the Chief of Police was the biggest toad in the puddle." That, of course, explained Mr. Ronald's letter to me; he knew that I was Chief of the Police and actually supposed that I had taken a hand in the business!

Incidents of Mounted Police Life

"Piegan Frank"

"Piegan (pronounced Paygan) Frank" was a Blood Indian, whom I engaged as a scout soon after I went to Lethbridge in 1888. As the Blood Indian Reserve was close by, it was necessary that we should know something of the movements of the Indians, for it was the policy of the Government to keep them on their Reserve as much as possible, and in order to do that we used to employ a couple of scouts, who could visit the Reserve and bring us news at first hand. An interpreter was attached to the Head-quarter Post, as very few of the Indians could speak English, but it happened that Frank could understand and speak it fairly well. He applied for the job, was recommended by the Indian Agent, and was consequently engaged at ten dollars a month and rations. Scouts were required to mount themselves, but they were very particular in exacting the issue of a saddle and revolver. This was the outward and visible sign of their high calling as Mounted Police Scouts.

One afternoon I was busy in my office and heard the sound of wheels outside. In a minute or two it was reported to me that Piegan Frank had brought in two prisoners, but that it was not exactly clear what was the charge against them. They came into my office, a young man and a woman, nicely dressed, well mannered, good looking, and obviously in the courtship stage. The young man had hired a buggy for the afternoon, and was taking his best girl out for a drive in the country when that villain Frank came across them and ordered them back to the village, for no earthly reason whatever except to show his authority.

As he had his revolver drawn, they thought it best to do as he told them, and turned their horse's head round without any delay.

I apologised profusely for the Indian's behaviour, and the young couple were very nice about it, and were not disinclined to look upon the whole thing as a joke. Before they left my office, however, I ordered Master Frank to hand in his pistol and saddle and then to go straight back to his Reserve and to tell the Agent he had been discharged because he was no good.

The sweethearts then resumed their drive.

I did not set eyes on Piegan Frank again for many years, not, I think, until 1900, when he applied to me for a job.

We were very short-handed at that time, so many of our men being in South Africa, and I happened to have a vacancy which the Indian could very well fill. I established him in camp in the detachment grounds at Kipp, a place half way between Lethbridge and Macleod, where the trail crosses the Old Man's River.

He was always on the look out for me when I made my weekly journeys between the two places, and attended strictly to business.

In June of 1900 the superintendent of the Canadian Pacific Division of that company's Crow's Nest Pass line, stationed at Cranbrook, B.C., informed me that the East-bound train of the previous evening had found a cart wheel laid across the rails near Kipp, and that an Indian had been seen in the distance walking south. As a matter of fact, there were some camps of Indians, hay-makers, in the vicinity. The superintendent said that he had been talking to the sergeant in charge of the Pincher Creek Detachment, who had suggested that it would be a good plan to have a Mounted Policeman travel on each passenger train within certain limits, and the superintendent thought the suggestion so good that he brought it to my notice.

Had the sergeant in question been within hailing distance I should have given him the rough edge of my tongue for talking such rubbish, particularly when he knew how short-handed the Division was; but to the superintendent I wrote and asked, in effect, "If the constable in police charge of a train in the course of his journey sees something suspicious by the roadside and desires to investigate, will he have authority to stop the train for that purpose? If not, he might just as usefully be lying on his bed in his barrack room."

It did not surprise me that I did not receive a reply to that letter, although I enlarged on the effect that might be produced upon the passengers by red coat, accoutrements, boots and spurs and all the paraphernalia of war, and the matter rested until I next drove to Lethbridge on the Saturday following.

At Kipp my scout was, as usual, waiting for me. "Frank," I said, "someone putting things on rails mile and half west of here. You go and find out who does it. Move your tent over there." "Yassir," said Frank, and I continued my journey. Next week, as I did not want a bad railway accident to occur within my district, I drove back on Monday, instead of Tuesday, a day earlier than usual, and thus I had no expectation of seeing Frank at the river crossing, but there he was, beaming. "Injun chil'n," he reported, "put iron brake-shoe on rail, and then go and sit on hill and see sparks fly when train comes."

He had learned this from a little boy named "Shines-in-the-night," and presently the little chap went with Frank and me to the spot and showed us how he and two companions, a little older than himself, had placed the brake-shoe on the rail and some stones in front of it, and how they had then retired up the hill to enjoy the fireworks.

The other two boys were called "The Lizard" and "Slapmouth," and Frank had orders to bring them all into my office at Macleod on the following Wednesday. He was to notify the Rev. Mr. Owens, who conducted a Church of England Mission on the Blood Reserve, that I should like him to be present, as I intended that these boys should go to his school, and he was to tell all the relations and friends of the boys in question that the poor little fellows were in the hottest kind of water, and that it looked as if the penitentiary doors were opening to admit them. The difficulty with the Indian parents was that they would not send their children to school and keep them there, and now I had a grand opportunity of disposing of some of the young rascals, and did not intend to let it go. Frank rubbed the fear of God into the parents and relations in great shape, so that, when my solemn investigation began at two o'clock on Wednesday afternoon, the poor Indians were ready to agree to anything in order to save their progeny from prison. The two older boys tried to put the entire blame upon "Shines-in-the-night," but the brake-shoe (a heavy lump of iron) was in court, and I told the boy to lift it. He was barely strong enough to raise it, much less to carry it, and so that story did not go.

The end of it was that the boys' parents undertook to let the Rev. Mr. Owens have the care of the children until they should become eighteen years of age, and he agreed to receive them into his Mission School and to look well after them.

To prevent any further mischief of the same sort, I stationed an Indian scout to watch the railway across the Reserve so long as any Indian camps remained in that neighbourhood, and there were no more complaints.

CHAPTER XIX

HUMOURS AND UNCERTAINTIES OF THE LAW

It was during the period of the prohibition liquor law in the early days, when permits were difficult to obtain and beer of any sort, whether lager or other, was expensive to import, that hop beer came into fashion, and all sorts of people took to making it. The Slavs and Hungarians used to get gloriously drunk and rowdy on it at their marriage feasts, and the Inland Revenue Department used to try to prevent the manufacture and sale of the beverage. The only interest that hop beer had for the police lay in the question as to whether it was intoxicating or not.

A case came before me wherein it was abundantly susceptible of proof that the accused had purchased so much hop beer on a certain day, from a certain person, for a certain price, and had become drunk thereon. The question was, Was the vendor liable under the prohibitory law for selling an intoxicant? The drunken man would never have admitted that his condition was not brought about by some beverage other than the hop beer pure and simple, and there was to my mind only one way of ascertaining the properties of the beer.

I instructed my sergeant-major to buy a couple of dozen bottles of the same brew as had been sold to the drunken men, and then to see if he could find someone who was willing to have a prolonged drink at the expense of someone else. There was no difficulty at all about the latter proposition. A very ready volunteer was found at once, and he was shut up in an empty barrack-room with two dozen bottles of hop beer and such accessories as he needed to contribute to his convenience and thirst.

He managed to wade through eighteen bottles, and then was unquestionably drunk.

At the trial which ensued, Sergeant-Major Jarvis gave evidence as to the intoxicating nature of the beer, and Mr. C. C. McCaul, K.C., rose to cross-examine him, somewhat in this wise:

"Now, Sergeant-Major, you have sworn that this beer (indicating the exhibits before the Court) is intoxicating. Why do you say that?"

Answer: "Because I know it to be so."

"Have you any special means of knowing it to be so?"

Answer: "I have, sir."

"Well, then, will you be good enough to tell this Court how it is that you are able to be so positive?"

Answer: "Because I have seen a man get drunk on it."

"I think the Court would like to have more details than that; I know I should."

Then the sergeant-major told the story. I never met anyone who could enjoy a laugh against himself better than Charley McCaul. He said to me afterwards: "It was too bad to let me drag all that evidence out of the witness and tie the rope round my own client's neck!" I cannot for the life of me remember now what it was, but he beat me, after all, on a point of law. He took the case to the higher Court at Regina, and the conviction was quashed, with a proviso that no action should lie against the J.P.

* * * * *

Humours and Uncertainties of the Law

Another amusing case arose out of a conviction which I made against a certain resident of Lethbridge for the unlawful possession of intoxicating liquor.

Notice of appeal was given, and Mr. McCaul was counsel for the appellant. The main witnesses for the prosecution were Sergeant Ross and a constable named Stribble. In the interval during which the appeal was pending, Sergeant Ross came to me one morning and said that the convicted defendant in the case was trying to persuade Stribble to desert and that Stribble did not want to go. The defendant's agents, it seemed, were rather persecuting Stribble, and were promising him all sorts of inducements to leave the country before the appeal could be heard. Being assured that Stribble had no desire at all to desert, I instructed Sergeant Ross to tell him to appear to comply with his persecutors' wishes, and to fix a date, about three days ahead, for making his venture.

Sergeant Ross and I, in the course of our many rides together, had come across a piece of river bottom about six miles out of the village, and we had agreed that it would make a nice site for a small farmer to settle on. It was situated on the east side of the Belly River, and its eastern bank was rather precipitous and covered with brush. A tent, therefore, pitched close to the bank would be out of sight to anybody on the bench land, although it could, of course, be seen from the opposite side of the river. I arranged with the quartermaster-sergeant to give Sergeant Ross a tent, stove, furnishings and rations, and these were all carried down to the place in question, and everything was prepared for Stribble's residence. I arranged also to give him a weekly pass, and he was to amuse himself there as best he could.

At the appointed hour on the date arranged, Stribble, dressed in plain clothes, met his friends on the Benton trail. When it came to the scratch they did not keep any of the promises they had made him. They gave him a couple of dollars, a kick on the posterior and started him off. He had before him a walk of 100 miles before he would be able to buy a morsel to put in his mouth, and there were no settlers along the road, so that two dollars would not be of much use to him. However, the dirty crew of whom I am writing cared nothing for that. They thought they had sufficiently involved the man with the Police Force to make it impossible for him to return, and followed him along the road for two or three miles to see that he did not change his mind. When he found that he was no longer being followed he turned aside to his tent and went to bed.

When the appeal came on for trial, as it did in course of time, and Constable Stribble walked into the room in response to the call of his name, the appellant's face was a study. McCaul had been led to believe that this witness would not appear, and a hurried consultation took place between counsel and client, neither of whom could give any explanation of this unexpected episode. Stribble simply repeated the evidence he had given at the original trial, and confirmed Sergeant Ross's evidence as he had done before. McCaul, with a view to discredit his testimony-in-chief, began his cross-examination by asking if he were not in some difficulty in connection with the Police Force. Stribble never pronounced the word "Sir," he never got beyond the first consonant, and his answer to McCaul was, "No, S'."

"Let me understand this correctly. Is there not a charge pending against you under the Mounted Police Act?"

Answer: "No, S'."

There was nothing more to be said; the man's character could not be blackened. There was no reason why the Court should discredit his testimony, and the appeal was dismissed.

* * * * *

The following is a copy of what appeared in the *Western Law Times,* vol. I, p. 86, in the late nineties, the city in question being Calgary:

"GUILTY OR NOT GUILTY?

"A learned Judge of French extraction, not of the Manitoba bench, lately pronounced, within 5,000 miles of this city, the following remarkable sentence on a man accused of stealing a horse:

"'Prisoner, de evidence is conflicting, but I find you guilty and sentence you to tree months in the guard-room. De evidence, as I say, is very conflicting, but if I was sure, if I was quite sure, dat you stole dat horse I would give you two years in de Manitoba Penitentiary.'"

The barrister who habitually furnished the law reports to the paper was away from Calgary on a holiday at the time of the foregoing deliverance, and on his return his attention was drawn to the report in question. He did not want to be mixed up in a blood feud with the learned judge for all time, and decided to take the bull by the horns. He walked into the judge's chambers one morning with a copy of the *Law Times* in his hand and said, "Judge, I hope you don't think that I was capable of putting a damned report like this in the paper?" The judge took the volume from him, read the report carefully, shut the book with a slam, and handed it back to him, saying, "You can tell dat man dat I can talk as good Engleesh as he can!"

* * * * *

I remember, some years ago, when Colonel Macleod was judge of the Southern Alberta District, that he convicted a Blood Indian of horse stealing, and sentenced him to undergo one month's imprisonment with hard labour in the Lethbridge guard-room. The Indian, on having the sentence interpreted to him, burst into a hearty laugh without any apparent reason or explanation, and it looked perilously like contempt of court, but the judge took no notice, and the Indian was taken away.

The police had had in various places, at different times, so much trouble with Indians who tried to escape that a General Order existed in the Force to the effect that convicted Indian prisoners should always wear a ball and chain. This meant an iron ball at one end of a chain, the other end of which was shackled to the prisoner's ankle. He thus had to bear the weight of the ball in his hand. The cause of the merriment in court appeared the next day, when my sergeant-major (who could talk Blackfoot) brought the Indian to me, and said he wished to be relieved of his ball and chain.

I explained that the order had not originated with me, and that I could not vary it. To that the Indian replied that he had been given hard labour for a month and he wanted to work, and work hard, but he couldn't do so while carrying that ball about. He said he had expected to be sent to the penitentiary for three years, and as he had only got one month he wanted to do as much work as he could in that time. He considered himself far too fortunate to want to run away.

I took off the chain, and he was as good as his word, for he worked like a Trojan as long as he stayed with us.

* * * * *

The two stories next ensuing are rather apt illustrations of the disquieting ease with which even a well-worked-up case may fail in court through the incompetency of counsel.

Humours and Uncertainties of the Law

In the spring of 1898 the Milk River patrol between Writing-on-Stone and Pendant d'Oreille detachments was in the habit of noticing on the open prairie a particular bunch of cattle which was invariably by itself. It consisted of from twelve to fifteen head of both sexes, but one cow had a calf which had, by some oversight, escaped the branding iron. The calf had, too, what was called on the range a "switch tail," which means that the end of the tail had in all probability been bitten off early in life by a timber wolf or a coyote. The calf was thus quite noticeable, and the patrol never failed to turn aside and see if the animal were still unbranded, wondering always how long she would continue to be so. One day the patrol came across the bunch as usual—the cow was there but the calf was gone. Somebody had got her. An immigrant of two or three years' standing had recently taken up a homestead on the Milk River, and thither the patrol went first to make inquiries. They heard the bawling of a calf, and found the little switch-tailed heifer shut up by herself in a log corral.

The next step was to drive the bunch of cattle to the corral. The cow recognised and answered her calf's voice as soon as she came within hearing distance, and when the bars of the corral were taken down the calf ran to her mother, who suckled her and licked her and made much of her, as cows do with their progeny. If the calf had not been her own the cow would not have allowed her to suck. In the language of the range, the cow and calf "claimed one another." The immigrant from the United States was charged with theft and was taken into custody.

The case was tried at Lethbridge a few weeks later before my old friend, Mr. Justice Scott. Mr. Conybeare, the Crown Prosecutor, was away from home, and his office was filled by a legal gentleman from Macleod. It was a very plain, straightforward case, and the principal witness, a constable named Arrowsmith, gave his evidence very clearly and well. I was sitting by the side of the counsel for the Crown, and when the witness had described the reunion of the mother and daughter, I whispered to him, "Ask him what that means." The answer would have come like a flash, "It means motherhood on the part of the cow," but in spite of its being such an obviously pertinent question, the counsel, incredible as it may seem, refused to ask it. He was stupidly afraid of giving rise to some cross-examination as to whether a range cow had never been known to suckle a calf not her own. There are such instances, of course, now and again, where a cow has lost her calf and a calf has lost her dam, for then a cow's udder is paining her, and she is glad to have it relieved even by a strange calf. This was a morning session of the Supreme Court, and as I was due to start on my thirty-two mile drive to Macleod at two o'clock, I left the court and went about my business. The following Saturday, in accordance with my weekly practice, I was returning to Lethbridge from Macleod, and at the crossing of the Old Man's River, which was about half-way, met the judge, who was taking advantage of my teams to journey to Macleod and there hold his court during the ensuing week. As soon as we met he said, "Well, I had to let that calf thief go." I asked, "How was that? I thought Arrowsmith gave good evidence." "So he did," he replied, "but no one told me what all that meant. I am not supposed to know the manners and customs of animals. I have to confine myself to the evidence which is given before me by witnesses, and nothing was said to show that the fact of the animals claiming one another constituted relationship between them." "I asked W—— to ask the question," I remarked, "but he would not, and so a well worked up case has fallen through."

About six years later, before the same judge at Medicine Hat, I was confronted with a somewhat similar difficulty. A rancher, living at a place called Medicine Lodge, reported that a suckling colt had been stolen from him. The mare was left, but the colt was gone, and it went without saying that the colt did not voluntarily leave its dam. A smart young corporal named McLean constituted the Mounted Police detachment at Medicine Lodge, and he took the case in hand. In the course of his search he looked one afternoon into the premises of a settler (away from home at the time), who had always had a somewhat unsavoury reputation, although we had never been able to prove anything against him. I had known of him in the Macleod district years previously.

Corporal McLean found, in an out-of-the-way spot, a corral enclosing a mare and a colt which answered the description of the lost one. The mare had her hind heels tied together. McLean put his horse in the stable and sat down to await the owner's return. He came, after a while, with a rack load of hay, and McLean asked if he could stay the night, as his horse was rather tired, etc. After supper the settler began to unload his hay, and McLean took off his coat to help him. The settler protested that he was under no obligation to do that, but McLean said, "I can't very well sit here and see you work without lending a hand." The reason for McLean's presence being unwelcome appeared when the rack was about half unloaded, and the freshly killed carcass of a sheep was found. There were very few sheep owners in that part of the country; the settler had none of his own, and it was quite easy subsequently to ascertain that no one had given or sold a sheep to this man, but nothing was said at the time nor was his explanation of the possession of the carcass questioned in any way.

Early next morning McLean fetched the owner of the colt, who identified and removed his property, and then criminal proceedings were initiated against the settler, who was admitted to bail pending his appearance in the Supreme Court. In due time the case was brought up before Mr. Justice Scott, the prisoner being defended by the late Mr. P. J. Nolan, K.C.

I was, as usual, sitting by the counsel for the Crown, and heard Corporal McLean tell in detail the story which I have here outlined. When he had described how the mare's heels were tied I said to counsel, "Ask him why that was done." He replied, "I don't think it is necessary." I said, "It is so far necessary that, if you don't ask such an obvious question it will appear to the Court that you are afraid to ask it and Paddy Nolan will make the most of it." There was a look of smug complacency on his face, and I turned from him and, in a stage whisper directed at the witness, I asked, "Why?" The judge was busy taking his notes, and after he had finished he looked up from his book and said, "Did I hear someone ask 'Why?'" By this time I was so mad at a possible failure of justice, knowing what the judge would expect, and remembering my former experience in a somewhat similar situation, that I said to counsel in a tone of voice loud enough to be heard by a good many other people, "If you don't ask the question you'll lose your case." This rather shamed him into it, and he asked the witness, "What could be the object of tying the mare's heels?" The answer came without a moment's hesitation. "The mare knew that the colt was not her own and would not have allowed it to suck if her hind legs had been free."

The accused in that case "went over the road" (as the Western expression is, meaning that he went to the penitentiary) for two years.

Humours and Uncertainties of the Law

In the month of December, 1907, complaint was made to us that, at a little settlement some fifty-five miles south-east of Calgary, certain people were butchering cattle which did not belong to them.

Two brothers named Runnion were said to have sold quite a lot of beef in the town of High River to householders at two cents a pound less than the butchers were charging. That of itself was hardly suspicious, for farmers, having no shop rent to pay, could always undersell the butchers who had that expense to meet. The Runnion Brothers were Mormons, the sons of a Latter Day Saints bishop, who had recently come into the country from the United States.

Detective-Sergeant Nicholson was detailed from another division to work on the case, and being unknown in the district, went to the village in question and put up at the hotel there with the avowed object of looking for land to purchase.

In the course of his peregrinations he found evidence of quite a number of cattle having been killed on the Runnion Brothers' homestead, although there were only two hides on the corral fence. This gave rise to a mental inquiry as to where the hides of the other beasts were.

At about three o'clock on the morning of January 12, 1908, the weather being fortunately propitious, he hid himself in a straw-stack about half a mile from the Runnions' corral and watched the brothers drive an animal into the corral and kill it. Presently three Indians drove up in a wagon, into which the beef was loaded, and the Indians drove off in the direction of their Reserve. About ten o'clock in the forenoon he saw the brothers cut three head of cattle out of a bunch belonging to another man, who was pasturing them in a field near their place, and drive them on to their own homestead.

Mounted Police Life in Canada

To readers who are ignorant of the conditions of life on the Western prairie it is, I think, necessary to explain how it was possible for peripatetic cattle to be gathered and stolen in such an easy way as has been described. In the early days a man who owned any cattle, whether many or few, first of all selected a brand, which he registered as his own. He burned his brand with a red-hot iron into the skin of his animals and turned them out to run at large on the public domain. He had nothing to pay for this, and as long as Providence was careful of his interests, his cattle grew and prospered at no expense to himself. They might, and did, suffer to some extent from the depredations of timber wolves and coyotes, and they might be overtaken by a severe winter which would freeze and starve the poor brutes to death, but their subsistence was not costing the owner anything, and he did not care how much they suffered. If he found them dead in the spring he was "out of luck," and that was all there was to be said. There are still owners who have more cattle than they can pasture on their own land, and they allow their animals to run at large in the same way. That is how the presence of these estrays was accounted for.

Not far from the Runnion premises there was living another American immigrant who had only been a short time in Canada, and had worked for the Runnions for about a month during November and December, 1907. Him Sergeant Nicholson approached "delicately," and in course of time induced him to talk.

He said that he had worked for the Runnion Brothers from November 15 until December 15, 1907, and that during that time they had killed at least fifteen head of cattle which did not belong to them, the killing being for the most part done in the night-time. He said: "During the first week in December they killed a roan steer branded. I helped to skin this animal.

The hide was cached in the stable under some hay, and I believe it is there still. Every night during the first two weeks in December they killed an animal, and I believe there are at least forty hides cached about the premises." He told the sergeant that a lot of beef had been traded to Indians from the Blackfoot Reserve in exchange for coal from the Indians' mine and for wood.

In the course of a night or two, Sergeant Nicholson investigated the stable, and therein found some hides and beef hidden. The hides were frozen stiff, and could not, in that condition, be opened out to show what brands they bore. A warrant to search the premises and a warrant to arrest the men were issued in Calgary, and to avoid possible trouble, we made rather elaborate preparations to effect the arrest. Wholesale stealing of the sort described could, obviously, not have continued for any length of time without arousing the suspicion at least of some of the neighbours in those parts, and it was a reasonable inference that, if they did not profit by the nefarious proceedings of the Runnions, they were at least in sympathy with them, and might be expected to help them in a difficulty.

A fellow-countryman of the brothers, who was employed as stock detective, when necessary, by the Southern Alberta Stock Growers' Association, told us that if these men should happen to be able to do so, they would "put up a fight," as he knew them to be bad characters. That being so, I did not propose to take any chances.

Sergeant Nicholson was instructed to get in touch with the Runnions as a possible purchaser of their place and to arrange, if possible, that he could stay in one of their houses as a paying or non-paying guest after the brothers had been removed.

As it happened, we had no trouble. Edgar Runnion was arrested in High River on January 18, whither he had gone to sell some beef, and John was found by a mounted patrol at his farm on the following day, and both brothers were sent at once to Calgary. After this, Sergeant Nicholson and some members of the patrol, assisted by Mr. A. F. Fagle, the hired man, of whom mention has been made, made a comprehensive search for hides. Those of the stolen animals were all hidden away—some in the stable under the roof, some rolled up tightly and buried in a hole in the ground, some covered with a load or two of manure, and some had disappeared altogether. Those in the hole and under the manure were frozen so hard that they had to be chopped out with an axe. These hiding-places were all indicated by A. F. Fagle, who had placed the hides there under orders from his employers, Each hide was tagged with a linen luggage label, showing where, when and by whom it was found. There were ten of them altogether, two had the brands cut out, and one bore no brand at all, so that it was impossible to tell who the owners were. The thawing out of these hides and the clipping of the long hair, so as to expose the skin bearing the brand, occupied several days, and then it was necessary to persuade the several owners, scattered all over the country, to come to Calgary to identify their property and to give evidence that they had never parted with their property in the animal under discussion.

This case was of such magnitude and importance to the stock industry that the Stock Growers' Association retained the services of the late Mr. P. J. Nolan, the eminent K.C., to assist the Crown Prosecutor, and then we had to find out who the people were who had obtained beef from the prisoners by purchase or by trade. This was not an easy matter, as in the village of Brant district most of the settlers were Mormons and friends of the Runnions, and shielded them as much as possible. Another difficulty was that comparatively few of the witnesses could tell, even approximately the respective dates of their deals. It was easy to obtain, through our detachment on the Blackfoot Reserve, statements from the various Indians who traded sometimes wood and sometimes coal for beef, and on February 18 the accused were arraigned on a charge of stealing seven hides, the property of seven different owners. They pleaded "not guilty." Their counsel applied to have John Runnion tried separately, and the reason for this appeared when, in his defence, he claimed the protection of the Court, and took the blame of the whole business upon his own shoulders. He swore that Edgar was not implicated in the killing of any of the animals. He said that Fagle and he had buried the hide in the hole, and claimed that Fagle helped him to slaughter the beasts. He also admitted that he had killed seven head altogether.

Edgar swore that he knew nothing at all about the hides and the story that had been told in court; that his brother did all the trading, and that the witnesses were mistaken when they said they had traded with him as well as with his brother when they obtained beef for coal; further, that Fagle was mistaken when he said that he and Edgar buried the hide in the hole.

His wife swore that while she was taking her clothes off the line she saw John and Fagle drive out and bury a hide in a hole; she said her husband was away at the time. She remembered Indians coming once or twice, but could not say if her husband was at home on either occasion.

Fagle had been one of the last witnesses called by the Crown, and gave straightforward evidence as to what he knew, but in preference to taking the oath he asked to be allowed to affirm. When asked his reasons, he replied that he believed in a Supreme Being and in a hereafter, but did not believe in punishment after death for deeds done in the flesh. That made the judge look askance at the witness and his evidence, for he was a son of a Church of England clergyman, and had joined the Church of Rome, so that it was not to be wondered at that he would be horribly shocked by Fagle's religious convictions.

Notwithstanding that he had heard the Indians speak of both brothers in connection with their bartering, calling the younger one "Paul," the judge said in his charge to the jury, "I think the whole question consists in the comparative credibility of John and Edgar and Mrs. Edgar on the one side and of Fagle on the other.

"If you believe Fagle you will convict this man. If you believe the others you will acquit him. If you have a fair, honest, reasonable doubt in your minds as to the guilt of the accused it would be better to acquit him."

There was not a word of comment as to the Indian testimony. The jury followed the advice given and acquitted Edgar, while John withdrew his original plea and formally entered a plea of guilty. He was sentenced to two years in the penitentiary.

However gratifying to the Runnion family this settlement may have been, it is unnecessary to say that the police could not accept it as final. It argued a good deal of assurance for foreigners to come into a white man's country and think that they could play fast and loose with law and order in the way these Latter Day Saints had been doing. They were fairly well-to-do people, and had no need to steal other people's cattle. I have never heard of a Mormon bishop who was not well off, not to say rich; and the Runnion Brothers had money enough to establish themselves comfortably on their farms and to buy out the brand and a herd of cattle numbering about 160 head. In the country from which they came money has an influence which it does not have under the British Crown, and these Mormons may have had an idea that it could protect them from the consequences of their evil deeds.

I came across an instance of this some years ago in Montana. In Cascade County there lived a very fine old man who was by way of being wealthy, and was very much liked by everyone who knew him. He had a nephew, a worthless scamp, of whom he was inordinately fond, and to whom he was by far too indulgent. This young rascal conceived the idea of coming to Canada with a *chère amie,* of whom his uncle highly disapproved, and the pair of them were actually seated in a north-bound train at Great Falls waiting for it to pull out. The old gentleman, distressed beyond reason, heard of this escapade at the last moment, and boarded the train to expostulate with his troublesome relative, but all to no purpose. The train was about to start, and the old fellow had to get out. His distress must have made him temporarily insane, for he walked off from the car a few paces and took pot shots at it with his revolver. Fortunately there were very few passengers, and beyond the damage done to the car itself no one was hurt besides the fugitive girl. One of the bullets found its billet in the back of her neck, and the train started. It was a 200 mile run to Lethbridge, and on arrival there the unhappy passenger had to be taken to hospital, where she died within twenty-four hours.

A United States sheriff came, of course, to investigate the circumstances, and a charge of murder was in due course laid against the uncle. The old man, after many weary months, was acquitted, not being held answerable even for manslaughter, but it was a poor man that regained his freedom.

To return to Edgar Runnion. As soon as the court

stenographer's notes were transcribed, I preferred a charge of perjury against Edgar Runnion, and called three Blackfeet Indians to prove that Fagle was witness to a trade which they had made with the accused at his farm. They all swore that an Indian named "Sarcee Medicine Pipe" traded a pair of moccasins to Edgar Runnion in exchange for some beef. They were asked why they called the accused "Paul," and they said because his brother called him so.

The jury brought in a verdict of guilty, with a strong recommendation to mercy, on account of the man's family, and the judge, who was made of sterner stuff than the judge in the previous case, gave effect to it by saying, "Had it not been for the recommendation of the jury to mercy I would have inflicted a severe sentence, as I do not like this matter of perjury. The accused is sentenced to eight months' imprisonment, with hard labour in the guard-room at Calgary."

So after all the young "Saint" got off pretty easily.

CHAPTER XX

SOME EARLY REMINISCENCES

PRAIRIE FIRES

PRAIRIE fires used to be the bane of our existence in the early days, for the simple reason that we had to put them out—there was no one else in the country to do it. Many of these fires were started by locomotives, and the rest in most cases by criminal negligence.

A careless camper would fail to extinguish his camp fire, or possibly, after lighting his pipe, would throw the lighted match on the prairie and set fire to the grass.

The most furious fire I ever saw occurred in the month of February, 1889. In the course of the forenoon I noticed a column of smoke arise from the valley of the St. Mary's River at a point about seven miles distant from Lethbridge, and sent a constable to see what it was. Our herd of horses were at pasture, in charge of a constable in the same valley at a point to the eastward of the smoke, and I was apprehensive of their safety in case a wind should spring up.

Within an hour of my constable's departure the wind rose from a gentle breeze to a furious gale. It blew from the west in the direct line of our horses. It was about twelve miles to where our camp was, and Sergeant Ross and I galloped out, but the fire crossed our path like a flash. It was a beautiful grazing country with long grass known as "bunch grass," and this made the fire burn more fiercely.

A bunch of grass would be lighted at the roots, the wind would catch it up all blazing as it was and carry it 50 and 60 feet at a leap. There it would set fire to another bunch, which would be similarly caught up and flung ahead, to repeat the same process. Long before we could reach our herd the fire had passed away out of sight, and when we came to the horses we found them bunched up together behind a mound or butte, which was blackened on the windward side, but green on the lee side. Here there was a little pear-shaped patch of grass, just big enough to contain the herd, and it looked as if they had had the sense to shelter themselves there. The constable in charge was busy saving the house, etc., of a settler who was away from home, and he arrived just in time to do so. As the feed was gone we had to take all our horses into barracks and to feed them with hay.

Another instance which occurred in April of the same year is a notable illustration of the difficulty in judging the distance of a prairie fire. Mr. Howell Harris, the manager of the Conrad Brothers' and I. G. Baker's ranches, came to me one evening and asked for assistance to put out a large fire, supposed to be from twelve to fifteen miles north of us, which was threatening his range. It certainly was a very alarming fire to look at, as there was a line of flame which extended over a great many miles. I happened to be very short of men just then, but went myself with a party of nine, taking with us a wagon, oats, canned corned beef and some tea, etc. We had first to find a ford across the Belly River, then to climb the opposite bank upon a road of our own making, and next we headed straight for the centre of the line of fire. We left barracks at eight o'clock in the evening, and travelled until three o'clock next morning. We seemed then to be just as far from the fire as when we started, but were fortunate enough to find some water, so we halted for an hour to rest and to feed the horses; then, as we were not rationed for a lengthy trip, and as there was great uncertainty about the supply of water, I decided to go home.

We reached the Belly River at eleven o'clock, and rode into barracks just as the people were sitting down to their midday meal. We afterwards found that the fire was burning in an arc, and that the centre was really farther from us than either end. We must have travelled over fifty miles.

As we neared our journey's end the wind gradually freshened, and after two days of such encouragement the fire came within striking distance. It was then credibly said to be within seven or eight miles, and I went out again with another party at 9 P.M. In spite of the distance, as estimated, we had to ride fifteen miles before we reached it, and by the time we had put it all out it was 5.30 A.M. We reached home, having travelled nearly forty miles. These fires were for the most part extinguished by means of gunny sacks, the business ends of which were saturated with water, and with these the fire was flogged out. Old brooms, too much worn for prolonged household work, were very useful, too, and we used to preserve our old brooms for the purpose. The wetting of the sacks necessitated a supply of water, and thus a barrel of water was carried in a wagon, so that progress could not be very rapid.

It was a happy time when the settlers had become so numerous that our duty was mainly limited to warning them to turn out and fight any fire in their own vicinity.

Suppressing Illicit Liquor Traffic

No history of Mounted Police work would be worth its salt unless it could give some instances of the manner in which the law prohibiting illicit liquor was enforced in the early days.

During the first half of the year 1889 we paid particular attention to the unlawful importation of the poison that had been in the habit of coming into the country from Montana. There was no railway in that section connecting the two countries, and the liquor must, perforce, travel by wagon or by pack-horse; yet, for a man who understood how to carry it on, the illicit trade was the most profitable business in the country. The stuff itself was known as "Forty Rod," "Red-Eye," "Rot-Gut," and other similarly expressive names, and it was invariably of overproof strength, so that it might be doctored by the retail vendor. In most cases it was little other than coloured alcohol.

In December, 1888, Staff-Sergeant Ross received information that about 100 gallons of this stuff was "cached" on the prairie a few miles to the south of the town of Lethbridge, and after diligent search, found them. He was unable at the moment to provide transport for more than thirty gallons, which he brought into barracks, and being assured that if he left the balance where it was he would see it again no more, he broke up the rest of the kegs and let the liquor run out on the prairie. It was a provision of the law that seized liquor could be so disposed of. We were never able to prove ownership, so the other thirty gallons went the same way, killing the weeds upon a barrack road.

I had occasion to remember this "find," for just at that time my groom came to me and said that my team was a little above itself and wanted more exercise than it had been getting lately. Would it not be a good plan to take them for a ten-mile run into the country to steady them down. I did not want the horses that afternoon, and told him to do as he proposed, dismissing the subject from my mind. I learnt some little time afterwards that the owners of the hundred gallons previously referred to had lost a ten-gallon keg of so-called brandy, which had fallen off the load, and my enterprising groom in some way came to hear of where it could be found. By means of my team and a buck-board he recovered the keg and sold it for a good round sum, putting the money, of course, into his own pocket.

I discovered subsequently what a thorough-paced blackguard he was in this way. My trooper, which had been bought for the Force in Ontario in 1885, was a well-blooded golden chestnut, bred, as I understood, in Kentucky. He had been used on a trotting race-course, and his paces were quite unsuited to the saddle. I had ridden him with Lord Lansdowne's escort in 1885, and again with Lord Stanley in 1889, and on the latter occasion one of the Staff asked me, when my old friend was playing the kitten, whether he was a young horse. I could only reply, "I wish he were." He was "aged" when he was bought, and could not be expected to last for many years longer.

Well, I had taken a great fancy to the horse, and allowed no one to ride him besides myself and my young son Percy, who was one of the best riders in the country. After many months of labour I had taught the old horse to canter quite pleasantly, and had always been very careful of his mouth. He showed his breeding in so many ways; no matter how long the day or how tedious the road, he always had a spare leg to fall back upon, and one day I had occasion to cross the St. Mary's River when the floe ice was floating down, and wasn't quite sure how the horse might take it, never having seen it before. He just cocked his ears and looked at it, and passed through without a second thought. My groom, as it transpired, resented not being allowed to ride the horse, and one day I received, forwarded from the Commissioner at Regina.

a very badly written, ill-spelt letter, in which he was informed that if he knew how Percy Deane was permitted to ride his father's horse he would not allow it.

Not very long after this it happened that my groom wanted a night pass, wrote it out himself, and brought to me to sign. I at once recognised the writing as being identical with that of the anonymous letter, and sent both documents to the Commissioner, with the suggestion that my groom should be at once transferred to some northern division, which was done. He was subsequently sent to the penitentiary for burglary.

The two following instances are good illustrations of the manner in which the detachments used to watch the illicit liquor dealers. Sergeant A. E. Macdonell, of Milk River Ridge detachment, about fourteen miles from the international boundary, was quite well aware that an old-time whisky smuggler, named Tom Percel, had a cargo of liquor in the proximity of the line, on the Montana side, which he was intending to run in whenever opportunity might offer. The 4th of July, American Independence Day, was approaching, and it could hardly be celebrated in gala fashion without a little stimulant, so on the evening of the 2nd, Tom decided to make his venture. At seven o'clock that evening Sergeant Macdonell started out on patrol, came across a fresh wagon track, followed it up, and overtook Percel, who had six five-gallon kegs of fire-water in his wagon. Macdonell escorted the outfit to Lethbridge, where Percel paid $100 fine, and where his wagon, horses and harness were seized, confiscated and sold by the Customs Department. Sergeant Macdonell was the richer by fifty dollars, as half the fine was payable to him as informer.

During the same month I had sent out a working party from barracks to construct a bridge over a bad hole in the Fort Benton trail, which our teams, carrying supplies, had to cross. It was about half-way between barracks and the Milk Ridge detachment, that is, at a distance of about thirty miles.

About twenty-five miles to the west of where this party was working a detachment was stationed on the St. Mary's River. This detachment was provided with a pack outfit, so that it could act as a flying patrol, and by means of its pack-horses carry its own small "A" tent, grub, etc., for a few days. The detachment was commanded by a live young corporal named Elliott, who never left anything to chance.

Corporal Elliott, in the course of his patrol, came across wagon tracks and, on general principles, followed them. The country at that time was overspread with smoke from bush fires in the foothills of the Rocky Mountains, and the surrounding view was accordingly very limited. At a particular spot on the trail Elliott noticed that the tracks of the wagon ahead of him grew rapidly fainter and fainter, and he reasoned from this that the load in the wagon had, for some reason or other, become decreased. On investigation he found that five ten-gallon kegs of whisky were reposing at the bottom of a bank, down which they had been rolled out of sight from the trail. He went on his way rejoicing, and presently rode into our bridge building camp, where he found a noted whisky-runner named "Red McConnell," with horses and an empty wagon.

McConnell, who was familiarly known to his confrères as "Reddy," had had a long and merry life at his trade, and had never yet been caught. They all had supper together, of course, and after supper McConnell hitched up his team and drove off into the smoke. Corporal Elliott went back to the kegs and watched them all night.

Bright and early next morning Red McConnell returned also to his kegs, and began to move them to a more convenient and accessible spot. Elliott allowed him to remove one, and "held him up" with the second in his arms. The poor man was helpless—nothing could be done except to obey the command to load the kegs into his own wagon and to drive them into Lethbridge and pay the $100 fine which was exacted from him. After this experience Red McConnell did not again operate in my district.

The Animals Contagious Diseases Act

Among our multifarious other duties, we were called upon to enforce the provisions of this Act, and a great deal of work it caused us from time to time, until at length the Dominion Veterinary Department took over and performed its own duties, some years subsequent to the time of which I am now writing. At the Parliamentary Session of 1897 the disease commonly known to stockmen as "big-jaw" or "lumpy-jaw," and to the veterinary profession as "actinomycosis," was added to the list of those scheduled in the Animals Contagious Diseases Act.

This complaint was very prevalent on the range, and it was contrary to the new law for an owner to dispose of an animal suffering therefrom. In October of that year some 500 head of cattle were shipped from Lethbridge in two trains to Hochelaga. Complaint was made to me by a local stockman that nine head of big-jawed steers were included in this consignment, and that they were all loaded into one car, together with nine cows. This car was the leading car of the train, and it was destined to carry its freight to the cannery.

The stockman who brought the complaint to me had been incited thereto by some of the men who had helped to load the cattle, and it was said that the nine steers were suffering from a very advanced stage of the disease. The lumps on the jaws had all burst, and the sores were exuding matter and blood, and it seemed to be a very exaggerated case. As the trains carrying the cattle had left before the complaint was made, it was fortunate that an Inspector of Brands was present, as he could, and did, give excellent independent testimony as to the condition of the suffering animals.

Being an appointee under North-West Ordinance only, he held no authority to interfere under the Contagious Diseases Act, which was a Dominion Statute, but his attention was drawn to the facts, and he took his own notes. The case was tried summarily before an Associate Justice of the Peace and myself, a charge being laid against one of the shippers (to whom three of the steers were said to have belonged) that he had disposed of the said animals knowing that they were suffering from an infectious disease. Oddly enough, no one would (obviously they could if they would) explain how it happened that the nine diseased animals forgathered in one particular pen. It seemed to be a remarkable instance of animal sagacity. With a small effort of the imagination one could imagine these poor suffering creatures calling aloud in their bovine language, "Unclean, unclean," singling themselves out from the madding crowd and, with self-sacrificing resignation, placing themselves on board the first car to hasten to the cannery.

I asked one witness how the cowboys had, in the course of conversation between themselves and the shippers, alluded to the diseased animals, and he replied, "Them with the wattles"; but not a solitary member of the combination would admit driving or seeing anyone else drive the infected steers into the No. 1 pen. It did not matter. The charge was proved beyond a shadow of doubt, and the defendant was ordered to pay a fine of one hundred dollars.

He gave notice of appeal, and as Mr. Conybeare was

acting for him, I had to request that some counsel should be appointed to uphold the conviction. The Crown Prosecutor of another judicial district was instructed to attend to this duty.

He duly arrived in Lethbridge in the month of March following, and the case was heard by Mr. Justice Scott. I looked up the learned counsel on his arrival, told him that all the witnesses were present and so on, and that he had a perfectly straight case to handle, and felt not a little surprise when he intimated that the sitting magistrates had taken considerably more evidence than was necessary to a conviction. I did not concede that point, but said nothing, as I had had no experience *then* of his capacity as counsel. When the trial came on it was, of course, incumbent upon him to prove his case *de novo,* and I was literally staggered when, after he had perfunctorily examined a couple of witnesses, he said, "That's the case for the Crown, my lord."

So much had been left undone that when Mr. Conybeare rose and said to the judge, "I submit, my lord, that there is no case for my client to answer," the judge simply queried, "You don't expect me to uphold the conviction upon such evidence as that, Mr. Blank, do you?" the man had no answer whatever to make.

The appellant, whom he was paid $25 a day to convict, was a stalwart of the Liberal party, which had been returned to power a couple of years previously, and the inference was irresistible that, in contemptuous disregard of his reputation as a professional man and of his obligations as a man of honour, he had deliberately wrecked the case for the Crown in the interests of a political partisan.

INDEX

Index

Index

Index

Printed by Cassell & Company, Limited, La Belle Sauvage, London, E.C.

7.5.1116

Printed in the United States

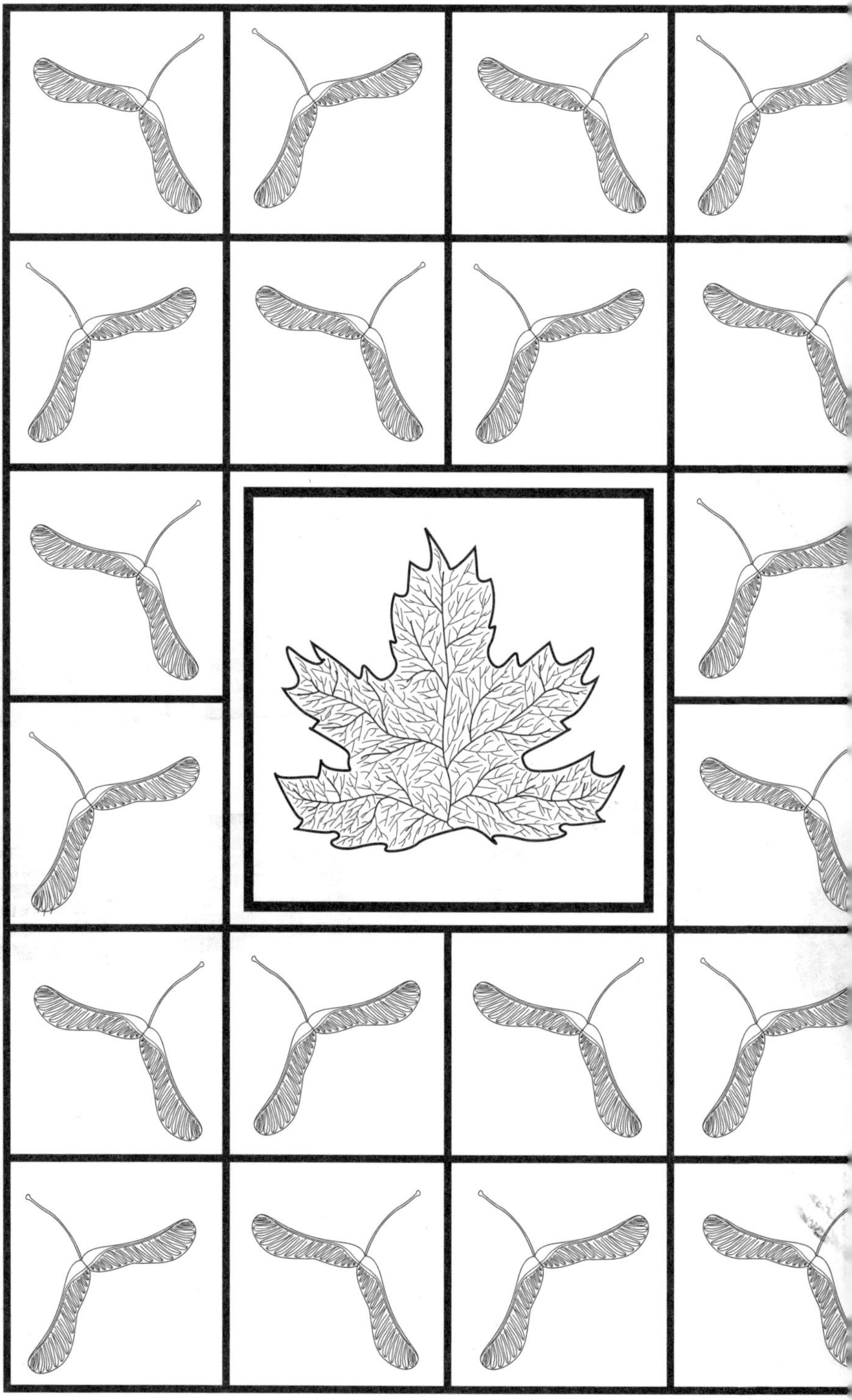